Praise for *Spiced*

In this timely and lively chronicle of psychoactive substance consumption, Professor Graham provides insights into human hopes and despair that touch all of us in one form or another. He does this at multiple levels: the personal, interpersonal, institutional, and larger societal. The treatment is comprehensive, historical, and penetrating into human and social vulnerabilities and remedies. All this is done with an integration of themes and principles from research into consumer behavior and marketing. Professor Graham makes his subject matter and purposes come alive with many actual stories, mini-case histories, and vignettes interwoven throughout the presentation of fascinating technical details of psychoactive consumption. The book is fun to read, yet haunting and sobering in its implications for people everywhere and public policy.

- *Richard P. Bagozzi, the Dwight F. Benton Professor of Behavioral Science in Management and formerly Professor of Social and Administrative Sciences, College of Pharmacy, both at the University of Michigan, Ann Arbor*

The list of psychoactive substances covered in *Spiced* is impressive. Including salt and sugar provides unique views about the consumption of hedonic molecules. The author's marketing background fills an important gap in our understanding of the global consumption of these powerful spices.

- *David J. Nutt, DM FRCP FRCPsych FMedSci, the Edmond J. Safra Professor of Neuropsychopharmacology and director of the Neuropsychopharmacology Unit in the Division of Brain Sciences, Imperial College London*

No one is better equipped than John Graham to tell the provocative story of ancient and contemporary spices – their global marketing, consumer use and abuse, and regulatory complexity. Efforts to improve consumer wellbeing require this kind of integrated review of how we got where we are. After reading this book, your perspective on these psychoactive substances, from the salt shaker on your table to contemporary discussions surrounding the legalization of marijuana, will be forever changed.

- *Linda L. Price, Philip H. Knight Chair, Lundquist College of Business, Department of Marketing, University of Oregon*

Other books by John and his coauthors

International Marketing, 17th edition

All in the Family: A Practical Guide to Creative Multigenerational Living, 2nd edition

Inventive Negotiation: Getting beyond Yes

Global Negotiation: The New Rules

China Now: Doing Business in the World's Most Dynamic Market

Doing Business in the New Japan, 4th edition

Spiced

Spiced

The Global Marketing of Psychoactive Substances

JOHN L. GRAHAM

CreateSpace

ISBN: 1537280597
ISBN 13: 9781537280592
Library of Congress Control Number: 2016914240
CreateSpace Independent Publishing Platform
North Charleston, South Carolina

Acknowledgements

Richard Bagozzi, Cristin Kearns Couzens, Stanton Glantz, Robert Lustig, Richard Haier, E.T. Hall, Gail Ho, Rod Jimenez, Franco Nicosia, David Nutt, Connie Pechmann, and Linda Price. Thanks to all for inspiration, encouragement, and helping to make *Spiced* better.

Also, Emily, Grace, Greta, Jack, and Mary!

Contents

Introduction

Spices and Biases

A strawberry, sugar cloys.

Marketing causes the consumption of spices. Yes, spices are the variety of life, but they aren't a necessity of life. We want them but don't really need them. Indeed, most spices, if consumed in excess, will actually kill you.

The realization is just now setting in – sugar, alcohol, and cocaine affect the brain, the person, and the public health in very similar ways. We also know that illicit drug dealers and tobacco companies market their products to the public in very similar ways. Despite these similarities, government regulation of these spices is a hodgepodge of path-dependent political decision making that yields destructive consequences for the public health and society in general. This must change. I have written *Spiced* to provoke new thinking and action.

I use the term "spices" broadly.[1] I take them to be imbibed substances of little or no nutritional value that provide pleasure to the brain, and therefore the person. I also call them "psychoactive substances" or hedonic (from the Greek word for pleasure) molecules. Examples range from salt to methamphetamine.

---

1   Richard Budgley, *The Encyclopedia of Psychoactive Substance* (St Martin's Press: New York, 1998).

My list in these pages is not exhaustive, but it does cover the major psychoactive substances widely consumed around the world.

The ideas herein are disruptive. The arguments will be many. After all, the book is about the marketing of products, from sugar to heroin to ecstasy, none of which is good for humans to consume. Yet virtually all humans in this country and on the planet regularly consume some of them. Often the health consequences are dangerous, even lethal. And because Americans are the champions of marketing and consumption in general, and these spices in particular, we suffer more than others around the world.

The principal cause of these unhealthy behaviors is marketing, my academic field. Throughout human history we have stumbled onto spices, told other people about them, and traded for them. We have also persuaded our neighbors to try them in the guises of spirituality, aphrodisiacs, medicines, and fun. We have murdered millions, fought wars, and incarcerated millions more over the production, distribution, and prices of spices. In many ways these psychoactive substances have dominated the cultural narrative of the nation, even the world.

I was so surprised when I began my research on this topic, because so many otherwise excellent books[1] about these substances completely ignore the topic of marketing. That is, the blame for irresponsible consumption is placed solely on the consumer as if the producers and sellers have nothing to do with their customers' behaviors. Wow! In his excellent book *Lethal but Legal,* Nicholas Freudenberg[2] refers to this other actor as the "corporate consumption complex." That's a bit too conspiratorial for my taste. But, perhaps he's right? The bottom line is that we are all being *spiced* – like a strawberry being doused with sugar – by a lack of our own self-control, our culture, and the companies that profit from our consumption.

---

1 For example, David Perlmutter and Kristin Loberg, *Grain Brain* (Little Brown: New York, 2013); Clayton J. Mosher and Scott M. Akins, *Drugs and Drug Policy* (Sage: Thousand Oaks, CA, 2nd edition, 2014); and Carl L. Hart and Charles Ksir, *Drugs, Society & Human Behavior* (McGraw-Hill: New York, 16th edition, 215).
2 Nicholas Freudenberg, *Lethal but Legal: Corporations, Consumption, and Protecting Public Health* (Oxford University Press: New York, 2014).

The purpose of this book is to provide a catalyst and a comprehensive context for the current and future discussion of controlling the marketing of these substances. Herein both the big picture and the moving picture[1] are presented. That is, we take a look at the *global* trade of spices through the *millennia*. Both views are crucial for effective policy making. Ideas used in other places and other times must enlighten our difficult choices in the coming decades.

In these pages I apply scientific analyses toward understanding the marketing of spices. That means looking at the numbers that yield informed decisions rather than political ones. The companies and their paid-off politicians will whine. But, perhaps reason can hold sway. Ultimately, this is a book about science and the public health versus politics and greed.

In marketing we also deeply understand that despite its immeasurability, imagery is immensely important. So I deliver the numbers, but use stories to bolster my cases. I mix entertainment with the most recent scientific findings and my own expertise in international consumer behavior.

I occasionally use the awkward term "hedonic molecules" and their chemical formulas to connote a scientific perspective. This scientific labeling is important because most of the commonly used names of these psychoactive substances are loaded with the symbolism of myth, religion, sex, racism, slavery, crime, corruption, and war.

My Biases

To avoid conflicts of interest, the secret is full disclosure.

WILLIAM HERNÁNDEZ REQUEJO

On this topic, or for that matter on any topic, there is no objectivity. So, it is important for you to understand and consider how life experiences slant my views. After forty years in the business, I am a world-class, award-winning

---

1　I thank Seth Crone for inventing this use of the term.

expert in international marketing. But my biases run deeper than that. Indeed, my very first memory is about a spice; and I was crying.

I must have been about 4 or 5 at the time. My parents had taken my older sisters and me to a Chinese restaurant in San Mateo, California, probably the Cathay Kitchen, which has survived the decades in the same location. I was pestering everyone to put mustard on my wonton. My mom said, "No, it's too hot." I persisted in my pestering, and finally my dad gave me what I wanted. The Ka-Me about killed me, the back of my throat was in flames. I yowled. My dad and sisters laughed. My mom got mad.

I order the discussion below based roughly on the chronology of the spices' introduction to mankind and to me personally, and with intoxicants following the substances with more subtle effects.

Salt. I don't remember my first experience with salt. It went on my scrambled eggs at home, but I never adopted my dad's Midwestern habit of salting his cantaloupe.

Sugar. My addiction to sugar was surely a direct result of shopping trips with my mom, taking a hot fudge sundae break at Blums on Fourth Avenue in San Mateo

Chocolate. Recall the hot fudge sundaes at Blums. Or, perhaps it was literally my mother's milk that did it to me. She had always consumed much chocolate over the years.

Caffeine. I'm still addicted, but down to a half cup of coffee a day. Both my parents enjoyed lots of coffee. I guess I picked up that habit at home.

Tobacco. Sixth grade – I stole a pack of Chesterfields from my dad's drawer. My pals and I smoked it in our tree fort. I also snuck cigarettes on occasion in my bathroom at home during high school. But, I resisted the dares to smoke in the boys' room at school. I smoked a pipe for a bit in college – to appear mature. Then I found myself smoking regularly during my full-time work senior year while driving a produce truck around the Bay Area. Two things kept me awake when I started my delivery route at three in the morning, peeling and eating oranges and smoking Winstons. Even with all that peeling and smoking, I still managed to doze dangerously at times. I also tried chewing tobacco and snuff, once each. Both turned my stomach. Nasty stuff.

My main role model, my dad, was a big smoker. When I started driving, I'd go to San Francisco International and pick him up. He was always easy to locate in a crowd by his hack. To this day I find cigarette smoke a pleasant aroma because it used to mean to me that Dad was around. Perhaps what cured me of tobacco was my father's exploratory surgery for lung cancer. I remember crying before he went into the OR. He ended up with a six-by-eight-inch, L-shaped incision on his back and a diagnosis of "we didn't find anything." They told him to stop smoking. Also, neither of the women I married smoked at all, so that helped too.

Alcohol. This one nearly killed me as a teenager. Thrice. My poker friends and I started filling flasks from our parents' liquor cabinets when we were 14. Binge drinking was the manly thing to do then. Often we got very sick. We did get into trouble with the police one night – we had the bourbon, mixers, and ice all sitting on the hood of a Buick out in the sticks somewhere when the patrol car drove up. Our parents raised hell, and worst of all they gathered at our house for their discussion of our delinquency. I had to apologize to the entire group.

The first near death incident had me driving drunk on a Thursday afternoon with four of the guys in my parents' '59 Pontiac station wagon. I spun out doing about forty-five and ended up on a neighbor's lawn, frighteningly sitting between two very large maple trees. Five feet either way and somebody would've been hurt. No seat belts in those days. I just drove off over the curb, leaving deep tire tracks in that nice lawn. Nobody was laughing.

Then came ΔΣΦ. In 1965 San Jose State had been named the best party school in the nation. What could be more fun than binge drinking? How about competitive drinking! The brothers taught us how to drink great quantities of all manner of beer, Red Mountain wine, and hard liquor really fast. Drinking games with coeds, consider the risks. With my fake ID I was elected president of the house as a sophomore. I "sort of remember" our national DSP convention that year in Phoenix. Another brother and I represented our chapter along with our alumni advisor. This thirty-year-old role model set the tone for the meetings when he opened his rather serious briefcase and demonstrated that it fit three quart bottles of vodka.

Spiced

Fortunately I lost only my driver's license that year, and not my life. My first accident involved me, my date, and my parents' '64 Chevy Impala T-boning a Datsun at the corner of Seventh and Julian. The Datsun ended up on the sidewalk. My date bruised her right arm, still no seat belts. But, nobody got hurt. The streets were wet, the Datsun ran a flashing red light, and my reaction time was assisted by a couple of beers. It could have been worse.

My second accident was worse. Three in the morning, a winding Crystal Springs Road – I woke up staring at a telephone pole coming my way very fast. I cranked the wheel left and skidded into the pole going sideways. Once the gravel settled I retrieved the remainder of the fifth of Jim Beam from the glove compartment and pitched it into the bushes. I drove the car home, parked it in the driveway, knocked on my parents' door, and said I'd got in an accident. My dad asked if I was all right. I responded that nobody got hurt. He said he'd look at the car in the morning. What he saw scared the crap out of him. He made me take him to see the damage to the pole. There was none, but that was the last time I touched that Chevy. I loved that car.

I likewise barely survived the first three years of college academically. God knows how many classes I missed, let alone how many brain cells I killed. I moved out of the fraternity house my senior year, and the competitive drinking stopped. However, I was perhaps on the road to alcoholism. Luckily two things threw me off it. First I got married and we soon had a daughter for whom I was responsible. Second, heavy drinking started to upset my stomach consistently. Indeed, one of the last drunks I joined was a Coronado Campaign. In the 1970s, when a US Navy frogman got engaged, his friends in the Teams celebrated by having a drink in every bar in Coronado starting with the Chart House, then the Hotel del Coronado, and so on, and so on until we got to San Diego Bay wherein we threw the betrothed. After we fished him out – it's not good to drown the prospective groom – I staggered home. My tolerant wife put me to bed shortly after which I puked all over the bedroom floor.

By the way, I still get calls from the national fraternity for contributions. I ask them what their policy is on arresting binge drinking. Their answers haven't yet resulted in me sending a check.

Based on these experiences I have concluded that the stupidest form of human being is a teenage boy. Look at the mayhem and death I might have caused in my own teenage years. I was very lucky. Additionally, you cannot have a war without teenage boys. The average age of Americans in the Vietnam War was nineteen. Indeed, perhaps the best way to end all wars is to try to draft men in their thirties. Few would show up. At the end of the book the teenage brain will come up again, as it has implications for how we address the burgeoning proliferation of hedonic molecules.

Finally, I've been witness to fights with alcoholism in my own family – one fight was successful, and one not.

Opioids. None until my first (and I hope only) kidney stone. The morphine at the ER didn't make me feel good. It just mitigated the pain.

Marijuana. When I was president of my fraternity in 1967 I hated the drug. It completely divided the brothers. Many thought smokers should be booted out of the house. Many others thought their consternation and castigation was a silly kind of conservatism. Good friends came to hate each other over this one. I really didn't care one way or the other, other than the conflict made my job of building unity very difficult.

My senior year I lived in a small house in San Jose on Seventh Street with three art majors and a business major. All four of these guys were smoking dope, but were generally respectful of my abstinence. However, one night after a lot of drinking they persuaded me to try it *just once*. Honest! Unlike Bill Clinton, I did inhale, but the high wasn't much distinguishable from the drunk.

My next experience with marijuana was in the Navy in 1973. I was appointed Drug and Alcohol Abuse Program Officer for Underwater Demolition Team Eleven (UDT-11) in Coronado. It became my job to deal with drinking and drug problems in my command – that is, to counsel and perhaps recommend treatment programs. At the time my best friend was an S-2 (antisubmarine warfare) pilot. He explained to me that when his squadron was assigned to the aircraft carrier *Kitty Hawk* off Vietnam, the officers drank scotch in their quarters and the enlisted men smoked dope on the fantail. Similar problems existed everywhere in the services then. Indeed, I'll never forget the commanding officer of Naval Special Warfare (in charge of all SEAL and UDT teams in the Pacific) visiting our unit at Subic Bay in the Philippines. A Captain and a role model for all of us, and he ended up with his face in his mashed potatoes, passed out drunk at the O-Club dinner party we held for him.

Upon my assignment, I was almost immediately ordered to a one-week training program at the Point Loma Naval Base for Drug and Alcohol Abuse Program Officers. I can remember the Lt. Commander in charge making the point that compared to marijuana, alcohol abuse was by far the greater problem for the Navy as an organization and for the individual officers and sailors involved. Binge drinking was injuring and killing personnel on ships and in ports around the world. Marijuana not so much. Abuse of both reduced human performance generally.

I left the Navy and got divorced about the same time. In the late 1970s I smoked marijuana on occasion. I even bought a "lid" (a plastic bag containing a few ounces) once. It lasted about three years before I eventually threw it out April 3, 1978. I know the date because I noted in my journal the night after an old friend's visit with me at Berkeley:

So what am I thinking about tonight? First, I guess I'm thinking about how doped up my thinking is tonight. I dropped Rick off at the airport and he wanted to smoke some dope on the way. He's got a bad habit, but I think it will clear away when he finds some direction in his life. I hope it happens soon. I guess my life does have more direction than his, at least at the moment. Professionally, I have some hazy idea of "where" I'm going. But, the most important thing to me right now is I am enjoying the "going" (a little self-centered of me – I was talking about Rick). Anyway my mind is a little fogged. It's an intoxication I find gnawingly uncomfortable, I think because I can't sense the effects, I just sense that something is missing. It's going to be a long, long time before I smoke dope again. I like clear sunny days too much and I think I like my mind the same way.

Cocaine. Never had it. On a vacation to Peru I did have a cup of coca tea. Not much to talk about.

The Continuing Alchemy. From among the limitless list of man-made spices I can admit to taking one amphetamine tablet my freshman year of college. It helped me pull an all-nighter to cram for a Philosophy final. I got an A on the final, but I had an A going into that exam anyway. I also witnessed my mother's diet pill addiction during the 1960s. The latter was a most unpleasant experience. During that year or so, my view of my mom completely changed along with her personality and behaviors.

So I have consumed many and become addicted to a few of these hedonic compounds. This certainly influences my thinking about them. As I have spent more than half my life studying and teaching international marketing my views have been fundamentally formed in that milieu. I am not a politician or a legal scholar, psychologist, physician, nutritionist, historian, epidemiologist, or a criminologist. I do borrow information and ideas from all these fields. My undergraduate degree is in chemistry – I suppose that influenced my use of "molecules" throughout the book. That is also how the drug-company folks describe their search – for new molecules. I have written another book, *Inventive Negotiation*, and have taught classes on Innovation Processes with an advertising-agency owner. I have consulted for no companies that produce or market hedonic compounds. Equity investments in Procter & Gamble, Kelloggs, Smuckers, Yum! Brands, PepsiCo, and Abbott Labs total less than one percent of my family's portfolio.

My purposes for writing this book are threefold: First, I am hoping to make a little money in my retirement. Second, I am very interested in promoting the public health, as that enriches all of us. Third, I seek to relieve the societal havoc (that is, the losses of personal freedom including incarceration and the violence and deaths) created by the path-dependent, hodgepodge of government restrictions on hedonic molecules.

One

MARKETING CAUSES CONSUMPTION[1]

We do not advertise to children under 12 years old.

THE COCA-COLA COMPANY

The best decisions are made in a context of full information. How psychoactive substances are marketed globally and how they have been marketed historically pertain to my arguments herein. The good news is that we actually know a lot about how spices have been marketed and de-marketed through history and around the world. For example, we can look back at the disastrous consequences of taxing salt in ancient China, Middle Ages France, and 20th century India. We can see quite clearly the futility of America's 20th century experiments with prohibition in the forms of the 18th Amendment to the US Constitution and the War on Drugs. We can also see the efficacy of alternative approaches to managing opioid addictions in the Netherlands and Switzerland.

Perhaps most important, during the last few decades we have learned details about how executives at many major American firms value their profits

---

1   I use this language unabashedly. There are of course a variety of other factors that influence consumption. For example, we are learning more and more how our genes influence our choices. But there can be no consumption without a product or service being produced and delivered. Obviously prices and promotion move things along as well.

1

over the public's health. Key have been the documents of the decision making within the tobacco companies laid bare in the lawsuits brought against them. And finally, we know that concerns about the public's health can win out over corporate self-interest and greed as we witness the continuing decline in tobacco consumption here in the United States.

Marketing 101

Beginning in the 1930s in this country we began to study the field of Marketing as a branch of economics. That work primarily informs managers of firms on how to efficiently satisfy the needs and wants of consumers, *at a profit*.

Here's some basics. Exhibit 1.1 shows how executives at Coca-Cola or at a cocaine cartel in Colombia view their daily tasks. We explain in our textbook, *International Marketing*:[1]

Exhibit 1.1
The International Marketing Task

Controllable by Firms	Uncontrollable Elements of the Domestic Environment and each Foreign Country
Firm characteristics	Competitive forces
Marketing research	Economic climate
4 Ps, Marketing Mix Decisions	Political/legal forces
Product	Structure of distribution
Place	Level of technology
Price	Geography and infrastructure
Promotion	Cultural/ethnic forces

Source: *International Marketing*, Cateora, Gilly, Graham, and Money, 2016

---

1   Philip R. Cateora, Mary C. Gilly, John L. Graham, and R. Bruce Money, *International Marketing* (McGraw-Hill: New York, 2016, 17th edition).

The successful manager constructs a marketing program designed for optimal adjustment to the uncertainty of the business climate. The column on the left in Exhibit 1.1 represents the area under the control of the marketing manager [who] blends product, place (channels-of-distribution), price, promotion, and research activities to capitalize on anticipated demand. The controllable elements can be altered in the long run and, usually, in the short run to adjust to changing market conditions, consumer tastes, or corporate objectives.

In the right-hand column are the array of uncertainties created by the domestic and foreign environments. Although the marketer can blend a marketing mix from the controllable elements, the uncontrollable factors are precisely that; the marketer must actively evaluate and, if needed, adapt. That effort—the adaptation of the marketing mix to these environmental factors—determines the outcome of the marketing enterprise.

So the marketers of hedonic molecules lose sleep over both kinds of issues. They are constantly (1) contemplating decisions about the marketing mix and (2) scanning the external environment for threats and opportunities. Their worst mistakes almost always are those of omission, so night-watchman vigilance of the shifting and swirling marketplace is crucial. They know their victories are due to a combination of good luck, good judgment, and creativity.

The Marketing Mix (Controllable)

The field of Marketing accepts as axiomatic that better products, broader distribution, lower prices, and creative promotion strategies (advertising and personal selling) lead to both higher top-line sales revenues and better bottom-line profits. For the mathematically minded:

$$\text{sales} = f(\textbf{product, distribution, price, promotion})$$

Of course, there are exceptions. Izod is my favorite. In the 1980s they pumped up their product line (alligator logos were on everything from polo shirts and perfume to automobiles), they broadened distribution to stores like Target, lowered prices, and their advertising budgets exploded along with their top-line sales. At the time I asked their Westcoast sales manager to talk to my Marketing class at University of Southern California (USC). He was a very happy man. I asked him to explain the boom represented by the ubiquity of the alligator. It was even mentioned as the uniform in the *Preppy Handbook*. His response was revealing, "Hell, I don't know. I'm just trying to keep up with the orders." Their mistake of omission? The company didn't see the incompatibility of ubiquity and the core characteristic of their brand, exclusivity. They blew out their brand, and the alligator sucked swamp water for most of the next twenty years.

So marketers of Coke and cocaine both have to worry about the right length of their product lines. Perhaps one of the greatest marketing mistakes ever was New Coke. Perhaps one of the greatest marketing miseries was the 1980s product line extension to crack cocaine. Controlling their distributors is a problem for both as well. Coke had to resort to the coercion of the courts to make waiters respond to your request for a "Coke" with "Is a Pepsi OK?" Cocaine cartels resort to the coercion of the Colt and machete to maintain purity standards. Both cut prices to boost consumption. One of the great marketing ironies is to see a street corner in Detroit with a Coke billboard and a Silent-Bob type coke dealer standing underneath.

The good news among these public health dirges is that the *four Ps* of marketing (that's what we call them in business school) – product, place (that is, distribution), price, and promotion – are also tools that can be used to reduce consumption of hedonic molecules. That is, if we play our cards right. Recall our formula above. Reasonable restrictions on product lines and distribution strategies, higher prices, and enforceable controls on promotion can all serve to reduce consumption of spices.

Please also notice the order of the list. Purposely represented in the sequence is a hierarchy of both the history and the use of the tools. First comes the making of a product that by itself has little value. Upon its delivery to a customer it attains an extrinsic value allowing a price to be set and/or negotiated. Finally, that extrinsic price can be manipulated via promotion. In the coming chapters the importance of this natural order of the *4Ps* will become readily apparent in setting strategies for reducing consumption of the various spices. If we think of the successful reduction of tobacco consumption in the United States manipulation of price and promotion have been salient.

Environmental Factors (Uncontrollable...Mostly)

The diagram also depicts both domestic and foreign environmental factors that provide the context for marketing-mix decisions. *Competitive forces* in the home market can be important. For example, the salt market in the United States is dominated by two producers, Cargill and Morton.

The *economic climate* for American sugar producers is a complex one, influenced by both government subsidies and the weather. Circa 2014 strong harvests yielded low prices. This caused a default by sugar producers on federal government loans that are usually paid back when prices are high. Despite the $280 million default the Department of Agriculture again made loans to the producers on their 2015 crop.

The fast liberalizing *political forces* of recent years have emboldened American distillers to renew their invasive television advertising. Now we see Captain Morgan ads during baseball game broadcasts. And kids do love pirates. Rrrrr!

The spice trade has always crossed national borders. So the *political, economic, and competitive forces* that make domestic marketing challenging serve to multiply the complexity facing hedonic-compound marketers. Certainly the recent $19 billion takeover of British icon Cadbury by Kraft featured political angst in the UK. The potential for higher prices and lost jobs due to the consolidation of the industry is high.

The global *distribution* of caffeine in the form of Red Bull has been particularly daunting because of the wide variety of restrictions across countries. The EU requires "high caffeine content" labels; Canadian labels recommend a limit of two cans per day; Norway restricts sales to pharmacies; France (until recently) and Denmark have banned the product completely.

When it comes to the *technological innovation* of e-cigarettes the Europeans have been much tougher on the tobacco marketers than the United States. The European Parliament has banned their sale to children, while only twenty-three American states have done likewise.

Geography and infrastructure, of course along with war, have limited the marketing of opium from Afghanistan.

Finally, *cultural differences* in part explain the different attitudes toward the regulation of marijuana and cocaine across the Americas. In Cusco, Peru, you can order a cup of coca-leaf tea in the best restaurants. And many Mexicans consider the carnage caused by the drug cartels in their country to be at least in part a consequence of American demand for the spices.

Beyond Marketing 101

Franco Nicosia loved race cars. He could talk both the technology and tactics of the track. His lectures in my doctoral course at Berkeley in 1977 were infused with car talk: "driving demand" and "staying on the bumper of the competition" and such. Indeed, his path-breaking model of consumer decision making resembles an automobile engine in many ways. His first PhD was garnered at the University of Rome in 1952 in commerce and economics. He came to Berkeley in 1959 to earn a second doctorate in Marketing in 1962. His cross-cultural background was also crucial to his work. Not taking American culture for granted, he asked questions like, "Why do American drivers go so slow?"

Among the classics[1] on his reading list for his course was a new paper of his with coauthor Robert Mayer in the new *Journal of Consumer Research*, "Toward a Sociology of Consumption."[2] The authors argued that beyond profit-yielding *purchases*, other consumer behaviors should be considered as

---

1 This is my term, not his. Most of the literature he had us read and discuss was not his. He did like this paper a lot, as did I.

2 Francesco M. Nicosia and Robert M. Mayer, "Toward a Sociology of Consumption," *Journal of Consumer Research*, 3(2), September 1976, pages 65-77.

well. In particular they added "*use* and *disposal*" to the list of concerns for managers and policy makers alike. Thus, the public health is part of the purview of marketers. He argued that brewers, in addition to worrying about sales, should also consider issues such as alcoholism, drunk driving, and even bottle and can disposal. He might have imagined a risky mix of reds – Ferrari and Chianti. Sadly we lost Professor Nicosia in 1997.

In 1979 I took the podium at Berkeley in the winter term to teach my first undergraduate class, Marketing 101. Right across the Bay, in San Francisco, the Federal Trade Commission (FTC) was holding hearings on advertising directed toward children. I sent all my students to listen in as a most excellent field trip. The combination of doctors, dentists, consumer behavior experts, and cereal industry witnesses fascinated. The consumer advocates argued for a ban on advertising to children, similar to the aforementioned policies of Coca-Cola and laws in other countries such as Sweden. The industry representatives argued against such regulations. There was no disagreement about the recent increases in the consumption of sugared cereals.

The fundamental controversy was over the cause of the increases. To the consumer groups the reason was obvious and well proven – industry advertising to children caused the unhealthful increases in consumption. Indeed, Coca-Cola's self-imposed ban of advertising to children clearly reflects their understanding that advertising does cause consumption. Alternatively, most industry experts responded with comments like, "The parents buy the Cocoa Puffs, not the kids;" and one of the biggest lies ever told, "Our advertising does not influence children to consume sugared cereals, our advertising simply influences kids to choose our brand when they seek cereal."[1] Really? That's not what the executives learned in their MBA classes! Their PR agents manufactured that little lie.

It was also quite interesting to witness the different testimonial styles of the academics versus the attorneys. The researchers piled up evidence to prove

---

1   This is certainly not the biggest lie ever told. That award goes to your Congressional representative when s/he tells you that donations do not influence her/his votes. Query your representative sometime about this and watch him/her squirm.

a point. Lawyers derogated with all possible derisions – small sample sizes, faulty statistics, and so on. Plausible or not, it didn't seem to matter. "If the glove don't fit, you must acquit!"

Ultimately the FTC waited too long to issue its rulings. The new Reagan administration attacked not only the suggested regulations, but also the FTC itself, temporarily refusing to fund the agency. Yes, the 1980s and 1990s were not kind to sociology and thinking like Franco Nicosia's. I took my first academic position at the USC in 1979. I watched with interest the 1930s brick School of Social Work being converted to a new School of Accounting. Our Arthur Laffer's Curve well represented the tenor of those times as well. The worship of free enterprise reigned and government regulation became a dirty word.

That's about the time a coauthor and I took up the study of infant formula sales in developing countries. Critics of the infant formula industry were staging a boycott of Nestlé products in the United States and in other developed countries. The gripe? Nestlé and its industry competitors were marketing too aggressively in less developed countries. This caused uneducated mothers to stop breast feeding which in turn resulted in widespread malnutrition of bottle-fed infants.

In 1981 the World Health Organization (WHO) passed a code on marketing breast-milk substitutes aimed at stifling objectionable industry marketing practices. The crux of the controversy again was the causal relationship between advertising and consumption. We looked at formula consumption in eighty-six less developed countries before and after a reported cutback in industry marketing efforts. We found a clear decline, confirming the advertising → consumption relationship and reported our findings in a peer reviewed journal.[1] Then the fun began.

After the article had been published we got a call from the journal editor informing us that two fellow academics were submitting formal criticisms to

---

[1] Mary C. Gilly and John L. Graham, "A Macroeconomic Study of the Effects of Promotion on the Consumption of Infant Formula in Developing Countries," *Journal of MacroMarketing*, 8(1), Spring 1988, 21-31. Separate comments on article by J.J. Boddewyn and B. Meade, *Journal of MacroMarketing*, 8(2), Fall 1988, 40-45. Our replies in *Journal of MacroMarketing*, 9(1), Spring 1989.

which we would be able to write a rejoinder. Here I provide the gist of the debate. The full published criticisms and rejoinder are cited below and included at www.Spiced.World/appendix. First, Professor Jean Boddewyn:

> Mary Gilly and John Graham have had the courage to tackle the difficult problem of unraveling the macro relationship between promotion and consumption of a controversial product – infant formula – in developing countries (LDCs)…However, I believe there are basic theoretical and operational flaws in their conceptualization, modeling, and analysis which vitiate their overall conclusion, namely, that there is a causal link between the promotion and consumption of that product…
>
> Although, I think their case is not proven, *partly* because of the real methodological and statistical problems which they could not avoid, but *mainly* because of serious theoretical lacunas, analytical weaknesses, and partisan attitudes on their part.

Excerpts from our response:

> Boddewyn's criticism is that our study proves nothing. The failsafe position of the infant formula manufacturers, the tobacco producers, and the alcoholic beverage industry is that one can never prove that the marketing of these products causes health problems. Attorneys worry about proof. The job of social scientists is to provide evidence, not to prove things. We mightily disapprove of Boddewyn's misleading out-of-context quotes which imply that we think otherwise. …
>
> Simply stated, Boddewyn's courtroom approach asks too much of any one study. Our question for him and the infant formula manufacturers is: "Do you have evidence to show that promotion does not have a causal effect on consumption?" If so, it should be put forward for scrutiny…
>
> Our findings support the theory that industry advertising and promotion can have a causal effect on primary demand for products. Boddewyn frequently cites the cigarette advertising controversy as

being analogous to the issue examined in our study of infant formula marketing. Curiously, he stands silent on the most recent studies in the marketing literature which support the causal relationship between industry advertising and primary demand for cigarettes.

When we first submitted our rejoinder, we included conjecture about Boddewyn testifying on behalf of tobacco companies. His eight-pointed fusillade of our article betrayed his "if-the-glove-don't-fit" rhetorical style. Moreover, none of the three blind peer reviewers chosen by the journal mentioned any of his eight points in their criticism. The editor replied that our conjecture was too inflammatory for an academic discussion. But, in fact we were correct back then in 1989. Boddewyn had testified on behalf of the tobacco industry as it fought government regulations even back in the 1980s. In Chapter 6 on Tobacco we provide new damning evidence about Boddewyn's credibility and integrity in these matters.

I close this section of the chapter with a little good news from the last century. In February 1996, in the *Journal of Marketing Research,* Richard Petty and John Cacioppo, two psychologists then at Ohio State University, published an important guest editorial. The title was "Addressing Disturbing and Disturbed Consumer Behavior: Is It Necessary to Change the Way We Conduct Behavioral Science?" Preparation of the article was in part supported by grants from the National Science Foundation. The authors are refreshingly succinct:

In 1960, 5 percent of the Gross National Product went to medical services; in 1990, this share grew to 12 percent. The economic costs of injury now total more than $100 billion annually, cardiovascular disease $135 billion, and cancer over $70 billion. Tragically, these economic costs are dwarfed by human and social costs, many of which are avoidable. According to the US Public Health Service, of the ten leading causes of death in the United States, at least seven could be reduced substantially if people at risk would change just five behaviors: compliance (e.g., use of antihypertensive medication), diet, smoking, lack of exercise, and alcohol and drug abuse. Each of these behaviors is inextricably linked with marketing efforts and the reactions of consumers to marketing campaigns. The link between consumer choices and social problems is clear.[1]

They go on to quote a colleague at Rutgers, Beth Hirschman:

There are currently 10 million alcoholics and 80 million cigarette smokers in the United States… Every year 25,000 people die as a result of alcohol related traffic accidents… All of these disturbing and disturbed behaviors result from consumption gone wrong.[2]

We will revisit and update these statistics in future chapters. Things have actually improved in many ways in recent decades, but the numbers still tell a horrific story.

Petty and Cacioppo go on to advocate a renewal of research in marketing to address the problems of public health. They talk a bit about how educational programs and cognitive approaches compete with emotions and hedonic urges limiting the abilities of consumers to control their own behavior. They also call for more research "to investigate the generality of successful health campaigns." But a key take-away from their paper is its appearance in one of the leading journals in the world informing the field of marketing.

Transformative Consumer Research (TCR)

Connie Pechmann is a genuine daredevil. You have to be a little nuts to get into hang gliding. You had to be a lot nuts to take on the tobacco industry back in the early 1990s. My colleague at The Paul Merage School of Business,

---

1 Richard C. Petty and John T. Cacioppo, "Addressing Disturbing and Disturbed Consumer Behavior…," *Journal of Marketing Research*, 33, February 1996, pages. 1-8. Also, I did not include their citation in the text for ease of reading. They referenced US Public Health Service (1991), Healthy People 2000: National Health Promotion and Disease Prevention Objectives, DHS Publication #PHS 91-50212, Washington, DC, US Department of Health and Human Services.
2 Elizabeth C. Hirschman, "Secular Mortality and the Dark Side of Consumer Behavior: Or How Semiotics Saved My Life," *Advances in Consumer Research*, 18, 1991, pages 1-4.

University of California, Irvine (UCI) has a nice smile and a nice family, and she loves to argue. Get her going in the wrong direction, and you have a big problem.

Perhaps it was her graduate school years in Tennessee, a tobacco state – a master's in Psychology, an MBA, and a PhD in Marketing all at Vanderbilt? She has been the tobacco industry's most formidable b-school opponent on the topic of advertising and tobacco consumption for the last two decades. She's done foundational work in the area and was recognized in 2005 for the most important article in the *Journal of Consumer Research*. Most recently she was selected as the editor of the *Journal of Consumer Psychology*, a top journal in her field. Her work has also garnered her the 2009 Pollay Prize for Research in the Public Interest from the University of British Columbia. She has been the frequent recipient of grants to study tobacco advertising, anti-smoking ads, and adolescents – totally more than $2 million. All this research productivity has made her an active consultant in anti-tobacco litigation.

And Connie is a leader in the newly defined field of Transformative Consumer Research (TCR). In this new networked century the consumer is fast gaining powers comparable to companies. One manifestation of the growing symmetry is the renewed interest in the field of marketing and consumer behavior that serves the public rather than private enterprise. Profits aren't depended upon to promote the welfare of consumers. Rather research is conducted with consumer welfare as the grail, recognizing that profits and shareholders' interests can be at odds with those of the publics the companies purport to serve.

The body of knowledge produced by what I call the TCR tribe is most valuable in the discussion of managing the marketing of hedonic molecules. It is well summarized in a book of that title[1] edited by Connie and her colleagues, David Mick (University of Virginia), Simone Pettigrew (University of Western Australia),[2] and Julie Ozanne (Virginia Tech). The battles to manage the market for spices can now be waged on a relatively equal footing with for-

1 The long title is *Transformative Consumer Research: For Personal and Collective Well-Being* (Routledge: New York, 2012).

2 Yes, tobacco was also grown in Western Australia during the last century and in Victoria to this day.

profit companies (both legal and illegal) that dominate the trade and information about it. One of my purposes in writing this book is to "highlight the socio-cultural and situational context" of this "disturbed consumer behavior."

The lesson of this literature is that important similarities across spices exist that can and should be exploited in the design of regulatory systems that maximize the public welfare, not the profits of a few. In one of the articles[1] in the book by Pechmann and her colleagues, successes and failures in managing alcohol and tobacco are compared. Both products pose significant health risks, including lethal side effects of use and agonies of addiction. Prohibitions of production and distribution have not worked to reduce consumption for either product. Limitations on distribution, for example, to children have not been effective. Higher prices through taxation have served to reduce consumption in both cases. Mass-media advertising can either promote or reduce consumption of both products.

The Great Corporate Copout

The competitive and profit-making priorities of major manufacturers clearly serve as rivals to the public health. Often in this book you will hear CEOs and other corporate executives excusing their decision making with statements in the genre of: "If we adjust our marketing mix as our critics demand, we'll lose market share to our competitors and the profits we owe shareholders." Such assertions are bogus[2] for at least two reasons. First, we've known for at least three decades that the causal relationship between market share and profits is weak at best.[3] Indeed, ask any finance professor if market share predicts future profits – it doesn't. Second, a CEO's responsibilities go beyond maximizing

---

1 Cornelia Pechmann, Anthony Biglan, Joel W. Grubb, and Christine Cody, "Transformative Consumer Research for Addressing Tobacco and Alcohol Consumption," Chapter 17 in David G. Mick, Simone Pettigrew, Cornelia Pechmann, and Julie L. Ozanne (eds.), *Transformative Consumer Research for Personal and Collective Wellbeing* (Routledge: New York, 2011).

2 Perhaps the more accurate term is "bull shit."

3 Robert Jacobson and David A. Aaker, "Is Market Share All That It's Cracked Up To Be," *Journal of Marketing*, 49(40, 1985, pages 11-22; Donald Peterson, award winning CEO of Ford Motor Company 1985 -1990 related to me in a personal conversation that he paid little attention to market share and focused on maximizing product quality.

shareholder value. On this second point, the following mission/purpose statements are revealing:[1]

> **Altria (Philip Morris)** – Our mission is to own and develop finan-
> cially disciplined businesses that are leaders in responsibly providing
> adult tobacco and wine consumers with superior branded products.
> **Hershey Company** – Undisputed marketplace leadership.
> **PepsiCo** – At PepsiCo we believe that business and society can thrive
> together. We are guided by Performance with Purpose: delivering top-
> tier results in a way that sustains and respects business, society, and
> the planet.
> **J.M. Smucker Company** –*Our Purpose…Helping to bring families to-
> gether to share memorable meals and moments.* We always have defined
> success by more than financial performance.

My favorite is the last.[2] Smucker's does italicize "bring families together" but
they immediately mention financial performance next! This, of course, begs
the key question. If they have to choose between the two, which will dominate their calculus? We know from Michael Moss's excellent food industry ex-
posé and the University of California, San Francisco (UCSF) Legacy Tobacco
Documents Library that profits almost always dominate the decision making.
Both will be discussed in great detail in the chapters to come.

American business schools are to blame for this depreciation of the public good. Almost nowhere in our curricula do we dispute the "greed is good"

---

1 All downloaded from the corporate websites on November 22, 2013.

2 I have to add a note about my personal relationship with the company (in addition to owning
some shares). Smucker's is the purveyor of Eagle Brand Sweetened Evaporated Milk, perhaps my
most dangerous addiction. It is the only ingredient in "danger pudding." Simply put an unopened
can in a covered pan of boiling water for three hours. Refrigerate. Open the can at both ends and
push the caramel slug out like cranberry sauce. Slice and serve with roasted almonds and whipped
cream. It's called "danger pudding" for two reasons. First it's a matter of immediate kitchen
safety – if the water boils out of the pan the closed can will explode. Second, it's about the worst
thing a guy like me can consume given its sugar and dairy ingredients. By the way, if you want
to save some time you can skip the nuts and whipped cream, and just eat it out of the can with a
spoon. Deadly! See Jill Conner Browne's *Sweet Potato Queens Book of Love* (Three Rivers Press:
New York, 1999) for details.

mantra of Wall Street. When Adam Smith published *The Wealth of Nations* in 1776, the market competition concept really took hold. In his book, the Scottish philosopher created perhaps the most influential sentence ever written in English: "By pursuing his own interest he frequently promotes that of the society more effectually than when he really intends to promote it." With a stroke of his pen Smith solved the age-old conundrum of group vs. individual interests. And, through his associates such as Benjamin Franklin, he inseminated that philosophy into the fundamental structure of the most dynamic social system ever devised by mankind. Thus, in no other country on the planet are individualism and competitiveness more highly valued than in the United States.

Unfortunately, almost all business scholars around the country disregard the central nuance in Smith's epiphany. He says *frequently*, not *always* or even *most of the time*. Through his use of the term *frequently*, Smith granted that competitive behavior can have negative consequences for society and organizations, and cooperative behavior can be a good thing. This subtlety in his lesson is most often ignored by our colleagues in the finance departments of our business schools and on Wall Street. Gordon Gekko actually should have said, "Greed is *frequently* good."

Executive decision makers at corporations often describe their fiduciary duty as maximizing shareholder value. Yet the seminal judicial decision expressed in the 1919 *Dodge v. Ford Motor Company* case allows consideration of other responsibilities. That is, the court specifically stated, "a business corporation is organized and carried on *primarily*[1] for the profit of the stockholders." As Smith's use of the word "frequently" is crucial, so is the court's use of "primarily." *Primarily* and *solely* are not synonymous. Indeed, the term "primarily" directly implies an order of things, and here most clearly recognizes the existence of other fiduciary duties, such as corporate social responsibility.

Nor do all CEOs and corporate directors dismiss Smith's subtlety. In Bill George's wonderful book *Authentic Leadership*,[2] he argues that the job of cor-

---

1 Stephen Bainbridge, "Room for Debate: A Duty to Shareholder Value," *New York Times*, April 16, 2015, online.

2 Bill George, *Authentic Leadership* (Jossey-Bass: San Francisco, 2003).

porate chief executive depends on six constituencies. Without surprise, the former CEO of Medtronic lists shareholders, employees, customers, vendors, and the larger community. What is unique, even revolutionary, in his list is his own family.[1] Sir Mark Moody-Stuart, former Chairman of Royal Dutch Shell, comments[2] on the view that corporate executives have a legal fiduciary duty to maximize profits:

> I believe that this is a distortion of the duties of directors. During my years at Shell I was familiar with the Shell Business Principles, promulgated in the 1970s which list obligations to what would now be called stakeholders – customers, employees, governments, and so on The responsibility to shareholders, according to these principles, is to provide an acceptable return to protect the value of their investment. No one has sued us yet, although I suppose in this litigious world it may yet come to that. (page *x*)

Perhaps the most important lessons of corporate governance and the exercise of fiduciary duties in the current century have been harvested from the internal communications of companies regarding their own research on the impacts of their marketing efforts. Much of this new insight has been gained through the government lawsuits against the tobacco companies and their mandated provision of damaging evidence including e-mails and research reports.

Perhaps Nestlé and the other infant formula producers saw in their own data their culpability in the infant formula crisis. Indeed, in accordance with the WHO mandates they began curtailing their marketing efforts while bringing a law suit against their critics. Too bad Nestlé didn't "open its kimono" on the issue of infant formula marketing and consumption earlier, or at least when we requested back in 1989.

---

1 Philip R. Cateora, Mary C. Gilly, John L. Graham, R. Bruce Money, *International Marketing* (McGraw-Hill: New York, 2016, 17th edition).

2 Sir Mark Moody Stuart, "Forward," (ed.) Oliver F. Williamson, *Peace through Commerce: Responsible Corporate Citizenship and the Ideas of the United Nations Global Compact* (University of Notre Dame Press: Notre Dame, IN, 2008).

Organic Chemistry 101

Finally, as a segue to the remainder of the book I have a little quiz for you. Which of these chemicals is the most dangerous for the public health?

$NaCl$ $C_{17}H_{19}NO_3$ $C_{11}H_{15}NO_2$

$C_{12}H_{22}O_{11}$ $C_{21}H_{30}O_2$ $C_{13}H_{16}ClNO$

$C_7H_8N_4O_2$ $C_{17}H_{21}NO_4$ $C_{18}H_{25}NO$

$C_8H_{10}N_4O_2$ $C_4H_4N_2O_3$ $C_{20}H_{25}N_{30}$

$C_{10}H_{14}N_2$ $C_9H_{13}N$ $C_{11}H_{17}NO_3$

C_2H_6O $C_{10}H_{15N}$

Yes, they all look pretty similar – carbon, hydrogen, nitrogen, oxygen and a little sodium and chlorine here and there. Actually, the only kind of person that would appreciate this annoying quiz is someone who teaches organic chemistry, ORGO as my daughter calls it. My point here is that all these spices are simply chemicals – by themselves they have little meaning beyond their ability to attract us humans, or more accurately, just entertain our brains. In any case, I will explain my answer in Chapter 12.

Two

Salt
Primary chemical ingredient: Sodium Chloride, NaCl

*The farther backwards you can look, the
farther forward you are likely to see.*

Winston Churchill

Let the world be sprinkled with salt, not deluged with it.

Carl Jung

Salt was first. It was probably the first spice you tasted. It was certainly the first spice to be marketed. Philip Curtin,[1] an expert on the history of global trade reports for example, "Several interior peoples in tropical Africa... founded their trade diasporas based initially on salt deposits but then moved on to become specialists in long-distance trade in a much greater variety of products." Indeed, going back even further in time, according to Rachel Carson in *The Sea Around Us*,[2] "When the animals went

---

1 Philip D. Curtain, *Cross-Cultural Trade in World History* (Cambridge University Press: Cambridge, 1984).
2 Oxford University Press: Oxford, 2003).

ashore to take up life on land, they carried part of the sea [salt] in their bodies, a heritage which they passed on to their children and which even today links each land animal with its origins in the ancient sea."

Salt is an essential ingredient of the human body. Too little salt, and you may suffer a series of symptoms – diarrhea, reduced urination, a lack of sweating, a general malaise, exhaustion, muscle cramps, headaches, nausea, mental confusion, muscle twitching, seizures, coma, and death. The last one is particularly inconvenient.

However, salt becomes a spice – that is, something you don't need – when you consume more than your body requires for healthy function. The National Academy of Sciences and the Centers for Disease Control (CDC) recommend that average Americans consume a minimum of about **500 mg** of sodium per day. This recommendation is a bit maisleading. It doesn't mean you can just eat some sodium. In its pure, elemental form sodium is a soft white/silver metal that explodes in water – a little on your tongue and you're dead. Take a look at the entertaining *Jackass*-type view of boys throwing sodium into a pond (http://www.youtube.com/watch?v=MTcgo46nxNE) if you doubt my memories from Chemistry 101.

So the only way to safely ingest sodium is in its compounded form. Ninety percent of the sodium consumed is as it combines with chlorine (another poison by itself) and forms sodium chloride, $NaCl$, commonly known as table salt. The other ten percent include items in your pantry such as baking soda, also referred to as sodium bicarbonate or $NaHCO_3$ and sodium benzoate or $NAC_7H_5O_2$, a preservative in many foods.

When you read the back of a bag of Doritos here in the States the government mandated "Nutrition Facts" tell you how many milligrams (mg) of sodium are included in a single serving. Please see Exhibit 2.1 to sort out the differences between salt and sodium, the metric system, and needs versus recommended dosages of salt, and the average American overdose.

Exhibit 2.1
Sorting out Salt, Sodium, and the Metric System*

	mg. sodium	mg. salt	teaspoon salt
Minimum daily needs (everything else is spice, that is, something we want, but don't need)	at least 500 mg	1250 mg	0.2 teaspoon
Maximum daily intake (recommended by the CDC for the nearly 150 million Americans that are older than 51, African American, have high blood pressure, diabetes, or chronic kidney disease)	less than 1500 mg	3750 mg	0.6 teaspoon
Maximum daily intake (recommended by the CDC for the other 150 million American adults not listed in the categories above)	less than 2300 mg	5750 mg	1.0 teaspoon
Average American daily intake (an overdose)	about 3400 mg	8500 mg	1.5 teaspoon

*Please don't confuse sodium and salt. Recall that salt consists of atoms of both sodium (Na, atomic weight = 23) and chlorine (Cl, atomic weight = 35.5). Thus, sodium contributes only about 40% of the weight of any amount of salt.

So that 500 mg of salt you *need* per day translates to about 1250 mg (or a fifth of a teaspoon) per day of salt. But of course, most Americans are not average, so recommended salt consumption varies by individual weight and activity, climate (heat and humidity), and a variety of other factors.

The federal government's new (circa 2011) Dietary Guidelines for Americans is a more generous **2300** mg of sodium per day, or one level teaspoon. Unfortunately, the average American consumes more than 3,400 mg/ per day of sodium. That's almost seven times that required and almost 1.5 times the recommended amount. Excessive consumption of salt **as a spice** also can lead to a series of nasty symptoms – hypertension, asthma, urinary stones, premenstrual syndrome, osteoporosis, edema, congestive heart failure, and, yes, death. And marketing is the primary cause of this excessive consumption.

History

The human race (*homo sapiens*) is about 200,000 years old. We know that for the first 190,000 years our hunter-gatherer ancestors really had no use for salt as a spice. Their daily dietary *needs*, probably that same 1250 mg/day as listed above, was supplied from the their Paleolithic diet of meats, fowl, fish, berries, nuts, greens, and roots.

Just 10,000 years ago humans began to farm and stay in one place. This changed everything. We grew grain and other crops and our meat came from animal husbandry – chickens, pigs, and cattle primarily – and fishing. The crops we harvested delivered no salt. The animals we slaughtered did, but because they were no longer allowed to roam for their own salt, we had to supply it.

A second quality of salt allowed humans to live even more stationary lives. Humans learned that salt could preserve meat and fish, and even human flesh. 5000 years ago Egyptians mummified their dead by gutting them like big tuna and covering them in salt. Because salt attracts the water that supports bacterial growth, the flesh of the humans and meat for consumption dried and did not rot. Storing their dead really didn't help much. But being able to store an ample catch or kill smoothed out the vagaries of climate and allowed for population growth and the formation of cities and nations.

Mark Kurlansky has written the definitive book on the topic – *Salt: A World History*.[1] It's a wonderful read. Of course the salt trade goes back further than recorded history. He tells the fascinating story of Lake Yuncheng in Shanxi Province, China. It's a hot, dry, desert sort of place in northern China. The average high temperature in July is over 90°F. Tourists today commend the fun of floating in the salt lake and the adjacent black mud baths. But, 8000 years ago they killed the tourists there. That is, wars were fought over the salt naturally created in evaporation pools around the ancient lake. Indeed, much older human bones have been found around the lake suggesting salt was gathered there millennia earlier.

So salt's scarcity (the geographical fact that only 5 percent of the land surface of the planet lies within ten miles of a salt supply) brought crowding, wars, and roads. Not only did civilization gather around salt resources, but the trade in salt literally defined patterns and systems of human exchange. The first roads that

---

1 Mark Kurlansky, *Salt, A World History* (Penguin: New York), 2002.

crossed the continents, including the hills and valleys of the United States, started out as mere game paths beaten down by herds traveling to salt sources. Indeed, one of the greatest concentrations of salt in North America is in western New York, near Buffalo. The city's name comes from the great herds of American bison that gathered in the area, supported by the salt at the surface of the earth there.

In 1825 the Erie Canal was completed, primarily to provide cheaply transported salt down the Hudson River for New York City. And from that great harbor salt was transported around the world. Barges loaded with trade goods filled those salt barges on the way back to Buffalo and ultimately the Great Lakes hinterland. This is all reminiscent of perhaps the first paved road in history, the Via Salaria, built by the Romans to bring salt from the marshes and salt works at the Adriatic mouth of the Tiber River. In our modern times, salt also clears our roads during winter snow storms – 25 percetn of salt produced in the United States is used for that purpose.

Scarcities have often been associated with violence. Governments have often sought to control the distribution of salt through monopolies and prices. The Chinese funded the construction of their Great Wall using a salt tax. The French Revolution was in part caused by an unwieldy and unfair tax system on salt called the *gabelle*. The British monopoly of the salt trade yielded not only the Erie Canal as a sort of countervailing American marketing power, but also a Mahatma Gandhi led protest of salt taxes in India in 1930.

Particularly in the 19th century, salt also was a crucial supply element for armies. Horses, men, and meat all needed salt to support the long marches of the time. Among Napoleon's preliminary planning for conquest was the salting of provisions for his marches to Spain, Egypt, and Russia. During the American Civil War prime targets of Union invasions were the coastal salt works of the Confederacy. Another important use of salt in that war was its medicinal qualities for dealing with the garish wounds of the time. The Union blockade became more effective with the destruction of salt-producing resources.

Finally, we cannot leave the topic of salt's history without a brief discussion of its religious, mystical, and cultural qualities. Salt is almost universally held to be sacred, and often it has been imbued with the power of purity. Ancient Greeks consecrated it. Jews offered salt as sacrifice and include it in modern rituals. Covenants have been sealed in salt throughut both books of the Bible. Jesus referred to his disciples at "the salt of the earth." *The Last Supper* by da Vinci depicts Judas spilling a bowl of salt, this an omen of bad luck. Both Christians and Buddhists throw salt over their shoulders for good luck. Salt is used in Shinto, Hindu, and Native American rituals.

In ancient times, salt was associated with life itself – not only in giving immortality to Egyptian pharos but also from the saltiness of sperm. Welsh Jungian psychologist Ernest Jones reported in a 1912 essay:

> In all ages salt has been invested with a significance far exceeding that inherent in its natural properties, interesting and important as these are. Homer calls it a divine substance, Plato describes it as especially dear to the Gods, and we shall presently note the importance attached to it in religious ceremonies, covenants, and magical charms. That this should have been so in all parts of the world and in all times shows that we are dealing with a general human tendency and not with any local custom, circumstance, or notion. [1]

Jones went on to describe the relationship of salt to sex and fertility in Spain, France, Germany, Egypt, Borneo, India, and among Pima tribesmen in the United States. He pointed out that the Romans called an aroused man *salax*, from which the word "salacious" is derived.

Thus, salt has influenced our use of language in deep ways. Places are named for the mineral – Salzburg, Greenwich (*-wich* is an Anglo-Saxon suffix for salt works), and Salt Lake City. The Roman legionnaires were paid in salt, thus the term salary. Salad, sauce, sausage, and salsa are also derivatives of the Latin term *sal*. These lead us directly to the modern importance of salt as a spice.

Consumer Behavior

The history of the salt trade is a story about a necessity. The problem was how to get enough of it, both for the preservation of other foods and for the maintenance of a healthy physiology.

1 Ernest Jones, "The Symbolic Significance of Salt in Folklore and Superstition," an essay in Stanton Marlan (ed.) *Salt and the Alchemical Soul* (Woodstock, CN: Spring), 1995 (originally 1951), pages 1-47.

The modern problem is different. As mentioned previously, according to the CDC the average body needs about 500 mg of sodium per day for healthy physiology. A bowl of Special K with reduced-fat milk, a honey laden piece of wheat toast, and a glass of low-sodium V8 juice delivers a bit more than that. That's all you need for the day. Any other salt you consume that day is strictly a matter of spice, not necessity. Want, not need. In fact, if you happen to break your fast at Denny's and choose their Lumberjack Slam containing about two teaspoons of salt you've got your required sodium for the whole week, that is, if you don't sweat or urinate.[1]

Salt consumption varies around the 1.5 teaspoon average along with a variety of demographic and geographic variables, such as body weight, gender, age, ambient air temperature and humidity. Culture appears to play a role too. As can be seen in Exhibit 2.2 Japanese, Chinese, and Finns consume more than Americans, for example. Only in Kenya is the average sodium intake at a healthful level among the selected comparators. The consumption in Kazakhstan makes the other, dangerous end of the scale that includes 187 countries.

Exhibit 2.2
Comparing Sodium Consumption around the World 2010

Country	mg/day	Country	mg/day	
Kazakhstan	5980	UK	3610	
Japan	4890	US	3600	
China	4830	India	3580	
Italy	4420	Germany	3540	
Brazil	4110	Netherlands	3320	
Finland	3850	Saudi Arabia	3200	↑dangerous amounts for
France	3770	--------------------	-----	some, unhealthful for all
UAE	3670	Cuba	2640	
Sweden	3650	Kenya	1480	

Source: The best international data on salt and sodium consumption by country can be found in John Powels et al., *Global Regional and national sodium intakes in 1990 and 2010*; "A Systematic Analysis of 24 h Urinary Sodium Excretion and Dietary Surveys Worldwide," *BMJ Open*, 3, 2013, online, pages 1-19. The measuring methods are reflected in the title.

1 Much of the excess salt we consume is eliminated from the body via urination or perspiration.

Most of the salt we consume is as a hedonic compound. Mostly what salt does as a spice is to hide bitterness. Or to put it another way, salt enhances the flavor of almost everything. Later in the chapter we will discuss in some detail the current controversy over these numbers, but the common theme of this book – that excess consumption of spices is bad for both individuals and the public health – holds true for salt.

The creepiest aspect of the salt story has just become clear in the last few years – salt addiction. Michael Moss makes the point concisely in his tome:

> The craving people get for salt [can be] at levels so high it causes disease…While at Frito-Lay, [Robert] Lin and other company scientists spoke openly about the country's excessive consumption of sodium and the fact that, as Lin said to me on more than one occasion, "people get addicted to salt."[1]

Dr. Robert I-San Lin was the chief scientist at Frito-Lay between 1974 and 1982 and Moss adds another pithy quote from Dr. Lin on the topic of salt: "I feel so sorry for the public." The brain scanning and other scientific evidence for Lin's assertion that the hedonic consumption of salt can be addictive (similar to sex, opium, and cocaine) is stacking up.[2] Moreover, at least one study has shown that the hedonic consumption of salt is a learned behavior, and infants and children are particularly susceptible to the problem.[3]

Corporations teaching kids to consume hedonic molecules will come up again in the book, particularly with respect to coffee and caffeine in Chapter

---

1 Michael Moss, *Salt, Sugar, Fat* (New York: Random House), 2013, page 305.

2 See M.J. Morris, E.S. Na, and A.K. Johnson, "Salt Craving: The Psychobiology of Pathogenic Sodium Intake," *Physiology & Behavior*, 95(4), August 2008, pages 709-21; and W.B. Liedtke, et al., "Relation of Addiction Genes to Hypothalamic Gene Changes Subserving Genesis and Gratification of a Classic Instinct," *Proceedings of the National Academy of Sciences*, 108(30), July 26, 2011, pages 12509-14. I note with some humor that the second author of the first article above is Dr. Na!

3 Leslie J. Stein, Beverly J. Cowart, and Gary K. Beauchamp, "The Development of Salty Taste Acceptance Is Related to Dietary Experiences in Human Infants: A Prospective Study," *American Journal of Clinical Nutrition*, 95(1), January 2012, pages 123-129.

5. The good news in the salt-addiction story is that the hedonic consumption of salt can be licked (pun intended). At least one scientist working in the area found that the amount craved associated with high salt consumption faded away after <u>twelve weeks</u>. At the end of the period subjects' taste buds became more sensitive and required half the salt for the same sensory stimulation.[1]

For completeness we now briefly turn to the consumption (or production) of salt at the macroeconomic level. Of the more than 277 million metric tons of salt produced globally, the major producers are China (72 million), the United States (45 million), Germany (19 million), India (17 million), Australia (13 million), and the rest of the world (~100 million). Because production costs are generally quite low, the primary cost of salt is in its delivery. Thus, many nations produce what they need or buy from nearby sources.

Eighty percent of the salt produced in the United States is from five states – Louisiana, Texas, New York, Kansas, and Utah in that order. More than seventy percent of the salt produced in the US is by five companies – Cargill, Morton International, North American Salt, American Rock Salt, and Detroit Salt.

Of the 55+ million metric tons of salt produced in and imported to the US about 47 percent is used as feed stock for industrial chemicals (for example, plastic, paper, glass, polyester, rubber, fertilizers, bleach, soaps, and dyes), 4 percent as ingredients in water conditioning, 25 percent in road deicing, and 5 percent in agriculture.[2] Only 5 percent is food-grade and is used in that industry. Actually, salt has uses in the food industry beyond flavor enhancement. It is also used as a preservative (in curing, color enhancement, and extending shelf life) and as an emulsion, water-binding, and texturizing agent.

Marketing

I mentioned in the last chapter the *4Ps* of marketing: product, place (distribution), price, and promotion.

---

1 Moss, pages 283-4.

2 Most of these statistics are taken from the US Geological Survey, *2011 Minerals Yearbook* (Department of the Interior: Washington, DC), 2013.

Product. Most of the salt we consume is the ordinary table sort, whether from mines or evaporation ponds around the country. It's well represented by the blue cylinder of Morton salt you probably have sitting in your cupboard. It includes a bit of calcium silicate to prevent caking – so it pours. You may have the iodized version. Sometimes iodine compounds are added for people or places that are deficient in that nutrient.

Then there is the expensive gourmet stuff. The clearly hedonic compounds. They're mostly versions of sea salt in differing textures, that deliver unique taste characteristics via their local chemicals where they're produced and/or their granulation. The popular varieties include coarse salt, finishing salt, flake salt, fleur de sel, grey salt, grinder salt, kosher, organic, smoked sea salt, kala namak (from India), and French, Hawaiian, and Italian sea salts. Colors range from white to pink to red to black. But my favorite form is Himalayan Pink salt blocks. It looks much like a chunk of marble, white with pink ribbons. You can buy it in a variety of shapes including cookware, tableware, and even shot glasses for tequila shooters, or a nine-by-nine-by-two-inch block on which to serve sliced apples and other hors d'oeuvres. The food and drink touching the block delicately absorb the enhancers and subtle flavors.

Most recently salt producers such as Cargill and their food-industry customers have been experimenting with different forms of salt crystals and other technologies toward reducing the amount consumed while delivering the same flavor-enhancement characteristics. It ends up that the majority of salt on the typical potato chip is simply swallowed without effect in the mouth. Finer grinds have been shown to deliver the taste with less salt. Other innovations that seem to help are changes to the crystal structure, mock salts, potassium chloride (KCl), and multiple emulsions. Yum!

In 2010 Pepsi told investors that such techniques may open up new salt-averse markets such as school lunchrooms, but so far the innovations have mostly stayed in the lab. We quote from an article in the *Wall Street Journal* in that year:

> The ingredient is a new "designer salt" whose crystals are shaped and
> sized in a way that reduces the amount of sodium consumers ingest

when they munch. PepsiCo hopes the powdery salt, which it is still studying and testing with consumers, will cut sodium levels 25 percent in its Lay's Classic potato chips. The new salt could help reduce sodium levels even further in seasoned Lay's chips like Sour Cream & Onion, PepsiCo said, and it could be used in other products like Cheetos and Quaker bars.[1]

And apparently PepsiCo has produced on its promises to investors. Four company employees report in the *Stanford Journal of Public Health*, a student-run journal:

Reducing sodium intake will require consumer demand for reduced sodium products in addition to action from governments, the media, and industry. PepsiCo has pledged to reduce sodium by 25 percent in key global food brands in key markets by 2015 (with a 2006 baseline), and has successfully reduced sodium in products in many countries without compromising product taste. Much of this reduction is stealth, and not directly communicated to the public to prevent consumers from rejecting the product based on preconceptions of poor taste. In the U.K., Walkers has significantly reduced sodium in its products since 2005. In 2011, Frito-Lay in the US reduced sodium by nearly 25 percent, on average, across its entire flavored potato chip portfolio. In Canada, Quaker instant oats products have been reformulated with a 15 percent to 25 percent reduction in salt. In Brazil, sodium was reduced in one of PepsiCo's most popular snacks, Fandangos, by more than 30 percent. The public health impact of reducing sodium levels in PepsiCo's portfolio is limited by the amount of sodium PepsiCo products contribute to the diet.[2]

---

1 Betsy McKay, "PepsiCo Develops 'Designer Salt' to Chip away at Sodium Intake," *Wall Street Journal*, March 22, 2010, online.

2 Eleanore Alexander, Derek Yach, George A. Mensah, and Gregroy L. Yep, (Stealth Prevention: PepsiCo Tackles Salt as NCD Prevention Strategy," *Stanford Journal of Public Health*, May 22, 2012, online.

Most of this is wonderful news. The company has even made progress with its world's best seller. In 1986 one ounce of Lay's Classic potato chips contained 200 mg of sodium, in 2010 180 mg, and in 2013 170 mg. But I find very disturbing the self-proclaimed "stealth" of PepsiCo's actions. Certainly in the business schools we teach the importance of maintaining competitive advantage. Indeed, beyond holding close to the vest their trade secrets, perhaps PepsiCo and Cargill have also applied for patents, and so on to protect their innovations in manufacturing technology? But the public health is more important than corporate competitive advantage. When Jonas Salk was asked by Edward R. Morrow, "Who owns the patent on this [polio] vaccine?" Salk famously responded, "Well, the people, I would say. There is no patent. Could you patent the sun?" PepsiCo, Cargill, and the others should be sharing this technology widely, even with their competitors. There are many other ways to compete without holding hostage the public's health.

Place (Distribution). The salt companies listed above distribute their products via three types of firms: food retailers (salt for your table and/or your recipes at home), food processors (as an ingredient in the meat, cheese, and bread you buy), and restaurants. The CDC reports that of the salt consumed by Americans, 65 percent enters our diet from processed food purchased in retail stores, 25 percent from restaurant meals, 6 percent is added at the table (salt shakers), and only 5 percent during home cooking. They continue, "Many foods that contribute a significant amount of sodium in the diet do not taste particularly salty, such a breads and cheeses. Some of these foods are deceptively high in salt; others are lower in salt content but frequently consumed."

Among the foods that deliver the most salt to Americans the big three are no surprise: sandwiches, burgers, and pizzas (totaling 25 percent). It's perhaps more than a coincidence that the word sand<u>wich</u> has the Anglo Saxon suffix for salt imbedded in it. A McDonald's Quarter Pounder with Cheese, a Subway Philly-Cheese Steak Sandwich, and a Carl's Junior Santa Fe Chicken Sandwich all include about a half teaspoon of salt. As far as I can tell, Carl's 1/2lb. Thickburger El Diablo is the fast-food champion of salt at over one teaspoon (2790 mg of sodium). The Cheesecake Factory delivers a 4379 mg Bacon-Bacon Cheeseburger. Lord only knows how much salt is in the Burgerizza at the Atlanta Braves stadium – it's a $26 bacon cheeseburger sandwiched between two eight-inch pepperoni pizzas. Most surprising to me, corn and potato chips aren't so bad. They're responsible for only putting 2 percent of the salt in American diets.[1] We will return to this last point in the next chapter on sugar. Other ingredients, such as sugar, render chips another kind of culprit.[2]

Price. You might say that table salt is dirt cheap at about 60¢ per pound in the dark blue cylinder of Morton's you find on your grocery shelf. There's not anything in the store much cheaper. If you're PepsiCo the salt you buy for your Doritos is less than 10¢ per pound or $200 per ton. It would be interesting to know the costs associated with the modified salts used in PepsiCo's new Doritos formulations. But remember, they're holding their cards close to the vest on this "stealth" innovation. Morton's Kosher sits on the supermarket shelf at about $1.15 per pound, their Mediterranean sea salt $2.50 per pound, and their Lite Salt (about ½ KCl by weight) $4.25 per pound. The designer salt prices are all over the place. On the Internet you can order the nine-by-nine-by-two-inch block of Himalayan Pink for $56.

We should mention that prices vary for bulk salt according to world prices and particularly the severity of winters. A blizzard in Chicago requires tons of the stuff to help clear the roads. Global warming forces the producers to worry about declining sales particularly in the United States where about 25 percent is for road deicing. That business is already quite volatile from year to year.

Of course, the food processors use price promotions (coupons, deals, and so on) as marketing tactics in the supermarkets. But such marketing decisions are based mostly on competitive factors, not the cost of their cheapest ingredient.

Finally, if we apply the 60¢ to the 2.75 million metric ton of food grade salt sold in the United States that gives us a total annual market value of about $3.6 billion.

---

1 *Strategies to Reduce Sodium Intake in the United States* (The National Academies Press: Washington, DC), 2013.
2 Moss, pages 328-9.

Promotion. We described in the last chapter that promotional decisions and expenditures made by marketing executives are primarily about personal selling and advertising. Promotion also subsumes sales promotions (things like free samples and event sponsorship) and public relations.

The firms involved in marketing spices are all very concerned about negative publicity and public relations. But, while the biggest companies spend billions on advertising, they only spend tens of millions on public relations. In many cases, some of those PR or perhaps their R&D (PepsiCo spends about $500 million a year on R&D) dollars go to support "scientific" studies that cast doubt on mainstream public health research findings. We will revisit this nasty little practice in coming chapters. Of course, other kinds of PR expenditures also help the corporations in often unsavory ways – lobbying and political contributions. In the 2012 campaign cycle PepsiCo spent over $4 million on lobbying and political donations on both sides of the aisle, including $35,000 to Obama and $25,000 to Romney.

The salt producers, such as Cargill and Morton, both advertise to their food industry customers, but almost exclusively in trade publications. Most of their promotional dollars go to their sales forces that make calls on the food distribution and processing companies. *Modern Family*, the ABC TV hit, is well known for its product placement advertising including that by Toyota, Audi, and an entire show built around the then new Apple iPad. As I was writing this chapter this faithful Pritchard clan fan noticed two separate segments where salting chocolate milk was featured. Perhaps Cargill at work? Perhaps it was just my imagination?

Alternatively, the food processors and restaurant chains spend big bucks on attracting customers to their salted products. Consider the power of the advertising budgets of those in the top twenty corporations in the world: Nestlé $2.9 billion, Kraft $2+ billion, McDonald's $1.6 billion, PepsiCo only $2.1 billion.[1] See the 2016 Super Bowl lineup of salted products in Exhibit 2.3 – PepsiCo is the clear Super Bowl winner.

---

1 *Advertising Age*, 2012.

Exhibit 2.3
2016 Super Bowl Advertising of Salted Products

Company	Product	Spend	Sodium in single serving
AB-InBev	Budweiser	$35 million	9-20 mg
Coca-cola	Coke	$10 million	45 mg
Heinz	BBQ sauce	$5 million	390 mg
Mars	Skittles	$5 million	10 mg
Mexican Avocados		$5 million	80 mg
Nestlé	Butterfinger	$5 million	100 mg
PepsiCo	Doritos	$5 million	210 mg
	PepsiCola	$5 million (+ halftime show)	30 mg
Taco Bell	Quesalupa	$5 million	890 mg

Source: *Advertising Age*, 2016.

Consequences of Consumption

So most Americans overdose on salt. The US Centers for Disease Control (CDC) specifically state the following:

1. As sodium intake rises, so does blood pressure.
2. High blood pressure increases the risk for heart disease and stroke.
3. If all Americans followed the recommended limits for sodium, national rates for high blood pressure would drop by a quarter, saving tens of thousands of lives per year.
4. Reducing average population sodium intake to 1500 mg/day may save $26 billion in health care dollars and reduce cases of hypertension by sixteen million.

The CDC's statements combined with my comments about marketing presume the following causal chain:

1   2   3   4

marketing (4 Ps) → *salt consumption* → *hypertension* → *CVD* → *premature deaths and lost $s*

There is a great deal of scientific evidence to support most of these causal presumptions. Certainly most medical experts would agree with relations 2, 3, and 4 above. Regarding relationship 1 above, it is an axiom in marketing that consumption is in part caused by marketing. Indeed, PepsiCo has demonstrated that developing and using different forms of salt (that is, changing the product) leads people to consume less salt while not affecting sales of their potato chips. Thus, it is logical to conclude that reducing the marketing efforts for salt will improve the public health and reduce the associated health care expenses.

Of course, not everyone agrees with this thinking. For example, take the Salt Institute, "a North American based non-profit trade association dedicated to advancing the many benefits of salt particularly to ensure winter roadway safety, quality water, and healthy nutrition."[1] They maintain, "A growing body of research shows salt is GOOD for you, but LOW-salt diets may HARM you" [in the original capitalization]. They cite their own set of scientific research, with which the CDC experts would not disagree. But, the Salt Institute, which is supported by the salt sellers' profits, is entirely mute on the question of the negative health and economic impacts of salt overdosing. Shame on their strategy of trampling the truth via their strategic omissions. They and their salt-producing contributors apparently missed the word "frequently" in Adam Smith's "invisible hand" statement.

As of this writing, things have gotten a bit strange with respect to mainstream scientific opinion on recommended limits on salt consumption. Please recognize that another important health authority, the World Health Organization (WHO) recommends adults consume no more than 2000 mg sodium/day. In 2013 the CDC commissioned a committee of the Institute of Medicine (IOM), a division of the National Academy of Sciences to review the scientific evidence on consumption rates below 1500 mg/day. Credible studies were demonstrating negative impacts of

---

1 See Salt Institute.com.

consumption rates too low. The IOM is right in the middle of the mainstream of American healthcare sciences – a most credible, unbiased source. The IOM committee[1] came back with conclusions that the CDC does not like.

1. Reducing sodium intake to less than 1500 mg/day for the 150 million Americans in the "at risk groups" listed in Exhibit 2.2 – those fifty-one and older, and so on – is not supported by the evidence.
2. The IOM committee still agrees that 3400 mgs/day of sodium is too much. But, they see no evidence supporting the 2300 mg/day CDC recommendation.

The CDC has so far disputed the IOM recommended changes in their consumption guidelines. This is much more than an acrimonious dispute between acronyms. But, what numbers are finally agreed to among the scientific groups, the bottom line is simply that *Americans on average consume too much salt*. This provides the segue to the next topic – how best to reduce that consumption.

Exhibit 2.2
Comparing Sodium Consumption around the World 2010

Country	mg/day	Country	mg/day	
Kazakhstan	5980	UK	3610	
Japan	4890	US	3600	
China	4830	India	3580	
Italy	4420	Germany	3540	
Brazil	4110	Netherlands	3320	
Finland	3850	Saudi Arabia	3200	↑dangerous amounts for
France	3770	--------------------	-----	some, unhealthful for all
UAE	3670	Cuba	2640	
Sweden	3650	Kenya	1480	

Source: The best international data on salt and sodium consumption by country can be found in John Powels et al., *Global Regional and national sodium intakes in 1990 and 2010*; "A Systematic Analysis of 24 h Urinary Sodium Excretion and Dietary Surveys Worldwide," *BMJ Open*, 3, 2013, online, pages 1-19. The measuring methods are reflected in the title.

1 *Sodium Intake in Populations, Assessment of Evidence*, Institute of Medicine (Washington, DC), 2012. Also see Theodore A. Kotchen, "The Salt Discourse in 2013," *American Journal of Hypertension*, 26(10), 2013, and the associated pages commentaries on both sides of the controversy, pages 1177-1200.

Ways to Control/Reduce Salt Consumption

Fortunately we have a 500-page tome on the topic produced by another blue-ribbon committee of the IOM in 2010 under the title of *Strategies to Reduce Sodium Intake in the United States*. I do find two points of concern in reviewing the makeup of the committee. First, there are no Transformative Consumer Research (TCR) marketing experts included. This is a surprising omission. Second, including Dwight Riskey (according to Michael Moss,[1] a genius at selling salted products for PepsiCo for twenty-five years) on the panel of reviewers of the report certainly adds to the balance of the group. It also seems a bit risky because folks with long success in industry are frequently [I use this adverb for its irony] biased in unsavory ways and they are excellent persuaders that can dominate a largely academic group.

I love the beginning of the report:

> While numerous stakeholders have initiated voluntary efforts to reduce sodium consumption in the United States during the past 40 years, they have not succeeded.

The report makes three fundamental recommendations:

1. The US Food and Drug Administration should establish a national standard for salt content in foods and monitor progress.
2. The industry should voluntarily act to reduce the sodium content ahead of the standards.
3. Other government agencies and NGOs should support these efforts.

The problem with these recommendations is their obvious obsolescence. Five-hundred pages and about all they recommend is more of the same formula for failure of the last forty years. Really?

I do find two parts of the report very interesting, yes, even humorous. First, among the challenges to change reported is, "Food industry representatives at the public workshop also said that sodium reductions that create

---

1 Moss page 216-320.

changes in product taste will result in a loss of market share to competitors' more flavorful products" (page 167). This statement implies two things: (1) market share is more important to corporation than the public health; and (2) this screams for government regulation to level the competitive playing field. Even more intriguing is the explanation why a salt tax is a bad idea:

> Public policy advocates have recently been making the case for insti- tuting taxes on certain foods that are suspected to be leading causes of obesity. These types of taxes, often referred to as "sin taxes," are typically excise (i.e., per-unit) taxes imposed on particular products that are believed to be harmful to society. By increasing the prices that consumers pay for these potentially harmful products, this theory suggests that consumers will reduce their purchases, substitute more healthful alternatives, and thus improve public health. Although these taxes are typically proposed for foods such as calorically sweetened beverages and high-fat snacks to reduce their consumption due to concerns about obesity, it has also been suggested that foods high in sodium could be taxed to reduce their consumption due to concerns about diseases associated with high sodium intake. There is insuffi- cient evidence to demonstrate the effectiveness of a sodium tax or to ensure that it will not result in unintended consequences. Past research has shown that consumers are not very responsive to small changes in food prices (i.e., food prices are relatively inelastic). Thus, *the tax rate on high-sodium foods would have to be fairly substantial* to induce a sufficiently large change in food purchases in order to have a major influence on health. This has already been demonstrated by the fact that states that have implemented taxes on soft drinks have not seen a substantial effect on sales. Furthermore, if consumers do alter their purchasing patterns in response to the tax, it is uncertain whether they would substitute more healthful alternatives. The issue of substitution is even more of a concern for a salt tax because sodium is an ingredient in numerous foods, some of which are otherwise nu- tritious. This is in contrast to a targeted tax on particular products

such as sugar-sweetened beverages that have no nutritional benefits. Finally, *sales taxes in general are regressive and affect lower-income households disproportionately* more than higher-income households, which could have the unintended consequence of crowding out purchases of other more healthful products and activities. Thus, given these concerns, other recommended strategies have the potential for a more direct reduction of sodium intake without the potential for unintended consequences on other purchase decisions by households. (pages 248-249).[1]

I include this argument in its entirety as a great example of academic mumbo jumbo. While it sounds like good research-based analysis, its mistakes of omission render it stupid. Why would anyone spend all this print and paper to argue against a consumer salt tax. Such a beast has always pissed-off consumers, and even caused national insurrections. No, you don't tax the consumers, you tax the food processors and restaurants as suggested by studies omitted by the IOM.[2] You make their use of unhealthful amounts of salt unprofitable. The Morton's twenty-six ounce blue cylinder would remain at 99¢ on the grocery shelf. Increase by ten-fold the price per ton to the corporations, the PepsiCos and McDonalds of the world. They can afford it.

Unintended consequences are a gamble in all innovations and policy changes. Such unintended consequences can be good or bad, particularly for one group versus another. Because we don't know what they are, that makes the odds for good or bad consequences about even. But the salient point here is that the current consequences are awful — tens of thousands of avoidable American deaths and billions of dollars in healthcare costs per year.

---

1   I italicized two key statements. I eliminated the research citations to make the segment more readable. You can easily find them in the IOM report, Strategies to Reduce Sodium Intake..., 2010 cited above.

2   Crystal M. Smith-Spangler, Jessie L. Juusola, Eva A. Enns, Douglas K. Owens, and alan M. Garber, "Population Strategies to Decrease Sodium Intake and the Burden of Cardiovascular Disease," *Annals of Internal Medicine,* 152(8), April 2010, pages 481-487.

Finally, I laud the IOM reporting of success stories in other countries. The successes in Canada and European countries are mostly a matter of labeling regulations, government public health advertising, and some industry collaboration. In Ireland regulations were passed in 2013 to control advertising of salt and other products. It will be quite useful to follow the efficacy of such approaches.

Marketing Miscreants

I close each individual spice chapter with a fun feature I call "Marketing Miscreants." I thought about calling it the "Gordon Gekko Award" or the "Anti-Salk Award," but I clearly want to place the blame on marketers and their often unvarnished greed.

It ends up that even marketers (I am one) have a code of ethics. It's imbedded in the AMA (American Marketing Association) definition. Like most such statements this has evolved over the years. Circa 2016 the AMA website specifies: **"Marketing is the activity, set of institutions, and processes for creating, communicating, delivering, and exchanging offerings that have value for customers, clients, partners, and society at large.** (Approved July 2013)" In this discussion "communicating" and "value for customers" are key terms. As the *Webster's* definition implies, some Marketing Miscreants are just ruthless, others are law breakers.

When I started this chapter, having just read Michael Moss's excellent book I was focused on choosing PepsiCo's Roger Enrico[1] for the Salt chapter. He headed Frito-Lay in the early 1990s, just after experiencing a heart attack while in Turkey. As chip king of the world he did "encourage the creation of more healthful snacks." But, he also worked with food-marketing genius Dwight Riskey to substantially bump PepsiCo's market share and the overall consumption of salty snacks. Indeed, I wonder if the combination of his successes in increasing salt consumption and his own heart attack helped him make the decision to leave operations at PepsiCo and instead teach management in company training programs? Ultimately he did become CEO of

---

1   See www.notablebiographies.com, find Roger Enrico.

PepsiCo during 1996-2001. And, as I mentioned earlier, the salt content of Lay's Classic Potato Chips was reduced during his executive tenures. Finally, I also realized that with regard to salt, PepsiCo and their chips are not the primary problem. The salt load in sandwiches is. So Mr. Enrico is off the hook.

Marketing Miscreant – Salt

Andrew Puzder has served as CEO of CKE Restaurants since 2000. Carl's Jr. and Hardee's are under his purvey. Carl's Jr. markets the saltiest sandwich among the top-ten fast food companies, the aforementioned 1/2lb. Thickburger El Diablo. The ingredients include "Black Angus burger, Jalapeno Poppers, Pepper-Jack Cheese, Fiery Havanero Sauce, Bacon Strips and Sliced Jalapenos on a Fresh Baked Bun." That's 2790 mg sodium. The CDC recommends no more than 2300mg. Indeed, one wonders how soon the burger will carry New York City's newly mandated warning label[1] for such salt bombs? Value? Nutrition? Healthful?

How about communication? Communication implies information. The ads I assume are approved by Mr. Puzder deliver a lot more than information. The juxtaposition of their Spicy BBQ Six Dollar Burger and a most salacious Paris Hilton in a skimpy black swim suit straddling a black Bentley rubbing herself with a soap soaked sponge and holding a squirting hose was perhaps the first to associate getting sex and eating a hamburger. The 2005 airing of the ad on sports programs, *Desperate Housewives*, *The O.C.*, and *The Apprentice* caused an uproar. The Parent Television Council's Research Director, Melissa Caldwell complained, "This commercial is basically softcore porn..." Puzder's response at the time was a miscreant classic: "This isn't Janet Jackson – there is no nipple in this. There is no nudity, there is no sex acts – it's a beautiful model in a swimsuit washing a car." [2] The ad is on YouTube.com: you can be the judge. I'd vote for Caldwell's interpretation.

---

1   Benjamin Mueller and Michael M. Grynmaum, "Health Board Back Warning of Menu Items with High Salt Content," *New York Times*, September 10, 2016,page A26.

2   Caleb Silver, "No Apologies for Sexy Paris Hilton Ad," *CNNMoney*, June 1, 2005, online.

What would really be interesting is to see Puzder's correspondence with the ad agency. Also, I note that *The O.C.* premiere in 2003 delivered very nicely in the twelve to seventeen audience bracket.[1]

You might excuse this one ad as Puzder's mistake? It must have sold hamburgers, because he's continued the campaign. Perhaps part of the appeal is the very Freudian and subconscious association between salt and sex mentioned earlier in the chapter. The 2013 installment showed super-model Heidi Klum as a Mrs. Robinson in a *Graduate* sort of character, seducing a young man with Carl's Jim Beam Bourbon Burger. Now Puzder is implying with the ad, "If you eat a Carl's Jr. burger, you get not only sex but also alcohol."[2] And he's saying it to kids. How old do you think the boy is in the ad? You can see his pubescent mustache attempt on YouTube.com. Also, on the topic of marketing to kids Puzder admits, "We decided the people we wanted to target were young, hungry guys. You set your target at a group that is cool or appealing and you get a much broader scope of people. We target hungry guys, and we get young kids that want to be young hungry guys."[3]

Kids, booze, sex, and salt – Pudzer's miscreant mix.

---

1   de Moraes, Lisa "The Beautiful People of 'O.C.' Deliver Some Ugly Numbers," *The Washington Post*, August 7, 2003, online.

2   In a more recent campaign the company now hawks a Moonshine Burger. Really?

3   Stephanie Clifford, "Carl's Jr. Tries to Go After the Young, and Hungry, Skateboarding Fan," *New York Times*, March 17, 2009, online.

Three

SUGAR[1]
**Primary chemical ingredient: sucrose and/
or high-fructose corn syrup, $C_{12}H_{22}O_{11}$**

If I don't die of a heart attack, that means I left pie on the table.

Sugar is my addiction. I have to blame my mother (or perhaps Mother Nature) for developing it. I was breast fed.[2] The first few days after my birth my mom's breasts produced colostrum, which gradually changed to mature breast milk. Colostrum is watery and very sweet. After three to four days it becomes thicker and creamier. Breast milk not only quenches thirst and hunger, it provides the proteins, *sugar*, minerals, and antibodies babies need. But the sweet taste is there from the very beginning. The sweetness gets the newborn's attention, creating a craving for the breast. The nutrition and mother-child bonding favors survival. Breast feeding has also served the maternal bonding by separating births – a return to fertility and ovulation is often delayed for the period lactation.

---

1 The two most important books on this topic are Robert H. Lustig, *Fat Chance: Beating the Odds against Sugar, Processed Food, Obesity, and Disease* (Penguin: New York, 2012; and John Yudkin, *Pure, White, and Deadly: How Sugar is Killing Us and What We Can Do about It* (Penguin: New York, 1972, 1986). In my conversations with him Robert Lustig praises Yudkin's prescience. I agree.

2 Some argue that eating habits are determined in the womb!

Upon weaning our nourishment comes from our diet. Of course, Gerber's baby foods include sugar as an ingredient. Also, you may recall from the Introduction that my mother and I also bonded at the ice cream parlor. The correct balance of nutrients (carbohydrates, fats, fiber, protein, minerals, and vitamins) is essential. Salt is a mineral, sugar a carbohydrate. Carbohydrates provide fuel to the cells and body. Our bodies literally burn them, breaking down and mixing them with the oxygen we breathe yielding water and carbon dioxide, much like chopped wood in your fireplace. Glucose ($C_6H_{12}O_6$) or blood sugar is derived from digestion of the more complex carbohydrates (see Exhibit 3.1 below) and it directly fuels the muscles and importantly brain functions.

Exhibit 3.1
The Vocabulary of Sugars

Almost all sugars (also called carbohydrates) share the general chemical formula $C_nH_{2n}O_n$. While simple sugars share a common formula $C_6H_{12}O_6$, their chemical structures differ affecting their reactions in the body.

Monosaccharides (simple sugars), all three $C_6H_{12}O_6$
Glucose (dextrose or blood sugar), from fruits and plant juices and the body breaking down compound sugars and starches
Fructose, from fruits, sugarcane, honey, hydrolyzed cornstarch
Galactose, from milk

Disaccharides (compound sugars) $C_{12}H_{22}O_{11}$
Sucrose (table sugar), glucose-fructose linked, from sugarcane and sugar beets, on your table
HFCS (high-fructose corn syrup), glucose-fructose linked, from corn
Maltose, glucose-glucose linked, from grains
Maltitol, a hydrogenated form of maltose, a "sugar alcohol" with a formula of $C_{12}H_{24}O_{11}$
Lactose, glucose-galactose linked, from milk

Polysaccharides (starches), corn, potatoes, wheat, rice, complex chains of simple sugars

---

In prehistoric times, fishing, hunting, and gathering provided all the essential nutrients. The salt and carbohydrates (starches and sugars) came from the plants and animals we killed and ate. Widespread farming, circa 10,000

BC, began to change the nutritional balance, lengthening life while yielding worse health.[1] Then around AD 1500 refined sugar entered the global diet and the public's health took a steep nosedive. Even as our longevity continues to increase, the fifty-year-old of today is much more likely to be obese and suffer from cardiovascular disease and diabetes than the fifty-year-old of just fifty years ago. Why?

We are designed to thrive without refined sugar in our diet. Yes, our distant ancestors evolving on the East African savannah occasionally enjoyed the sweetness of seasonal fruits or perhaps honey. But neither was necessary for good health. Almost all the carbohydrates humans consumed were in the form of meats, fruits, and roots. While glucose is essential, sugar has always been a hedonic compound, a matter of wanting, but not needing. Moreover, eliminating 22.7 teaspoons of refined sugar from your daily diet – the average American consumption – would, without question, make you remarkably more vital. Of course, that's easy to say. For a little fun you might watch John Oliver's take on the topic: https://www.youtube.com/watch?v=MepXBJjsNxs.

History

So sugar has always been around. Unlike the wars and riots over salt, nobody ever killed anyone for the sake of sugar, at least not directly. Sugar became a villain when it was refined from sugarcane into sucrose, the crystalized white stuff on your kitchen table.

The first historical reference to sugarcane dates back to the 8th century BC in China. The paleobotanists tell us that the cane was native to Southeast Asia (India and New Guinea). The Indians during the fifth-century reign of the Imperial Guptas first refined the juice into white crystals making it easier to store and ship. They called it *khanda*, thus the derivation of our word "candy." Once the Chinese got hold of the recipe during a trade mission to India in about 647, the business really took off in South Asia and the Middle East.

---

1 Spencer Wells, *Pandora's Seed: The Unforeseen Cost of Civilization* (New York: Random House), 2010. seed.

Spiced

The Europeans' first taste is reported by the chroniclers of Alexander the Great's incursions into India in the fourth century BC. But, Europe was a most primitive place, and generally without the frost free climates sugarcane demands. In the twelfth century the Crusaders brought sugar home and the Venetians dominated the European trade before the voyages of Columbus.

In California fourth graders focus on the state's history, beginning with the Native American experience there. California history is a hobby of mine and I was drafted by my son's teacher to talk about Columbus, Cortez, and the discovery of California. Most folks think the goal was gold. But, the greater motivation of European exploration and exploitation of the Americas was the pleasures of the palate – spices.

Now how to make this point to forth graders? I made silver-dollar-sized pancakes and served them, asking for their opinion. Without syrup they weren't well received. Then I served up a homemade Toll House chocolate-chip cookie to each. Yes, the sugar got their attention and goodwill. The lesson, the Spaniards did get their gold and silver, but even more important, they got the vanilla, chocolate, and sugar that went into the cookies "you just ate."

I might have also read the following passage to make my point about the European sweet tooth of the time, but I thought it a bit strong for fourth graders: Paul Hentzner, a German visitor described Queen Elizabeth I in 1595 [1]: "Her face oblong, fair but wrinkled, her eyes small, yet black and pleasant, her nose a little hooked, her lips narrow and her teeth black, a defect the English seem subject to, from their too great use of sugar."

More precisely, what the European powers gained from their colonization of the West Indies and Brazil was the land and climate they needed to cultivate sugarcane, independent of the Muslim and Asian masters of the spice trade. The consequent carnage of the Native American populations by cannon, muskets, measles, and pox is well known. The European solution to the lack of local labor and demands of growing and harvesting sugarcane in the tropics of the Americas was a second carnage. West African slavery.

---

1   From Paul Hentzner, from www.britannia.com/history/docs/hentzner.html, printed in William J. Bernstein's excellent book, *A Splendid Exchange: How Trade Shaped the World* (New York: Grove Press), 2008, 207.

Sugar

During the three centuries of the triangle of trade – manufactured goods to Africa, slaves to the Americas, sugar and rum to Europe – some 12 million Africans were enslaved and shipped. About 2.2 million (18 percent) died from starvation, suicide, and disease during the horrific two-month voyages. African and some American scholars refer to this most shameful profit making as *Maafa*, the Swahili word for "great disaster." That pretty much repudiates my earlier off-hand statement, "Nobody ever killed anyone for the sake of sugar, at least not directly."

Moreover, the Africans' dying continued once they made it to land. Preceding the "blood diamond" protests of the twenty-first century, abolitionists in the 18th century employed a "blood as sugar" meme. Elizabeth Abbott in her excellent book, *Sugar: A Bittersweet History*, quotes Quaker William Fox exhorting his fellow English and American citizens that for every pound of sugar, "we may be considered as consuming two ounces of human flesh."[1] We doubt that a pious Quaker would read a saucy satire in French, but Voltaire's portrayal of human depravity written three decades earlier sounds similar. The Frenchman described the brutality of New World sugar production in the words of one of his characters in *Candide*: "When we work in the sugar mills and we catch our finger in the millstone, they cut off our hand; when we try to run away, they cut off a leg. Both things have happened to me." [2]

In Chapters 5 and 8 we will again visit disgraceful eighteenth and nineteenth century Western trade practices involving other spices, tea and opium.

During the Napoleonic Wars the British blockade of continental ports forced a huge increase in the production of sugar from beets that could be cultivated in a cold climate. Imagine how a shortage of pastries played out in

---

1   Fox's 1791 pamphlet is perhaps the single most influential abolitionist document ever published. Two-hundred-thousand copies of his *An Address to the People of Great Britain on the Consumption of West India Produce* were circulated across both countries.

2   Voltaire, *Candide* (Philip Littell's undated translation, USA: Renaissance Classics) 1759, 72. Thanks to Rich Cohen for alerting me to these pithy quotes from Abbott, Fox, and Voltaire. See his "Sugar Love, A Not So Sweet Story," *National Geographic*, August 2013, 78-97. I suppose not just coincidentally *candide* is the Latin term for "sparklingly white" and is quite similar to the ancient India term *khanda* for "sugar".

Paris. By 1880 beets were the primary source of sugar in all of Europe. As an aside, when I first visited Moscow in 1989, they had a national shortage of sugar and soap. My Russian hosts were very unhappy and literally suspected a plot by Gorbachev to stir up dissent. Indeed, I wonder which was the worse shortage – what would you give up first, soap or sugar?

Consumer Behavior

Today the average American adult consumes about seventy[1] pounds of sugar per year, that's the 22.7 teaspoons per day we mentioned earlier. The American Heart Association recommends a healthful consumption rate of about one-third of that, or six teaspoons a day for women and nine for men.[2] Perhaps the most dangerous part of our consumption of sugar is that we don't notice eating it. Most recently a study at the University of North Carolina found that sixty-eight of the products in American grocery stores contain added sugars.[3] New product labeling regulations approved only this year by the Food and Drug Administration begins to require information about *added* sugars. This represents a huge improvement. Restaurants are increasing information on menus, but not added the sugar yet. McDonald's has just proudly proclaimed in a full-page ad in the *New York Times* that

---

1 The estimates of sugar consumption across sources vary substantially depending on assumptions made about waste. This number is a best estimate of the US Department of Agriculture. The industry ships the equivalent of 130 pounds per person per year, but the Department assumes very roughly that more than one-third is not eaten, but instead ends up in the trash can or goes down the drain. See Stephanie Strom, "US Cuts Estimate of Sugar Intake," *New York Times*, October 26, 2012, online.

2 As in the case of salt there is some disagreement within the medical research community on healthful sugar intake levels. See Andrew M. Seaman, "Added Sugars Abundant US Diets, Linked to Death," *Reuters*, February 3, 2014, online. Seaman's reports the Institute of Medicine recommendation at less than 25 percent of caloric intake of added sugars while the World Health Organization has adopted a more stringent standard of less than 10 percent. Comically, or tragically, depending on how you look at it, the Sugar Association concludes (www.sugar.org) you can eat as much as you want. What jerks! To be exact, what they say is, "Thus, it is difficult to conclude that total sugars intake is of sufficient public concern to be included in FOP (Front of Package) rating systems." They're still jerks, and dangerous ones at that!

3 Margot Sanger-Katz, "Revealing Just How Common Added Sugar Is," *New York Times*, May 24, 2016, page A3.

HFCS is being eliminated from its buns. That's all very nice, but the company says nothing about the amount of sugar in its online nutritional information. It only reports calories and carbs, and nothing about sugar content, let alone added sugar.

Two-thirds of Americans are overweight, and one-third is obese. Between 30 and 50 percent of Americans are dissatisfied with their weight.[1] Today some 100 million dieters are spending $20 billion a year trying to lose weight. Why is losing weight so difficult?

> *Sugar is not addictive. You get habituated to*
> *sugar, which is not being addicted.*

STEFAN CATSICAS, CHIEF TECHNOLOGY OFFICER, NESTLÉ

Bloomberg BusinessWeek tells us Dr. Catsicas is a a quadrilingual Swiss neuroscientist.[2] But he apparently doesn't understand English very well. Or perhaps he's a bit biased by his nice Nestlé salary? Sugar is an addictive compound. Some criticize this label as it equates eating disorders with hard-drug addictions. Certainly the sugar industry hates the idea of being lumped together with drug dealers. But that is precisely the conclusions drawn by a National Institute of Health sponsored study by three psychologists at Princeton:[3]

> From an evolutionary perspective, it is in the best interest of humans to have an inherent desire for food for survival. However, this desire may go awry, and certain people, including some obese

---

1 The estimates are all over the place on weight dissatisfaction among Americans. See David Garner, "Survey Says: Body Image Poll Results," *Psychology Today*, February 1, 1997, online and Rachel A. Millstein, et al. "Relationship between Body Size Satisfaction and Weight Control Practices among US Adults," *Medscape Journal of Medicine*, 2008 10(5), 119.

2 Matthew Campbell and Corinne Gretler, "Can Nestlé Sell the Problems and the Cure?" *Bloomberg BusinessWeek*, May 9, 2016, pages 50-55.

3 Nicole M. Avena, Pedro Rada, and Bartley G. Goebel, "Evidence for Sugar Addiction: Behavioral and Neurochemical Effects of Intermittent, Excessive Sugar Intake," *Neuroscience & Biobehavioral Reviews* 2008 32(1), 20-39.

and bulimic patients in particular, may develop an unhealthy dependence on palatable food that interferes with well-being. The concept of "food addiction" materialized in the diet industry on the basis of subjective reports, clinical accounts and case studies described in self-help books. The rise in obesity, coupled with the emergence of scientific findings of parallels between drugs of abuse and palatable foods has given credibility to this idea. The reviewed evidence supports the theory that, in some circumstances, intermittent access to sugar can lead to behavior and neurochemical changes that resemble the effects of a substance of abuse. According to the evidence in rats, intermittent access to sugar and chow is capable of producing a "dependency". This was operationally defined by tests for binging, withdrawal, craving and cross-sensitization to amphetamine and alcohol. The correspondence to some people with binge eating disorder or bulimia is striking, but whether or not it is a good idea to call this a "food addiction" in people is both a scientific and societal question that has yet to be answered. What this review demonstrates is that rats with intermittent access to food and a sugar solution can show both a constellation of behaviors and parallel brain changes that are characteristic of rats that voluntarily self-administer addictive drugs. In the aggregate, this is evidence that sugar can be addictive.

And, that is precisely my fundamental argument in this book – hedonic molecules such as sugar and cocaine should be thought of in similar ways. Craving, binging, and withdrawal are all terms I associate with my own rat-like relationship with sugar. So I use the term "sugar addiction" herein without hesitation. [1] For other opinions on this, check out: http://www.webmd.com/diet/ss/slideshow-sugar-addiction or http://ed.ted.com/lessons/how-sugar-affects-the-brain-nicole-avena. See also Exhibit 3.2 – funny, but not really.

---

1 James J. DiNicolantonio and Sean C. Lucan, "Sugar Season. It's Everywhere, and Addictive." *New York Times*, December 23, 2014, page A25.

Exhibit 3.2
You're a Sugar Addict If You...

1. ...look at the desserts before the entrees at a new restaurant.
2. ...choose Coke over Diet Coke.
3. ...answer "Grand Marnier crepes from a street vendor" when asked what you like best about Paris.
4. ...are obese, diabetic, and/or have had the gout.
5. ...can't get home from the grocery store without eating a half pound of the one-pound package of Oreos you bought there.
6. ...searched for, found, and bought Halloween packets of candy corn from Amazon in January.
7. ...examine at the check-out counter the M&M's brand extensions instead of the gossip magazines.
8. ...by accident take a bite of the free samples in a pet store.
9. ...eat two bags of Halloween candy before the 31st.
10. ...have a candy stash in your office desk.
11. ...own a T-shirt that says, "Eat dessert first, life is uncertain."
12. ...give people directions using Baskin-Robbins 31 Flavors as a landmark.
13. ...plan to have dessert only on Sunday nights, but have donuts for breakfast on Monday morning.
14. ...know what "danger pudding" is, and often consume the whole can yourself.
15. ...remember your mother's cooking only for her desserts.
16. ...are a connoisseur of flan.
17. ...have dessert thrice or more daily.
18. ...have candy to cure depression.
19. ...celebrate peaking at Mount Whitney with a one-pound box of See's Nuts & Chews.
20. ...your brown paneled garage door reminds you of a Hershey's bar.

Add to the list at www.Spiced.World/SugarAddict

Americans are having some success in beating the addiction – per capita sugar consumption has decreased by about fifteen percent from its peak in 1999. That's the good news. Two-thirds of that reduction is from cutting back on sugared sodas.[1] The bad news is that we're still far from meeting the recommendations of the American Heart Association.

---

1 Jean A. Welsh, Andrea J. Sharma, Lisa Grellinger, and Miriam B. Vos, "Consumption of Added Sugars Is Decreasing in the United States," *The American Journal of Clinical Nutrition* 2011, 94(3), 726-734.

So far we have just talked about *average* American consumption of sugar. However, studies have clearly demonstrated a variety of factors that influence consumption levels. The Centers for Disease Control reports per capita consumption rates are lower for females, older folks, whites and Latinos (versus African Americans), and higher-income groups.[1]

Per capita consumption varies dramatically around the world. A quick look at the data in Exhibit 3.3 suggests we are the champion sugar eaters on the planet. However, I would guess that Americans actually waste more sugar than Cubans, so perhaps they win this most dubious honor. Indeed, the Cuban government provides each Cuban citizen some ninety-six pounds per year for free! Both countries are in the throes of diabetes epidemics. At the healthy bottom of the list are China and India. The resulting lower obesity rates in those two countries can be readily seen just walking their streets.

Exhibit 3.3
A Comparison of Sugar Consumption around the World

Country	grams/day	Country	grams/day
US	126.4	France	68.5
Cuba	119.0	Italy	57.6
Germany	102.9	Japan	56.7
Netherlands	96.7	Brazil	47.6
UK	93.2	UAE	41.9
Finland	91.5	China	15.7
Sweden	86.1	India	5.1
Saudi Arabia	80.7		

Source: Euromonitor, 2015.

At the macroeconomic level, we also see national differences in sugar production and consumption. The world production of sugar in 2011/12 was

---

1   R. Bethene Ervin and Cynthia L. Ogden, "Consumption of Added Sugars Among US Adutlts, 2005-2010," CDC Report #122, May 2013, online.

168 million metric tons. Brazil was the biggest producer at 35.8 million metric tons, followed by India at 28.3, the EU at 16.7, China at 11.8, Thailand at 10.2, and the United States at 7.1 million metric tons. India was the biggest consumer of sugar at 26.5 million metric tons, followed by the EU at 17.8, China at 14.9, Brazil at 11.7, and the United States at 10.4 million metric tons. Thus, the United States imports about 3 million metric tons per year mostly from the Dominican Republic, Brazil, the Philippines, and Australia in descending order.

Marketing

Product. Out in California the prominent brand name for sugar on the shelf in the supermarket is C&H – "pure cane sugar from Hawaii," so the TV slogan went when I was growing up. Only about 16 percent of the sugar enters the American diet via packaged sugar brought into the home.[1] On the supermarket shelf you can see white granulated, golden, dark brown, washed raw (all the browns have a residual of molasses creating the color), powdered, baker's ultrafine pure cane, all with different uses and preferences in the homemaker's kitchen. Also included in that 16 percent are HFCS, honeys, other syrups, and molasses. Notable newer shelf space holders are organic coconut palm sugar and organic blue agave nectar. A variety of sugar substitutes are available adjacent to the sugar choices. We will discuss those a bit later in the context of how to reduce sugar consumption.

The syrups, including molasses are usually in the breakfast aisle. On our Sunday morning waffles we use Aunt Jamima Butter Lite – HFCS is the main ingredient. While reading the ingredients on the label, I just noticed that butter is not listed. As I read the label carefully, it says "Natural ***Butter*** Flavor… Contains No Butter. Indeed, **Butter** is the second biggest word on the label. I just love marketing [read as sarcasm]! Before I read the label just now, I had thought for the last twenty years that butter was an ingredient. I also had the

---

1   USDA estimates online 2014. "Table 20a – US sugar deliveries for human consumption by type of user."

impression that it contained some maple syrup as well. Some consumer behavior expert I am? But actually reading labels is one of the most important lessons of both the salt and sugar chapters.

Karo corn syrup is there on the syrup shelf too, and it's used mostly for cooking. The interesting part of the Karo label is the "**0g High Fructose Corn Syrup**" prominent on a bottle of corn syrup. Og sounds like a Flintstones character – of course, "0g means" zero grams. Obviously HFCS has developed a negative reputation at least for homemakers.

Perhaps the biggest change in the form of the sugar product used has been the replacement of sucrose by HFCS (a Japanese invention) in the food-processing and particularly in the beverage industries. Here in the States the real Coke aficionados often seek out the version produced by Mexican bottlers who persist in using sucrose. They claim they can taste the difference between the sucrose and HFCS versions. And, perhaps they can? Although the molecular formulas are identical, the structures and percentages of the molecules vary. Generally the HFCS is a bit sweeter. But despite the popular opinion, they are virtually the same thing once they get inside your body.

Often the food processors prefer HFCS over sucrose because its liquid form makes storage, transportation, and blending more efficient. Up until this last year, it has also been cheaper as we will discuss a bit later.

The conflicts between the HFCS folks and their critics and competitors (that is, the sucrose producers) are generating big bucks for PR firms. The Center for Science in the Public Interest (CSPI) sued Cadbury for calling HFCS "natural" since the enzymatic production process is relatively complex and includes a genetically modified enzyme. After a battle the company changed its label on 7Up cans from "all natural" to "100 percent natural flavors."

In advertising campaigns in 2008 and 2010, the Corn Refiners Association attempted to move the public's perceptions again, closer to sucrose and nature. One executive at CSPI called the HFCS claims deceptive, but in his testimony he added, "The special harmfulness [with respect to obesity] of high-fructose corn syrup has become one of those urban myths that sound right, but is basically wrong. Nutritionally, high-fructose corn syrup and sucrose may be identical."[1] Most recently the FDA has refused to allow a name change for HFCS to "corn sugar." And of course, we make no distinction between sucrose and HFCS in this chapter. They are equally bad news when it comes to the public health.

The geography of American production also makes a difference. Sugarcane is grown in four states that have tropical regions: Florida, Louisiana, Texas, and Hawaii. Sugar beets are grown in eleven northern states running from Washington to Minnesota. Of course, corn is grown just about everywhere – Iowa is the leading producer, but corn is grown even in Alaska. During the last decade the market shares of sugar have been about 25 percent cane, 25 percent beet, and 50 percent HFCS.

Perhaps someone, not me, will write an interesting book about the politics of the sucrose/HFCS conflict. In opposition you have two of the most politically powerful (in terms of political lobbying and donations) groups in the world – Cargill and Archer Daniels Midland (ADM) versus South Florida's Fanjul brothers and their sugarcane empire. We return to this topic again in the "Pricing" section below and in Chapter 14, our chapter on government control of hedonic compounds.

Place. The 84 percent of sugar that is not purchased by consumers at retail stores for home use is distributed through food processors, restaurants, and the like. To be a bit more precise the USDA reports:

Bakery, cereal, and allied products (think Cheerios and Oreos)	32%
Confectionary and related products (think Hershey's)	14%
Ice cream and dairy products (think Baskin-Robbins)	9%
Beverages (think Coke)	7%
Canned, bottled, and frozen foods (think Smucker's)	6%
Hotels, restaurants, and institutions (think McDonald's)	2%

The remainder of the deliveries is listed in the other category. So added sugar is ubiquitous in our food production and distribution systems. You can get a

---

1   Michael F. Jacobson, "Corn Refiners' Ad Campaign Called Deceptive," Center for Science in the Public Interest, June 23, 2008, online. Cspinet.org.

glimpse of the sugar content of the a variety of food and beverage products advertised in Super Bowl Fifty in Exhibit 3.4.

Exhibit 3.4
Sugar Content of Products Advertised During the 2016 Super Bowl (single servings)

Product	Serving size	Sugar (grams)
Budweiser beer	12 oz	0 g
Coke	12 oz	38 g
Pepsi	12 oz	40 g
Butterfinger	59.5 g (1 bar)	24 g
Heinz ketchup	17 g (1 tbsp)	4 g
Doritos	28 g	0 g
Mountain Dew	12 oz	46 g
Skittles	40 g	30 g
Quesalupa	~120 g	3 g

Sources: A variety of websites, corporate when data are available.

Start the day with a bowl of Special K with low-fat milk (17 g of sugar), a piece of whole wheat toast with jam (14 g), and a glass of orange juice (24 g, yes, they are actually growing sweeter oranges now). With just those 51 grams you've already exceeded the recommended limit of **38 grams for men**, and doubled it **for women at 25 grams**. Toward the middle of the day have a Quarter Pounder with Cheese (10 g), a one-ounce bag of Barbeque Sun Chips (3 g), a twelve-ounce Coke (38 g), and a scoop of ice cream (15 g). And you haven't even had dinner yet! A pack of six Oreos is another 30 g of sugar. Ouch.

Price. Sugar is cheap. For shoppers at the grocery store your standard granulated cane sugar is about 97¢ per pound. The other forms get more expensive. A twelve-ounce bottle of C&H Blue Agave Nectar I bought for $4.39, and the Coconut Palm Sugar was most expensive at $5.99 per pound.

If you apply the retail price of 97¢ per pound across all the sugar sold to the American consumer each year, that makes the production and distribution of added sweeteners (sugar, HFCS, honey, and so on) in the United States a $35 billion industry.

As can be seen in Exhibit 3.5, for the past decade the *world* wholesale price for granulated sucrose has been quite volatile, ranging between 10 and 33¢ per pound. Moreover, the world prices are really cheap compared to US domestic prices. Circa 2015 the world price is running 15¢ per pound and the US price is 24¢. Why the discrepancy? That brings us to the story of Alfy and Pepe Fanjul.

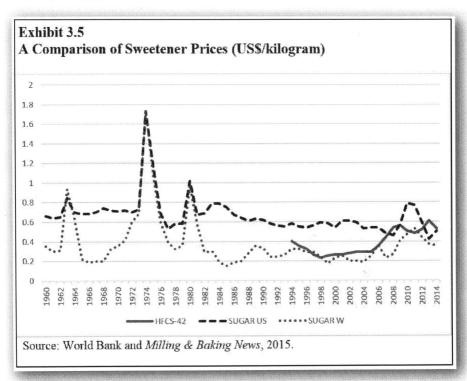

Exhibit 3.5
A Comparison of Sweetener Prices (US$/kilogram)

Source: World Bank and *Milling & Baking News*, 2015.

Alfonso Fanjul's blue eyes, Gordon Gekko haircut, and energetic smile communicate much about the man. His roots are in Asturias, the Celtic part of Spain in the far north. *Asturianos* are known for their unbridled pride, blues eyes, and freckled skin. Five-Hundred years ago the Moorish invasion of Spain stopped at the border with Asturias. The septuagenarian's slicked back hair well reflects his entrepreneurial acumen. His family controlled the Cuban sugar business before Castro took over. In 1960 his father, Alfonso Sr., and his sons immigrated to South Florida and began buying up sugarcane assets, both fields and refineries. Now the older son, Alfy Jr., controls the family businesses including the Domino and C&H brands, 12 percent of the land in Palm Beach County, and the largest sugar production facilities in the Dominican Republic.

Alfy Fanjul has at least two reasons to be smiling at the moment. First, as reported in the *Washington Post,* "Last week, the Fanjul family's influence over policy makers was on display when the US House passed a farm bill that would cut subsidies to many agricultural products while leaving unscathed the controversial, taxpayer-backed program that protects sugar profits."[1] The Fanjul clan has deftly balanced their contributions to Washington politicians – Alfy donates to the Democrats and his younger, taller brother, Jose (Pepe), to the Republican candidates. Alfy's coziness with the Clintons and President Obama has allowed his most recent travel to Cuba, thus his second reason to smile about new possibilities.

Prices for sugar in the United States make little sense until you put into the calculus the political heft of Fanjul brothers on Florida and national policy making. So the sugar industry in the United States has been supported by the federal government through a helter-skelter of restrictions on domestic sales, a roughly 100 percent tariff on sugar imports, import quotas, and price subsidies. The consequence of this scramble of government policies is that Americans often pay about three times the world price for sugar. While the unsavory manipulation of government policies regarding prices is derided my most, there is a silver lining. Higher prices for sugar in the United States have meant lower consumption of the

---

1 Peter Wallsten, Manuel Roig-Fanzia, and Tom Hamburger, "Sugar Tycoon Alfonso Fanjul Now Open to Investing in Cuba under 'Right Circumstances.'" *Washington Post,* January 28, 2013, online.

hedonic molecule. Moreover, we Americans are used to paying this 100+ percent "tax" on sugar – we just haven't noticed it.

During the last decade the wholesale price for cane sugar here has varied between 42 and 69¢ per pound. Beet sugar prices have ranged from 23 to 56¢ per pound during the same period. Prices for HFCS 55, the closest equivalent of sucrose, has skyrocketed during the decade, going from 19¢ per pound straight up to 39¢. As the cost advantage of the HFCS makers declines, and as consumers continue to eschew the product, the soft drink companies are beginning to consider using sucrose again. Archer Daniels and Cargill, the two biggest sellers of HFCS, slashed prices for the first time in 2013.

Finally, as in the case of salt, the food processors make short-term pricing decisions (discounts, price promotions, coupons, deals, and so on) based on competition in the super markets, and not so much based on the price variations of one of their least expensive ingredients.

Promotion. Since most (80 percent+) sugar is reaching American stomachs as a processed food ingredient, most of the promotional efforts involve the big food processors, beverage companies, and restaurant chains. And, most of the promotional dollars spent by those firms are in the form of mass-media advertising. Personal selling by both sugar and beverage firms to commercial customers such as McDonald's is also a very important aspect of competitive marketing practices, but those efforts are more difficult to track and analyze. So we will focus on mass-media advertising here. We do note, however, that the sugar producers' budgets for public relations and legal services have ballooned during the recent civil war between sucrose and HFCS producers.

Advertising. You will see in Exhibit 3.6 that six of the top twenty global advertisers are delivering sugar to their customers. That's almost $22 billion dollars globally and almost $5 billion domestically being spent on ads by only six companies to convince you to buy their sugared products. The six largest automobile manufactures spent less, only $15.5 billion in the same time period.

Exhibit 3.6 Top 20 Global Advertisers

Company	Advertising Expenditures 2014 ($ billions)	
	Global	United States
Procter & Gamble	$10.1	$2.9
Unilever	**$7.4**	**$0.8**
L'Oreal	$5.2	$1.5
Coca-Cola	**$3.3**	**$0.4**
Toyota	$3.2	$1.2
Volkswagen	$3.2	$0.6
Nestle	**$2.9**	**$0.7**
General Motors	$2.8	$1.7
Mars	**$2.6**	**$0.8**
McDonald's	**$2.5**	**$0.9**
Reckitt Benckiser	$2.4	$0.3
Naspers	$2.4	--
Sony	$2.3	$0.6
AT&T	$2.2	$2.0
Nissan	$2.2	$0.9
Johnson & Johnson	$1.9	$0.9
PepsiCo	**$2.5**	**$0.8**
Pfizer	$2.0	$1.4
Ford	$2.0	$1.1
Fiat	$2.1	$1.1

Source: *Advertising Age,* 2016.

Below we will go into some detail about the product and promotional strategies of one company, Coca-Cola.

Public Relations. These massive efforts to influence behavior and public opinion thoroughly dominate the debate on the public health. As we said in the last chapter, when the US corporations weigh shareholder interests against those of the public health, the choices almost always favor shareholders. Indeed, recently the large beverage companies spent $4.1 million fighting beverage tax initiatives in two small cities in California. Or consider the consequences of the US Federal Trade Commission's (FTC) attempts to regulate the advertising of sugared cereals to American children in the late 1970s. The maelstrom of public relations and lobbying by the industrial giants almost destroyed the FTC itself. Regulators have remained gun shy since.

Finally, we are just beginning to learn that Big Food has imitated some of the awful PR tactics of their brothers in Big Tobacco circa 1976:

> With an initial annual budget of nearly $800,000 ($3.4 million today) collected from the makers of Dixie Crystals, Domino, C&H, Great Western, and other sugar brands, the [Sugar Association] recruited a stable of medical and nutritional professionals to allay the public's fears, brought snack and beverage companies into the fold, and bankrolled scientific papers that contributed to a "highly supportive" FDA ruling, which, the Silver Anvil [a PR "oscar"] application boasted, made it "unlikely that sugar will be subject to legislative restriction in coming years."[1]

Several researchers report additional evidence of the sugar industry's PR attack on health science for the sake of increasing sales of the addictive white crystals.[2] In Chapter 6 on Tobacco I report on the roots of this devious approach to public relations. There is some good news on this front of the battle: "The Coca-Cola Company has finally been shamed into backing away from a research program that sought to deflect attention from the role of sugary soft drinks in the nation's obesity crisis."[3]

---

1   Gary Taubes and Cristin Kearns Couzens, "Big Sugar's Sweet Little Lies: How the Industry Kept Scientists from Asking: Does Sugar Kill?" *Mother Jones*, October 31, 2012, online.

2   Kelly D. Brownel and Kenneth W. Warner, "The Perils of Ignoring History: Big Tobacco Played Dirty and Millions Died. How Similar is Big Food?" *Milbank Quarterly*, 87(1), March 2009, online; Maira Bez-Rastrollo, Matthias B. Schulze, Miguel Ruiz-Canela, Miguel A. Martinez-Gonzalez, Financial Conflicts of Interest and Reporting Bias Regarding the Association between Sugar-Sweetened Beverages and Weight Gain: A Systematic Review of Systematic Reviews," PLOS Medicine, December 31, 2013, online; Michele Simon, "And Now a Word from Our Sponsors: Are America's Nutritional Professionals in the Pocket of Big Food?" EATDRINK Politics, January 2013; and *Union of Concerned Scientists*, "Added Sugar, Subtracted Science: How Industry Obscures Science and Undermines Public Health Policy on Sugar," June 2014, online.

3   "The Defense of Sugary Soda That Fizzled," *New York Times* editorial, December 5, 2015, page A22.

Consequences of Consumption

Obesity (since 2013 classified as a disease by the American Medical Association), diabetes,[1] elevated triglycerides, cardiovascular disease, non-alcoholic fatty liver disease, elevated uric acid levels, gout, and progressive dental decay are all *associated* with high levels of sugar consumption according to the US Center for Disease Control. Given their Jobian list of aliments I'm surprised the CDC didn't include death. A most recent report by Credit Suisse – yes, the bank – adds a few more ailments to the risk list: osteoarthritis, high blood pressure, high cholesterol, and cancer. Finally, for men there's low testosterone – one study found that for obese men losing 17 pounds increased testosterone levels by 15 percent.[2] Other experts aren't so circumspect and explain the *causal* links:

> The impact on health of sucrose and HFCS appears to be similar. [Dr. Richard Johnson, a nephrologist at the University of Colorado, Denver] explained... that although glucose is metabolized by cells all through your body, fructose is processed primarily in the liver. If you eat too much in quickly digested forms like soft drinks and candy, your liver breaks down the fructose and produces fats called triglycerides.
>
> Some of these fats stay in the liver, which over long exposure can turn fatty and dysfunctional. But a lot of the triglycerides are pushed out into the blood too. Over time, blood pressure goes up, and tissues become progressively more resistant to insulin. The pancreas responds by pouring out more insulin, trying to keep things in check. Eventually a condition known as metabolic syndrome kicks in, characterized by obesity, especially around the waist; high blood pressure; and other metabolic changes that, if not checked, can lead to type 2 diabetes, with a heightened danger of heart attack thrown in for good measure. As much as a third of the American adult population

---

1 While *Time* and *Newsweek* are fading from American newsstands, now you can buy a copy of *Diabetic Living* at the grocery checkout counter, next to the candy bars. Its circulation is growing fast and is currently over ½ million.

2 John La Puma, "Don't Ask Your Doctor about Low T," *New York Times*, February 4, 2014, A19.

could meet the criteria for metabolic syndrome set by the National Institutes of Health.

Recently the American Heart Association added its voice to the warnings against too much added sugar in the diet. But its rationale is that sugar provides calories with no nutritional benefit. According to Johnson and his colleagues, this misses the point. Excessive sugar isn't just empty calories; it's toxic.

"It has nothing to do with its calories," says endocrinologist Robert Lustig of the University of California, San Francisco. "Sugar is a poison by itself when consumed at high doses."

Johnson summed up the conventional wisdom this way: Americans are fat because they eat too much and exercise too little. But they eat too much and exercise too little because they're addicted to sugar, which not only makes them fatter but, after the initial sugar rush, also saps their energy, beaching them on the couch. "The reason you're watching TV is not because TV is so good," he said, "but because you have no energy to exercise, because you're eating too much sugar."[1]

For Dr. Lustig on video please see http://www.ucsf.edu/news/2010/03/3222/ucsf-lecture-sugar-and-obesity-goes-viral-experts-confront-health-cri. For a colorful portrayal of where the term "sugar rush" comes from, take a look at http://www.webmd.com/diet/ss/slideshow-sugar-addiction?print=true. Indeed, if you watched the commercials for the sugar laced products aired during the Super Bowl, the only exercise you're getting is via voyeurism.

The main motivation behind the Credit Suisse report[2] is to get a handle on the financial costs associated with the over consumption of sugar. *Forbes*[3] featured some of their primary points:

---

1   Rich Cohen, "Sugar Love, A Not So Sweet Story," *National Geographic*, August 2013, 78-97, quote from page 96.

2   Credit Suisse Research Institute, "Sugar Consumption at a Crossroads," online at https://doc.research-and-analytics.csfb.com/.

3   Dan Munro, "Sugar Linked to $1 Trillion in US Healthcare Spending," *Forbes*, October 27, 2013, online.

1. So 30 to 40 percent of healthcare expenditures in the United States go to help address issues that are closely tied to the excess consumption of sugar.

2. The 2012 Global Burden of Disease report highlighted obesity as a more significant health crisis globally than hunger and/or malnourishment.

3. More than half a billion adults (over the age of twenty) worldwide are obese.

4. The world average daily intake of sugar and high-fructose corn syrup (HFCS) is now seventy grams (seventeen teaspoons).

The irony of #2 is that when I was growing up the world worried about starvation – that is, of course still happening in some places, particularly war-torn ones. But now the threat of global gluttony is greater? One study reports: "Global food systems are not meeting the world's dietary needs, About one billion people are hungry, while two billion people are overweight."[1] And for a moment juxtapose #3 and #4 above to the global expenditures on advertising for Coke and the rest listed in Exhibit 3.6. The bankers' bottom line on this? The United States overdosing on sugar costs Americans some $1 *trillion* per year. Robert Lustig estimates the costs of the epidemic of "metabolic syndrome" at $1.4 trillion.[2] Also see UCSF's SugarScience Initiative (www.SugarScience.org) for the growing scientific literature on consequences of consumption worldwide.

Ways to Reduce the Sugar Consumption of the Average American

In an important 2010 report the CDC[3] focuses their strategies narrowly on sugar laced beverages. The report states:

---

1 David Stuckler and Marion Nestle, "Big Food, Food Systems, and Global Health," PLOS Collections, /PLos Med 9(6), online.

2 Robert Lustig, "Toxic Taste," *Leader's Edge*, June 25, 2014, online.

3 US Center for Disease Control, "The CDC Guide to Strategies for Reducing the Consumption of Sugar-Sweetened Beverages," 2010, online, the quote is from page 4.

Several social and environmental factors have been linked to the purchase and consumption of SSBs [sugar-sweetened beverages]. These factors include advertising and promotion, increased portion sizes, fast food consumption, television watching, permissive parenting practices, parental SSB consumption, and increased access to SSBs in the home and school.

Please notice the cause listed first. And please notice my use of the word *cause*. Advertising causes consumption. The CDC report continues with a list of seven categories of strategies for reducing SSB consumption. Most of these might be applied more broadly to other sugared products and, indeed, most of the hedonic compounds discussed in this book. In the CDC's presentation they provide their rationale, assessments of efficacy (including insights from other countries), barriers to implementation, action steps, program examples, and existing resources and, finally, seven tools for implementation:

1. Ensure ready access to potable drinking water.
2. Limit access to SSBs.
3. Promote access to and consumption of more healthful alternatives to SSBs.
4. Limit marketing of SSBs and minimize marketing's impact on children.
5. Decrease the relative cost of more healthful beverage alternatives through differential pricing of SSBs.
6. Include screening and counseling about SSB consumption as part of routine medical care.
7. Expand the knowledge and skills of medical providers to conduct nutrition screening and counseling regarding SSB consumption.

Many of these recommendations have been adopted around the country with some success and with some failure. Regarding #3, Michelle Obama and others have successfully campaigned against childhood obesity through the promotion of healthier vegetable choices. General Mills has reduced the sugar content of some cereals. PepsiCo has stopped selling full-sugar drinks in schools. A recent survey reports a reduction of calories – 6.4 trillion over five years – by sixteen large food processors. For example, Nestlé reduced the sugar content of Nesquik by 25 percent.

One innovation I have not run across is a sugar and salt free aisle in a major grocery chain. As I will detail in a bit, I can easily find the sugar (cereal and candy) aisle in my local Safeway. The big retailers know all about what they call category management. How about a category that attacks the metabolic syndrome epidemic?

A related effort has been the development and marketing of sugar substitutes. Anytime you order ice tea in California the server will bring you a choice of three: Equal (blue pack), Splenda (yellow pack), and Sweet 'N Low (pink pack). Perhaps Stevia's (made from the leaves of another South American plant) appearance on the finale of TV's *Breaking Bad* will boost its popularity? The support of Cargill (its maker) and Coke has already moved it up to number two in the $400 million alternative-sweetener market. Zero-calorie Diet Coke, with a market share of the soft drink market of about 9 percent uses Aspertame (as does Equal).

But circa 2016 consumers are eschewing alternative sweeteners as they are generally perceived as unhealthful. Some experts recommend avoiding them for another reason – they keep the brain locked in onto the craving for sweetness. Worse still, new research suggests that substitutes may "disrupt the body's ability to regulate blood sugar, causing metabolic changes that can be a precursor to diabetes."[1] Diet-cola sales have declined commensurately. In any case, sales of all these alternatives amount to about 1 percent of their real sugar competitors.

Michael Moss often mentions in *Salt, Sugar, and Fat* that a standard procedure for food processors is to add back one controversial ingredient when another is being hotly criticized in the public domain: "Any improvement in the nutritional profile of a product can in no way diminish its allure, and this has led to one of the industry's most devious moves: lowering one bad boy

---

1 Kenneth Chang, "Artificial Sweeteners Alter Metabolism, Study Finds," *New York Times*, September 18, 2014, page A4.

ingredient like fat while quietly adding more sugar to keep people hooked."[1] The fact that Diet Coke has 35 percent more caffeine than Classic Coke makes you wonder whether the extra caffeine has been added to make the craving [addiction] stronger given the reduction in sugar? We will take up this issue in more detail in Chapter 6 on caffeine.

Most recently chocolate candy makers have been using maltitol, the sugar alcohol listed in Exhibit 3.1 above, to replace sugar allowing them to advertise a "sugar free" product. This dirty dodge will be discussed further in the next chapter on chocolate.

Related to #4 above, Disney has banned junk-food advertising ads on its shows for kids. Beverage companies have agreed to post calories on vending machines and McDonald's now posts calorie counts on its menu boards. Several countries around the world have passed laws limiting TV advertising targeting children. The prominent example is Sweden's long lasting ban of all ads aimed at kids. Santa Clara County (a.k.a. Silicon Valley) and the city of San Francisco have banned sales promotions targeting children at fast food retailers – no more Happy Meals toys there.

The most prominent application of CDC recommendation #5 is New York City's attempt to tax sixteen-ounce+ sugared drinks. While the courts turned back that initiative, other municipalities (such as Berkeley, California) and countries (Mexico) are pursuing similar sugar taxes with some success.

In the United States some signs of progress are beginning to appear – the CDC recently reported a first-time moderation in obesity percentages of low-income preschoolers in California. Most recently the US Department of Agriculture reports that Americans shaved on average 100 calories from their diets between 2005 and 2010. And earlier we mentioned the 15 percent decline in per capita sugar consumption nationwide since its 1999 peak. In September 2014 Coke, Pepsi, and Dr. Pepper all agreed to reduce by 20 percent sugary drink calories by 2025. As I write this today, my morning paper reports "Behind a Drop in Calories, A Shift in Cultural Attitudes."[2] Indeed, I

---

1   Michael *Moss, Sal, Sugar, and Fat* (New York: Random House) 2013, xxvi.

2   Margot Sanger-Katz, "Behind a Drop in Calories, A Shift in Cultural Attitudes," *New York Times*, July 28, 2015, page A3.

greet with mixed emotions another headline: "Bye, Bye American Pie: Desserts are Disappearing."[1] Yes, perhaps the tide is turning. Indeed, bottled water now outsells regular sodas! Diabetes cases have declined by more than 18 percent since 2008. But still not fast enough boys. The war is still not over.

Among the options listed by the CDC I am most optimistic about the viability of two. First, disallowing commercial advertising to children is an attainable goal. It has been accomplished in other countries. Like Disney, Coca-Cola itself eschews the practice. We quote directly from the firm's *2012-2013 Sustainability Report*[2], "We take our responsibilities seriously regarding advertising and marketing.

- We do not advertise to children under 12 years old.
- We do not place advertising in media where the audience is over 35 percent children under 12 years old.
- This policy applies to television, radio and print, and, where data is available, to the Internet and mobile phones.
- We openly participate in audits by external organizations that monitor our advertising.
- We believe in commercial-free classrooms for children, and have joined with other beverage companies in implementing voluntary school beverage guidelines in Europe, the US, Canada, New Zealand, and Australia. We also have Global School Behavior guidelines which guide our actions across all countries."

According to Mark Pendergrast's tome on the history of the firm, these prohibitions of advertising to children have their roots in a legal action taken against Coca-Cola more than a century ago. In 1911 the firm had won a case regarding the caffeine content of the beverage but experienced uncomfortable criticism regarding its effects on children. Pendergrast reports, "After 1911, an unwritten law stated than no one under twelve years old would be shown

---

1 Bruce Horovitz, "Bye, Bye American Pie: Desserts are Disappearing," *USAToday*, February 26, 2015, online.

2 "At Coca-Cola, We Market Responsibly and Don't Advertise Directly to Children Under 12," *2012-2013 Sustainability Report*, online at www.coca-colacompany.com.

drinking in a Coca-Cola ad – a dictum enforced until 1986."[1] Perhaps the most important aspect of Coca-Cola's policy on advertising to children is their implied admission that advertising to children influences their behavior in unhealthy ways. I wonder if they have data to support their policy that they might share to convince their competitors to behave similarly?

The *Coca-Cola Sustainability Report* also comments on two additional important topics:

- We offer low or no calorie beverages options in every market [pertinent to the CDC recommendation # 3 above]
- We provide transparent nutritional information, featuring calories on the front of all our packages [this another important aspect of delivering product information to consumers]

The second CDC strategy that seems particularly viable is their #5, above regarding differential pricing. The evidence from Mexico's soda tax is beginning to demonstrate its efficacy in reducing consumption of sugar. Higher prices in Japan have caused a remarkable 30 percent decline in per capita consumption since 1973. I agree with the marketing/economic principle underlying the CDC recommendations, Mexico's actions, Japan's long-term success, and most recently, Hillary Clinton's campaign statements – higher prices reduce consumption. But, taxing consumers directly will not be the best approach. Instead, a heavy tax on bulk sugar purchases should be assessed on the food processors, the beverage producers, and the restaurants that use **sugar as an added ingredient**. One of Michael Moss's most astute observations is that the industrial users of salt and sugar are themselves addicted to the unhealthful white crystals. A federal tax on *sugar as an ingredient* will level the competitive playing field with respect to taste. It will also get the executives' attention as the tax will affect profits. Such a tax would have little effect on market share and top-line sales revenues, but it would increase costs. The profit focused users of bulk sugar will reduce their use of the more costly ingredient to maximize

---

1   Mark Pendergrast, *For God, Country & Coca-Cola* (New York: Basic Books), second edition 2002, 119.

their bottom-line incomes. Yes, American sugar and HFCS producers will be hurt, but it is high time to end their coddling by government. And once the American public understands that we already pay a 100 percent tax on sugar – to folks like the Fanjul brothers – is should be relatively easy to raise those taxes another 500 percent[1] for the sake of the public health.

Marketing Miscreant – Sugar

Focusing solely on the distribution channels defined by the USDA, you might expect that my villain for this chapter might come from the cereal, cookie, candy, or ice-cream tribes. Certainly the bias I formed by sitting with my students at the San Francisco FTC hearings on cereal advertising to children in 1978 might yield a candidate from Kellogg's or General Mills. I find the specific targeting of children by cereal makers in their product design and advertising a most egregious breach of social responsibility. Shame on Cocoa-Puffs and the rest. When I visited Safeway today I found the incredible array of sugared-cereal products shelved directly across from the incredible array of candy bars. The kids must love, and the parents must hate that aisle.

Open Happiness.

CocaCola advertising tagline circa 2016.

But looking across all the categories of marketing efforts by the companies makes easy my selection of Coca-Cola as the tribe from which to choose the Marketing Miscreant for sugar. Coke is the biggest-selling soft drink in the United States with a market share of 17 percent. And, recall that just one twelve-ounce can of Coke equals the American Heart Association's recommended level of thirty-eight grams of sugar in the daily diet. Recall that Coke spends more than $3 billion a year on advertising. And realize that sugared

---

1 John L. Graham, "How to Tax Sugar," letter to the editor, *New York Times*, May 27, 2016, page A20.

beverages deliver fructose most directly to the liver, thus the public health is dangerously damaged.

I might have chosen any of the Coca-Cola CEOs for my criticism. Certainly, Robert W. Woodruff, CEO from 1923 to 1954 has been most responsible for the firm's remarkable success. He is credited with reviving the financially distressed company in the 1920s. Perhaps even more important, he conceived and implemented the global expansion of the firm's operations.

While all the CEOs continued the miscreant behavior of John Pemberton, he instigated it with his invention Coca-Cola. This leads us to the definition of snake oil. Because it's the more entertaining source, I prefer *Wikipedia* over *Webster's*:

> **Snake oil** is an expression that originally referred to fraudulent health products or unproven medicine but has come to refer to any product with questionable or unverifiable quality or benefit. By extension, a **snake oil salesman** is someone who knowingly sells fraudulent goods or who is himself or herself a fraud, quack, charlatan, and the like... the name originated in the Western regions of the United States and is derived from a topical preparation made from the Chinese Water Snake (*Enhydris chinensis*) used by Chinese laborers to treat joint pain. The preparation was promoted in North America by travelling salesmen who often used accomplices in the audience to proclaim the benefits of the preparation.[1]

The *Atlanta Journal* on May 29, 1886 ran the first ad for the greatest snake oil in history. The copy read:

> *Coca-Cola. Delicious! Refreshing! Exhilarating!*
> *Invigorating! The new popular soda fountain*
> *drink containing the properties of the wonderful*
> *Coca plant and the famous Cola nut.*

---

1 There is a bit more on etymology at http://en.wikipedia.org/wiki/Snake_oil. The current high-finance clash over the stock value of Herbalife is reminiscent of the nostrums and patent medicines of a century ago.

Pemberton listed the ailments cured on the label: "…a valuable Brain Tonic and cure for all nervous affections – Sick Head-Ache, Neuralgia, Hysteria, Melancholy, and so on The peculiar flavor of COCA-COLA delights every palate."[1] Now, more than a century later, see the remarkable carry-through of message in the company's mission statement listed at www.Coca-ColaCompany.com:

- To refresh the world…
- To inspire moments of optimism and happiness…
- To create value and make a difference.

You may notice the veiled reference to shareholder value in the third point. Maybe they mean value for the consumer – what do you think? The advertising sizzle is in the first two. As I will explain in the next paragraphs, there is no actual refreshment, only the illusion of such. There is truth in the use of the word "moments," but "inspire?" Their most overt advertising strategy was to picture consumers having a Coke "when they were happy."[2] This is not inspiring moments of happiness, this is taking advantage of them, building an emotional association with the product through advertising imagery.

Mark Pendergrast tells us that John Pemberton had both a financial interest in creating a "patent medicine" but also a personal health problem he wished to solve – his addiction to morphine (opium). A druggist himself, Pemberton combined cocaine (from coca leaves) and caffeine (from cola nuts) with a little alcohol and carbonated water and found the mix to relieve his morphine cravings. At the time soda fountains were in drug stores because carbonated water was also seen as a kind of medicine. His early concoctions tasted poorly, so he began to add sugar, a lot of it. So the story of the invention of Coca-Cola involves five of the spices/hedonic molecules listed in my table of contents – sugar, caffeine, cocaine, alcohol, and opium. Nice!

As cocaine and alcohol began to be recognized as addictive drugs a public uproar festered. In 1907 the US Army banned sale of Coca-Cola because

---

1 See Pendergrast for details, 30-31.
2 Michael Moss, *Salt, Sugar, Fat* (New York: Random House), 2013, 97-98.

of those ingredients. Both were dropped from the formula leaving us with apparently a benign mix of sugar, caffeine, and carbonated water. Now we are beginning to better understand the addictive qualities of both sugar and caffeine. That brings us to Dr. Pepper, 10, 2, and 4, and the claims about "refreshment."

Dr Pepper was born in a drug store in Waco, Texas and received its US patent a year before Coca-Cola did. Like Coke it is now thought of as a soft drink (containing sugar, water, and caffeine), but when it was concocted it was clearly considered a patent medicine, nostrum, or perhaps another kind of snake oil. www.DrPepperMuseum.com tells us that during the 1920s, "… research was discovered proving that sugar provided energy and that the average person experiences a letdown during the normal day at 10:30am, 2:30pm, and 4:30pm. A contest was held for the creation of an ad using the new information. The winner of the ad campaign came up with the famous advertising slogan, 'Drink a bite to eat at 10, 2, and 4.'" For decades you could find those numbers on the bottle cap of every Dr Pepper.

What science is telling us now in the 21st century is that both sugar and caffeine deliver volatility in human energy levels,[1] and for addicted users the peaks reach only the average level for non-addicted humans. So in the moment, the addicted user can get refreshed to a normal level of energy, but overall the addicted user suffers deeper "blood sugar lows." So the promise that Coke "refreshes" is only true for the "moment," but over the course of the day the claim carries little credence. Moreover, Rob Lustig pointed out to me at lunch one day the enormous difference between happiness and refreshment. By the way, we did not order dessert.

The bottom line on sugar:

1. It is a hedonic compound – added sugar is something we want, but do not need.
2. We are addicted to the drug.
3. Corporations spend billions of dollars encouraging our addiction.

---

1 "Slide Show: The Truth about Sugar Addiction," www.webmd.com, online, February 5, 2014.

4. The health consequences are personal and family disasters and cost the country $1 trillion per year.
5. We are seeing some success in reducing consumption of sugar.

Finally, I find it humorously ironic that my own doctor now prescribes real live snake oil – Lisinopril is extract of viper venom – to treat my high blood pressure, not from drinking too many Cokes, but from eating too many break and bake Toll House chocolate-chip cookies and the like. And that leads us to the next chapter on chocolate.

Four

CHOCOLATE, ETC.
Primary chemical ingredient: Theobromine, $C_7H_8N_4O_2$

*The divine drink which builds up resistance and
fights fatigue. A cup of this precious drink permits
a man to walk for a whole day without food.*

HERNANDO CORTÉS

This is the fun chapter. I'll talk a little about "too much," but not too much. Most of the spices covered here won't kill you. Maybe you'll feel a bit guilty is all. Many may even help your health. Also, you are not likely addicted to them, with the exception of chocolate.

While I spend the most ink on the topic of chocolate, I also tell brief stories about the other important spices that drove the first global trade and exploration. Vasco da Gama (1497) headed east and Christopher Columbus (1492) west to break the Muslim monopoly of trade in spices from China, India, and the East Indies. Previous to the Iberian caravels it was camels that carried spices west along the Silk Road. Only the value of the spices to the European royalty can explain the *huevos* of the Spanish and Portuguese sailors of those flimsy 50-foot vessels of adventure. Compared to the other sailing ships of the time their smaller size and shallow keel allowed the caravels to maneuver up river in coastal waters. They could also sail closer to the wind and were speedier allowing for the long-distance voyages.

Exhibit 4.1 illustrates the global trade that has resulted from the creation, craving, caravel delivery, and consumption of chocolate and another eight[1] key spices. We also include the story of tulips, a visual spice. All these hedonic compounds once involved daring and death and depravity. Wars, slavery, and poverty have all been consequences of consumption of these spices. Yet global free trade has now delivered peace, posterity, and the petty prices you see in the last column.

Exhibit 4.1
Information about Spices

Common Name	Place of Origin	Date of Origin	Largest Producer	Shelf Price/oz.
Chocolate (Hershey's Unsweetened)	Mesoamerica	1100 BC	Western Africa	66¢
Cinnamon[i]	Sri Lanka	2000 BC	Indonesia	$3.52
Chili pepper	Ecuador	7500 BC	India	$2.83
Cloves	Indonesia	1721 BC	Tanzania	$4.99
Ginger	South Asia	pre-history	India	$4.42
Nutmeg	Indonesia	pre-history	Indonesia	$4.66
Pepper (black)	India	2000 BC	Vietnam	$1.74
Saffron	Greece	50,000 BC	Iran	$676.33 (this is correct)
Vanilla (extract)	Mexico	pre-AD 1500	Madagascar	$4.91
Tulips	Persia	AD 1000	The Netherlands	$7.99/dozen

Chocolate

Chocolate by itself is relatively benign as an addictive hedonic compound. Its mix with sugar, as we discussed in the previous chapter, makes it unhealthful.

---

1 My selection of ten common spices may certainly omit your favorite. Obviously I am biased by what I've been fed and what I can find in my local Safeway. Indeed, *Wikipedia* lists some 281 "culinary herbs and spices" ranging from Ajwain to Zedorary. By the way, the main distinction between the two is herbs are consumed fresh often from your garden, while spices are dried allowing for their long storage and shipment across the seas.

History. The seed pods of the cocoa tree grow on the trunk. Each pod is about the size of a cantaloupe and holds about forty seeds. The scientific name for the tree is *Theobroma,* which means "food of the gods." Apparently Cortés was right, or he just had a lot of influence. The cocoa seeds are bitter tasting as they contain both theobromine and caffeine.

The Olmecs, Mayans, and Aztecs of pre-Columbian Mesoamerica crushed the dried cocoa beans, mixed them with water and sometimes vanilla and/or chilies, and drank the concoction. This is what Cortés would have been reporting in the epigraph at the head of this chapter. While he was happy about the gold he was absconding from the Aztecs, the more valuable discovery was the "divine drink" he had held in his hands. The Conquistadors witnessed Moctezuma downing some fifty cups a day of the frothy liquid he called *xocolatl,* a native word for "bitter water." Sounds like addiction to me. The theobromine and caffeine content would have produced the buzz Cortés experienced and the addiction apparent in the Emperor's court.

The first commercial shipment of chocolate arrived in Seville from Veracruz in 1585. As in the case of sugar this ushered in enslavements of natives and West Africans to work in the growing harvesting of the cocoa seeds in the Americas. Sadly, love of chocolate also contributed to the *Maafa.*

Like druggist John Pemberton would do some three centuries later to avoid the bitter tastes of coca and cola, the Europeans dumped in sugar to make the chocolate drink more palatable. You can get a good idea of why this practice developed by trying a teaspoon of unsweetened baking chocolate from your pantry. Make it a half teaspoon.

The Europeans really pushed other innovations: In 1689 Jamaican Dr. Hans Sloane developed milk chocolate. Solid chocolate, invented in Italy at the end of the eighteenth century soon benefitted from Swiss, Dutch, German, and British ideas. The Cadbury brothers came out with their first chocolate bar in 1849. Many of the brands popular today are associated with this stream of innovations – Ghirardelli, Nestlé, and Lindt. The mass production processes developed by Milton Hershey added the characteristic of the low prices and cultural memes we see today in Exhibit 4.2.

Exhibit 4.2
Chocolate Quips

"All you need is love. But a little chocolate now and then doesn't hurt." Charles M. Schulz

"There is nothing better than a friend, unless it is a friend with chocolate." Linda Grayson

"Strength is the capacity to break a Hershey bar into four pieces with your bare hands - and then eat just one of the pieces." Judith Viorst, *Love & Guilt & The Meaning Of Life, Etc*

"My therapist told me the way to achieve true inner peace is to finish what I start. So far today, I have finished 2 bags of M&M's and a chocolate cake. I feel better already." Dave Barry

"Your hand and your mouth agreed many years ago that, as far as chocolate is concerned, there is no need to involve your brain." Dave Barry

"He showed the words "chocolate cake" to a group of Americans and recorded their word associations. "Guilt" was the top response. If that strikes you as unexceptional, consider the response of French eaters to the same prompt: "celebration." Michael Pollan, *In Defense of Food*

"Just the other day, I was in my neighborhood Starbucks, waiting for the post office to open. I was enjoying a chocolatey cafe mocha when it occurred to me that to drink a mocha is to gulp down the entire history of the New World. From the Spanish exportation of Aztec cacao, and the Dutch invention of the chemical process for making cocoa, on down to the capitalist empire of Hershey, PA, and the lifestyle marketing of Seattle's Starbucks, the modern mocha is a bittersweet concoction of imperialism, genocide, invention, and consumerism served with whipped cream on top." Sarah Vowell

"The 12-step chocolate program: NEVER BE MORE THAN 12 STEPS AWAY FROM CHOCOLATE!" Terry Moore

"Every now and then, I'll run into someone who claims not to like chocolate, and while we live in a country where everyone has the right to eat what they want, I want to say for the record that I don't trust these people, that I think something is wrong with them, and that they're probably - and this must be said - total duds in bed."
Steve Almond, *Candyfreak: A Journey through the Chocolate Underbelly of America*

"It was like having a box of chocolates shut in the bedroom drawer. Until the box was empty it occupied the mind too much." Graham Greene, *The Heart of the Matter*

"The Spanish ladies of the New World are madly addicted to chocolate, to such a point that, not content to drink it several times each day, they even have it served to them in church."
Jean-Antheleme Brillat-Savarin, *The Physiology of Taste* (1825)

"Researchers have discovered that chocolate produces some of the same reactions in the brain as marijuana. The researchers also discovered other similarities between the two but can't remember what they are." Matt Lauer

The global trade of chocolate has evolved into a mainstream of cocoa leaving Africa for European and American production facilities and consumers. The complex supply chain includes some five million farmers around the world, local and foreign cocoa buyers, shipping organizations, grinders, processors, chocolatiers, and distributors. The production and distribution of Cortés' "divine drink" now employs forty to fifty million people worldwide.

Consumer Behavior. Judging by the character of the quips you just read, you might conclude that Americans are the champion chocolate eaters. But we aren't. The Europeans take the cake in that regard. In 2015 the average German consumed 20.2 pounds[1] followed by the UK (18.9), Belgium (15.8), Switzerland (13.6), France (10.8), Netherlands (9.2), Italy (9.2), and Spain (4.5). You will notice the decline in consumption as you go south on the list. In decades past it has been more difficult to keep chocolate candy on the shelf in warmer southern Europe.

As part of my *International Marketing* textbook I have been monitoring chocolate consumption across these countries for the last two decades. Before 2010 the British consumed the most chocolate per capita – surely due to their penchant of global trade and Cadbury. The British press complained loudly about Kraft's (Mondelez International) purchase of Cadbury for $19.6 billion in 2010. Twenty billion dollars just wasn't enough for a national treasure!

Chocolate is much less popular in Asia – the average Japanese or South Korean consumes only four pounds per year. The average consumption in China is less than two pounds, but you can see the British influence in Hong Kong by their 7.5 pounds per capita per year. Mexican consumption reflects their history. Of course they do eat candy bars, but the majority of their one pound per year comes in the form of drink and spice. Chocolate is the main ingredient in their spicy and colorful meat sauce, *mole*. Mole generally lacks sugar but includes other tasty ingredients, such as cumin, onions, garlic, and chili. That makes it the most healthful way to consume chocolate.

Here in America we're up to 11.4 pounds per person per year. As you might guess most chocolate enters the human stomach via our consumption

1   These statistics vary from data source to data source. I am using www.mda.marketline.com numbers.

of candy – so we will feature how chocolate candy is marketed in the next sections. Obviously we consume chocolate as an ingredient in a variety of other foods – cookies, croissants, cakes, ice cream, milk, and most recently as a coating for Lays potato chips. Really.

Chocolate was originally consumed for its medicinal properties – treatments for diarrhea, cardiovascular ailments, and lack of libido. Regarding the last one author reports in the *New York Times* I read today:

> Spanish physician, Antonio Colmenero de Ledesma, wrote in the 17th century that chocolate "vehemently Incites to Venus, and causeth Conception in women, hastens and facilitates their delivery." The English doctor, Henry Stubbs, writing in the same era, extolled his countrymen's "great use of Chocolate in Venery, and for Supplying the Testicles with a Balsam, or a Sap." [1]

Indeed, it is a common gift on Valentine's Day here in the States. But in modern research we cannot find support for the good doctors' seventeenth century prescriptions.

A fundamental change in consumption patterns is now underway as consumers are more often preferring dark chocolate for its perceived health benefits vis-à-vis milk and white chocolates. In 2008 the percentage of dark chocolate bars purchased by Americans was 18 percent, now it's over 20 percent. The mix of sugar, theobromine, and caffeine in the typical chocolate makes it an addictive package. My own addiction to See's milk almond clusters is now shifting to dark almond clusters. I *am* flexible. And my wife no longer needs to worry about me mixing up the two in the See's bag and "accidentally" eating her dark.

Having just now bragged about my flexibility, I also must report that chocolate consumers are astonishingly brand loyal. My brand preferences for peanut M&Ms, Hershey's with almonds, and See's milk-chocolate almond clusters have remained constant for at least a half a century. Hershey's and Coke had the same cachet with American soldiers in World War II. I'll try to remember to report when we edit the book whether I've been able to make

1 Samira Kawash, "Sex and Candy," *New York Times*, February 14, 2014, A25.

the switch to the healthier dark chocolate options.[1] Of course, the repeat purchases associated with strong brand loyalty are the keys to corporate profits enjoyed by both the candy and cola makers. And a Hershey's chocolate bar is a national icon similar in character to Coca-Cola.

The other side of consumption is the global production of cocoa. About 70 percent comes from the West African nations of Cameroon, Cote d'Ivoire, Ghana, and Nigeria. Indonesia, Brazil, and Ecuador are also big producers. The top five cocoa bean importing countries are Netherlands, the United States, Germany, Malaysia, and France in that order.

Product. Four forms of chocolate are marketed to American consumers: dark, milk, white, and a bitter (unsweetened) powder for cooking. The bitter cocoa seeds are fermented after harvest to yield the chocolate flavor. Then the beans are dried, cleaned, roasted, separated from their shells, and ground to produce a thick chocolate liquor. The liquor is then separated into cocoa solids and cocoa butter. Bitter chocolate contains varying proportions of the solids and butter. Sweet chocolates contain cocoa solids, cocoa butter, other fats, and sugar. Milk is added to produce milk chocolate. White chocolate contains no chocolate solids, only cocoa butter.

Governments around the world have set a variety of standards for use of the various chocolate-category names. For example, in the United States milk chocolate must include at least 15 percent chocolate liquor and 12 percent milk solids. Standards in other countries vary as does the taste.

Cocoa solids contain the psychoactive ingredients theobromine and caffeine which are linked to serotonin levels in the brain. There is also some evidence of cardiovascular benefits (via antioxidants) of the consumption of dark chocolate – if only we could avoid the sugar content that accompanies it. The US Food and Drug Administration helps the cause a little by requiring dark chocolate products to include at least 35 percent chocolate liquor. One ounce of dark chocolate contains about 200 mg of theobromine and 15 mg of caffeine, while milk chocolate includes about 60 mg of theobromine and 6 mg of caffeine. Theobromine is a weaker stimulant than its chemical cousin,

---

1 As with most of my "will power" experiments, it lasted about a month. Now back to milk chocolate.

caffeine, and both hedonic molecules are in lower quantities in a Hershey bar than in a cup of coffee or a Coca-Cola. In the next chapter I will provide a detailed comparison of caffeine content across products.

A recent product development is also worth mentioning. Please recall my own bias on this issue – from childhood I have been in love with Hershey's milk chocolate almond bars. I've even taken my family to the Hershey's museum in, where else, Hershey, Pennsylvania. Even the light standards on their main street, Chocolate Avenue, are topped with two-foot silver kisses, Hershey's pull tab and all. Quite cute.

But my research on their product line extensions is now making me quite cranky. I was really excited to notice for the first time a "sugar-free" alternative for their chocolate bars and York Peppermint Patties. The biggest print on their package says "**sugar free**" – it's bigger than their most attractive HERSHEY'S logo. My brain went right to "it must taste bad," but I gave it a chance. The patties are quite good. But my chagrin emanates from the nutritional details. Hidden by the glow of the giant "sugar free" is a fine print qualification: "not a low calorie food." What they've done (and Mars and Nestlé have too) is replaced sugar with maltitol, a hydrogenated disarccharide (see Exhibit 3.1 in the last chapter), that behaves almost the same as sugar. Maltitol does include fewer calories – Hershey's Sugar Free Special Dark has about 113 calories/ounce and regular Special Dark has 131 calories/ounce. Not much of an improvement. Hershey itself reports on its website:

With HERSHEY'S SUGAR FREE Chocolate Candy, people with diabetes and those interested in cutting back on sugar have great-tasting alternatives for enjoying HERSHEY'S chocolate, TWIZZLERS Candy, BREATH SAVERS Mints and ICE BREAKERS Chewing Gum.

HERSHEY'S Sugar Free products are sweetened with sugar alcohols. Sugar alcohols (or polyols), such as xylitol, mannitol, sorbitol, erythritol, and lactitol, contain some calories and increase blood sugar levels to varying degrees. Our sugar-free products therefore are not necessarily low calorie foods. Typically, they have about 20 percent fewer calories per serving than the original version and similar amounts of fat.

Sugar alcohols are neither a sugar nor an alcohol. They are called "sugar alcohols" because part of its chemical structure resembles sugar and part resembles alcohol. Sugar alcohols occur naturally in foods and are found in plant products, such as fruits and berries.[1]

And *corn,* according to the Cargill website. I'd like to know what percentage of the ingredients in the sugar alcohols Hershey's buys is corn versus fruits and berries? Tell the truth!

I'm a consumer, even a faithful Hershey's customer, and I feel deceived by their "sugar free" labeling. Moreover, I note that in other countries such as Australia, Canada, and New Zealand that maltitol carries warnings about "laxative effects" at dosages of more than a couple of forty-one-gram bars a day. Nothing about that on the Hershey's website. I also like Cargill's warning label:

Maltidex™ maltitol
Maltitol is produced by hydrogenation of the disaccharide maltose. Maltitol is available as a crystalline powder and as maltitol syrup, which, besides maltitol, contains a narrowly controlled range of hydrogenated oligo-and polysaccharides.

Besides maltitol powder, Cargill offers a range of tailor-made maltitol syrups with varying maltitol content to suit the desired application.

Some Cargill products are only approved for use in certain geographies, end uses, and/or at certain usage levels. It is the customer's [Hershey's, Mars, and Nestlé in this case] responsibility to determine, for a particular geography, that (i) the Cargill product, its use and usage levels, (ii) the customer's product and its use, and (iii) any claims made about the customer's product, all comply with the applicable laws and regulations.[2]

---

1 http://www.thehersheycompany.com/brands/iconic-brands.aspx, accessed February 12, 2014.

2 http://www.cargillfoods.com/emea/en/products/sweeteners/polyols/maltidex-maltitol/index.jsp, accessed February 12, 2014.

The Google category "Maltitol Farts" leads me to believe that the unusual amounts of intestinal gas I'm experiencing as I write this is related to the three Sugar Free Hershey's Peppermint Patties I consumed about an hour ago. Nice.

Place (Distribution). The largest five candy companies deliver the most chocolate to consumers worldwide. In order they are Mars ($16.8 billion in global sales of Snickers and M&Ms), Mondelez ($15.5 billion – Cadbury and Oreos), GrupoBimbo ($14.1 billion, the Mexican company with my all-time favorite corporate name – in Spanish, Bimbo has no pejorative meaning, Ricolino, Marinela, and Sarah Lee are important Bimbo brands), Nestlé ($12.8 billion, think Crunch bars), and Hershey's ($4.6 billion in global sales, Kit Kat and Almond Joy). In the US the top three chocolate distributors are Hershey's (43 percent market share), Mars (30 percent), and Nestlé (6 percent).[12]

Price. As attested to in the Hershey's annual report and Exhibit 4.3 below the cocoa-futures contract prices are quite volatile within and across years, particularly vis-à-vis world sugar prices. While such volatility in prices at the wholesale level gives purchasing agents headaches, it's great news for marketers. It's easy to argue for immediate price increases down the distribution channel (from grocers to consumers) when the cost of your most important ingredient rises dramatically from 2008 to 2010. Then when cocoa prices crash in 2012 you don't bother to lower your selling prices much or quickly – the practice helps profits. I notice that Hershey's topline sales revenues in 2012 increased 9.5 percent over 2011 while cost of sales only increased 6.6 percent during that period. Indeed, Punchcard reports they raised their prices 10 percent in 2009, 2.4 percent in 2010, 3.5 percent in 2011, and 5.7 percent in 2012. And in the United States the virtual duopoly of Hershey and Mars makes it easier to maintain price increases vis-à-vis overall inflation rates and the volatility of cocoa prices.

---

2 Punchcard Investing, 2012, online.

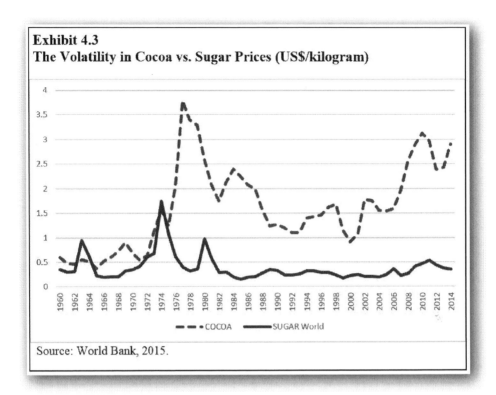

Exhibit 4.3
The Volatility in Cocoa vs. Sugar Prices (US$/kilogram)

Source: World Bank, 2015.

Finally, if we apply the 66¢ per ounce shelf price of Hershey's Natural Unsweetened Cocoa powder as roughly representative of the price/cost of delivering chocolate to consumers across product categories and multiply by the US annual imports of cocoa of 1237 metric tons (in 2012) that makes the chocolate business in the United States a $30 billion industry.

Promotion. You may recall that in the 2016 Super Bowl Nestlé advertised Butterfingers and Mars Skittles at about $5 million for thirty-second ads. Their global advertising budgets are huge (Nestlé at $2.9 billion and Mars at $2.6 billion) compared to Hershey's at only $782 million. But, in the States it's a different story. Nestlé has a broad line of products globally (Nescafe, Gerber, Hot Pockets, and Purina), where both Mars and particularly Hershey's are more focused on chocolate candies. The US advertising expenditures for the *chocolate duopoly* (almost sounds like a candy bar!) of Mars and Hershey's are $792 million and $640 million, respectively. Mars spends about

60 percent on television advertising, 24 percent on magazines, and 10 percent on the Internet. Hershey's spends almost everything on TV. And both target kids heavily.

Both companies spend more on marketing, sales, and customer service than on advertising, but their focus is on institutional customers. The ads target consumers directly, particularly in their homes on Saturday mornings.

Consequences of Consumption. Sugar is the real problem, and I discussed its bad side in the last chapter. But the theobromine and caffeine contents add to the addictive qualities of these products. Sleeplessness, heart burn, osteoporosis, and withdrawal headaches are on the list of potential negative health effects.

On the other hand, some studies suggest that dark chocolate and cocoa can help the circulatory system reducing cardiovascular disease, blood pressure, and body mass. Even better, a new study suggest that chocolate may improve memory![1] But, obviously, the high sugar content included in most of the chocolate products consumed render such pluses inconsequential at best.

Reducing the Consumption of Chocolate. Chocolate is not the problem – the sugar that comes with it is. Mexicans enjoy it in mole and hot drinks. The best thing we can do is to find new matches for chocolate consumption. Try sprinkling unsweetened chocolate powder on a banana, fresh raspberries, or warmed butternut squash. Send your recipes into recipes@Spiced.World and I'll post them on the website www.Spiced.World/recipes/. By the way, this is the strategy behind Hershey's recent purchase of the Brookside brand mixing dark chocolate with fruit juices such as pomegranate, blueberries, and açai.

Rounding Out the My Top Ten List of Good Spices
Here I'll spice up the topic with short anecdotes about each of these historically and culinarily important hedonic molecules. Many of these spices

---

1 Pam Belluck, "To Improve Memory, Consider Chocolate," *New York Times*, October 27, 2014, pagesA12, A18.

have antimicrobial properties associated with the warmer climates around the world where infectious diseases and spoiled meat are more prevalent. Ironically, the US Food and Drug Administration reported that about 7 percent of spices imported during 2007-09 were contaminated with Salmonella bacteria. Shipments from Mexico and India were most often contaminated.[1] Since noticed we assume these contamination numbers are falling in the last few years.

Historically, many are also associated with human fertility and libido, as were salt, sugar, and chocolate.

The United States imported 366 metric tons of spices (as defined and listed by the USDA) in 2012. Those numbers exclude salt, sugar, chocolate, coffee, and tea. That's about 19 percent of the world's total production. If we apply an average grocery shelf price of about $4.00 per ounce across all spices (including the hundreds not listed in this chapter) then that yields a rough measure of the industry revenues at about $46 billion.

Cinnamon. In Roman times cinnamon was shipped by barge from Indonesia to West Africa where it was carried north to Alexandria, Venice, and Rome. The Portuguese and then the Dutch carried it by ship more directly to Europe after 1500. And now it comes by ship to America mostly from Indonesia.

Over the centuries poets have associated spices with romance. John Keats wrote about cinnamon:

And she slept an azure-lidded sleep,
In blanched linen, smooth, and lavendered,
While he from forth the closet brought a heap
Of candied apple, quince, and plum, and gourd,
With jellies soother than the creamy curd,
And lucent syrups tinct with cinnamon;

---

1 Another more recent FDA investigation reports finding insect parts, whole insects, rodent hairs, and other things in 12 percent of imported spices. While these are repulsive, they really don't much affect your health. Se Gardiner Harris, "FDA Finds 12 percent of US Spice Imports Contaminated," *New York Times*, October 30, 2013, online.

Manna and dates, in argosy transferred
From Fez; and spiced dainties, every one,
From silken Samarcand to cedared Lebanon.[1]

Certainly cinnamon is also good on toast, just hold the sugar. No one has yet
scientifically tested the relationship between cinnamon and sex. Some studies do show potential positive effects on HIV-1, herpes, diabetes, cancer, and
Alzheimer's disease.

But, before you accept a *Jackass*-style "cinnamon challenge" to swallow a heaping tablespoon, first take a look at a YouTube.com version, and
second recognize that the European Union sets a guideline limit on cinnamon low enough to affect the taste of cinnamon pastries. The European
Safety Authority determined the toxicity of coumarin, a cinnamon component, to cause liver and kidney damage. This is certainly not what Keats
had in mind.

Chili peppers. The spicy and hot flavor of the chilies Columbus found
in the New World resembled the valuable black and white peppers of the
Spice Islands of Indonesia. The Portuguese traders would have passed them
along to Asia, and particularly India. Chili peppers are now integral parts of
both Indian curry powder and paprika, both important spices internationally and in the United States. Indeed, India is now the primary producer of
chili peppers worldwide. However, the hottest chili peppers are not produced
there, but rather here in the United States. The Guinness World Record folks
rank Smokin Ed's "Carolina Reaper" as the hottest. A chili pepper's spiciness
was once a matter of taste, but now it is a matter of chemistry – taste buds
have been obsolesced by high-performance liquid chromatography. Everyone
around the world accepts the Scoville Heat Unit (SHU) scale as grail for the
determining the concentration of capsaicinoids, the chemical compounds responsible for the sensation of heat. The names of the 10 hottest chili peppers
are really cool -- see Exhibit 4.4:[2]

---

1 John Keats, *The Eve of St. Agnes* (1819), 262-270 as quoted from the wonderful book by
Timothy Morton, *The Poetics of Spice* (Cambridge: Cambridge University Press), 2000, 109.
2 See www.CrazyHotSeeds.com, accessed February 17, 2014.

Exhibit 4.4
The Ten Hottest Chili Peppers

	Name	SHU score
1.	Carolina Reaper	2,200,000
2.	Trinidad Scorpion Moruga Blend	2,009,231
3.	Pot Brain Strain	1,900,000
4.	7 Pot Primo	1,900,000
5.	7 Pod Douglah	1,853,936 (7 digits – impressive)
6.	Trinidad Scorpion Butch T	1,463,700
7.	Naga Viper	3,349,000
8.	Other 7 Pot Varieties	1,000,000-1,300,000
9.	Bhut Jolokia (Ghost Pepper)	1,041,427
10.	Red Savina Habanero	500,000

Chili peppers, of course, are quite popular for flavoring foods. They generally contain a variety of good vitamins and minerals. Capsaicin[1], a key component of chili peppers is listed as effective in treating a variety of health problems – digestive tract, cardiovascular, arthritis, mastectomy pain, and headache.

It is also useful in keeping bears, elephants, and mammalian vermin away from humans, crops, and birdseed, respectively.

Cloves. One of the original globally traded spices, cloves are used in cooking throughout the world and in pickling in many places. Small concentrations of the little "black roses" work well.

As a kid growing up in California I can remember Clove Gum in the red package. Cadbury still produces it, and you can buy one-hundred sticks for $29.99 on Amazon. It wasn't one of my favorites, but the rumor was it hid bad breath. This was an important product attribute for a kid in junior high school. And there is the story of the Chinese leader circa 200 BC who required all that spoke to him to chew cloves first to freshen their breath.

In Indonesia cloves and tobacco are blended in the manufacture of kretek cigarettes. The name of the blend is onomatopoetic – it is related to the

---

1   For a list of medicinal purposes see http://www.webmd.com/vitamins-supplements/ingredientmono-945-CAPSICUM.aspx?activeIngredientId=945&activeIngredientName=CAPSICUM.

crackling sound the cloves make as they burn. Some 90 percent of smokers in that country smoke the mix. In 2009 the US government banned the sale of cigarettes made with cloves, that is, kretek cigarettes. In 2010 Indonesia filed a complaint with the World Trade Organization (WTO) regarding the prohibition. The WTO panel found the US law to be discriminatory. The US government appealed. The case now stands in arbitration. However, you *can* buy in the United States "kretek cigars," that is, the exact same sweet-smelling clove/tobacco blend with a filter, but wrapped in brown cigar paper. Ah, loopholes. Even in the twenty-first century cloves continue to be an important matter in international trade.

Cloves and clove oil have been used in traditional (Chinese and Indian) and modern medicine applications. Clove oil (its main component is eugenol), once a common dental pain reliever has now been downgraded by the US Food and Drug Administration. The buds do contain antioxidants and the oil is still used in some toothpastes, laxative pills, and as a dental pain reliever.

Ginger. My dad loved gingersnaps. It must've been a Nebraska thing. Ginger imparts a strong, hot flavor to foods and also serves as a preservative. In Western cuisine ginger is used with sugar in things like gingerbread and ginger ale. In the Koran ginger is granted heavenly status:

God will reward them for their steadfastness with robes of silk and the delights of Paradise. Reclining there upon soft couches, they shall feel neither the scorching heat nor the biting cold. Trees will spread their shade around them, and fruits will hang in clusters over them. They shall be served dishes, and beakers as large as goblets, silver goblets which they themselves shall measure; and brimming cups from the Fountain of Ginger.[1]

The cancer-tumor-reducing claims regarding ginger are largely unproven. It has been found in limited studies to be useful in reducing nausea from

---

[1] Andrew Dalby, *Dangerous Tastes: The Story of Spices* (Berkeley: University of California Press), 2000, 23.

seasickness, morning sickness, and chemotherapy. Of course, in folk medicine ginger is considered a wonder drug.

Nutmeg. Giles Milton writes in his prologue for *Nathaniel's Nutmeg*:

> The island can be smelled before it can be seen. From more than ten miles out to sea a fragrance hangs in the air, and long before the bowler-hat mountain hoves into view you know you are nearing land.
>
> So it was on 23 December 1616. The *Swan's* captain, Nathaniel Courthope, needed neither compass nor astrolabe to know that they had arrived. Reaching for his journal he made a note of the date and alongside scribbled the position of his vessel. He had at last reached Run, one of the smallest and richest of all the islands in the East Indies.
>
> …A forest of willowy trees fringed the islands mountainous backbone; trees of exquisite fragrance. Tall and foliaged like a laurel, they were adorned with bell-shaped flowers and bore a fleshy, lemon-yellow fruit. To the botanist, they were called *Myristica fragrans*. To the plain-speaking merchants of England they were known simply as nutmeg.[1]

After decades of bloody battles, the Dutch ultimately gained control of Run and the rest of the Banda Islands through the Treaty of Breda in 1667. The compromise included an island swap, Run for Manhattan (yes, the New York one). The Dutch laughed all the way to the bank at the time.

In this period cloves from these and adjacent islands were so valuable to Europeans that often the black rose buds themselves served as money. And nutmeg was more valuable than that. Nutmeg trees which also yielded mace grew on far fewer islands making them more precious. Nutmeg is sweeter and mace more colorful, and both were special culinary ingredients for the hedonic-compound-starved Europeans. They also served medicinal and preservative services as well. Obviously in the last four centuries prices have declined, but nutmeg particularly is a favored spice worldwide.

Health benefits from the consumption of nutmeg are not supported by modern research. What we do know is that nutmeg can make you nuts. That

---

1 Giles Milton, *Nathaniel's Nutmeg* (New York: Penguin), 1999, 1-3.

is, in high enough doses, the raw spice induces psychoactive responses, none of which sound like much fun – an excited and confused state, headaches, nausea, dizziness, memory disturbances, and hallucinogenic effects such as visual distortion and paranoid ideation. Apparently, a little is nice, a lot is not.

Pepper (black). The first century Roman poet Persius was already complaining about the power of pepper:

The greedy merchants led by lucre, run
To the parched Indies, and the rising sun;
From thence ho Pepper, and rich Drugs they bear,
Bart'ring for Spices, their Italian ware.[1]

Now it's married to the more common and far cheaper salt on American tables. Black pepper was until recent times much, much more precious. White pepper, its skinless and milder cousin, also comes from the same plants. Ground black pepper can lose its spiciness, its taste, through evaporation. Thus it is often served freshly ground.

The list of ailments black pepper *was thought* to cure is long: constipation, diarrhea, earache, gangrene, heart disease, hernia, indigestion, insomnia, joint and liver problems, lung disease, tooth aches, and more. Modern research provides no evidence for any of these curative claims. Indeed, imagine a product that would cure either constipation or diarrhea. If you are choosing between the salt and pepper at your table – and you should be – always grab the black.

Saffron. Nearly seven hundred dollars an ounce! Why does this cost so much? Pat Willard explains in his book, *Saffron: The Vagabond Life of the World's Most Seductive Spice*:

A cry lets out, the bells ring, and workers rush into the fields, shuffling up and down and across the rows of blossoms, gathering as many as they can before the midday sun wilts the crocus's petals and melts it sated heart. And it is the heart – the three plump trumpet-shaped

1 Quoted in William J. Bernstein's, *A Splendid Exchange: How Trade Shaped the World* (New York: Grove), 2008, 41.

stigmas and a bit of white style – that has for thousands of years been the prize. Such a fragile potency makes the harvest fast and brutal. The one or two weeks during which the flowers bloom – three blossoms for each corn, opening on succeeding mornings – require Herculean drive. Fingers gnarl and backs begin to ache. Eyes grow weary; skin stains a burnt hue. It is delicate work and has, so far, resisted modern machines and innovations. For that reason, saffron is most at home in rustic pockets of insular countries.[1]

The short purple crocus flower grows best in arid lands with Mediterranean breezes. Because its biology is complicated – it is a genetically monomorphic clone – it has propagated slowly. It is a domesticated flower requiring human help to reproduce. There are few places it grows, and the harvest is daunting.

Saffron's honey taste and hay-like fragrance make it attractive, but its rarity makes it culturally alluring. Over the millennia it has been used to treat some ninety illnesses. And, of course, it has also been thought to be an aphrodisiac. It helps that Cleopatra used saffron in her baths so that lovemaking would be more pleasurable. Modern research is pointing to several potential medical uses, but the evidence is still preliminary. I can find no mention of negative consequences of consumption.

Vanilla. Ice cream comes immediately to mind. Thus, Patricia Rain describes in her book, *Vanilla: The Cultural History of the World's Favorite Flavor and Fragrance* how vanilla ice cream first came to the United States:

> … a Frenchman, is believed to have introduced ice cream in Philadelphia. It was after the Revolution, and our young country still maintained strong ties with Europe and an eye for its latest culinary trends. French confectioners, often with credentials, were in demand. Ice cream became such a hit with the elite that George Washington bought Martha an ice-cream machine in 1784, Abigail Adams

---

1 Pat Willard, *Saffron: The vagabond Life of the World's Most Seductive Spice* (Boston: Beacon), 2001, 3-4.

produced it in her home, and Thomas Jefferson, a great fan of French cuisine, experimented extensively with ice-cream making.

Although they were flavors of the Americans, chocolate was a luxury largely reserved for drinking, and vanilla was unknown in the Unites States at this time. Refreshing and available at least part of the year, lemons provide *the* flavor of choice.

All this changed with Thomas Jefferson's request for vanilla pods from France. The irony of his request is the fact that the vanilla pods destined for Jefferson's pleasure traveled from Mexico or the Caribbean to France and then back to the United States, on sailing ships *during the middle of the French Revolution*! Was vanilla an expensive commodity? You bet! ...Jefferson's recipe called for eggs, a product that Philadelphia purists considered an "additive." His recipe was based on creating a French custard base, then freezing it....and was possibly the origin of the term, "French vanilla."[1]

Yum. Now I sitting here wondering what saffron-flavored ice cream would taste like?

Similar to saffron, vanilla production is labor-intensive making it the second most expensive spice. Like chocolate, historically vanilla came from Mexico by way of the Aztecs, then Cortés (thank you again, Hernando), and now is grown in Madagascar primarily. Once the beans are harvested and cured, they are macerated and percolated in ethyl alcohol and water, creating pure vanilla extract with about 35 percent alcohol. Like most spices vanilla was historically thought of as an aphrodisiac and more recently as an antidepressant. Modern studies to support these notions do not exist.

Tulips. An edible aphrodisiac like most of the rest? Actually, one of the first Dutch importers in the sixteenth century mistook a box of the bulbs arriving from Istanbul as Turkish onions. He cooked them up and enjoyed them. He also planted a few and much to his surprise, up came colorful flowers in the spring. The bulbs never did catch on as food although the Dutch did

1 Patricial Rain, *Vanilla: The Cultural History of the World's Favorite Flavor and Fragrance* (New York: Tarcher/Penguin), 2004, 65-66.

consume them is some quantities as starvation hit their country at the end of World War II.

Flowers and sex? We do give them on St. Valentine's Day, don't we?

The reason I include them in my list of important spices is the apparent psychoactive effects they have on humans, particularly Dutch humans. We all love flowers. But for the Dutch, flowers are more important than that. For them, it's more like a national fascination, fixation, or even a fetish for flowers. Why?

The answer is an instructive story about culture and international markets. The story starts with geography, goes through the origins and elements of culture, and ends with the Dutch being the masters of the exhibition, consumption, and production of flowers.

The rivers and the bays make the Netherlands a great trading country. But the miserable weather, rain, and snow more than two-hundred days per year make it a colorless place, gray nearly year-round. The Dutch caravels not only went to the Spice Islands for spice for the palate; they also went to the Eastern Mediterranean for spice for the eyes. The vibrant colors of the tulip first came to Europe from the Ottoman Empire on a Dutch ship in 1561.

The Dutch enthusiasm for the new "visual drug" was great. Its most potent form was purple lace on a background of white, the Semper Augustus. Prices exploded, and speculators bought and sold promissory notes guaranteeing the future delivery of such beauties' bulbs. This derivatives market yielded prices in today's dollars of $1 million or more for a single bulb, enough to buy a five-story house on the canal in central Amsterdam today. Not only did the tulip mania create futures markets, it also caused the first great market bust in recorded history. Prices plummeted when the government took control in 1637. While Semper Augustus has disappeared, you can still buy a close cousin, a Zomerschoon bulb (circa 1629), for $17.55 circa 2016.

The technology in the story comes in the name of Carolus Clusius, a botanist who developed methods for manipulating the colors of the tulips in the early 1600s. This manipulation added to their appeal and value. Because tulips were planted as bulbs, this meant that prized versions could be propagated only slowly, thus adding rarity to their allure. The tulip trade became international for the Dutch.

Every Easter Sunday, the Pope addresses the world at St. Peter's Square in Rome, reciting, "Bedankt voor bloemen." Thus, he thanks the Dutch nation for providing the flowers for this key Catholic ritual. The Dutch government, once every tenth year, sponsors the largest floriculture exhibition in the world, the Floriad. You can go next in 2022. Finally, at the Aalsmeer Flower Auction near Amsterdam, the prices are set for all flowers in all markets around the world. The Dutch remain the largest exporters of flowers (60 percent global market share), shipping them across Europe by trucks and worldwide by air freight.

The high value the Dutch place on flowers is reflected in many ways, not the least of which is their high consumption rate. The Dutch buy more flower stems per capita per year than anyone – 125 compared to American purchases of 75 per capita per year.

Rembrandt Van Rijn's paintings, including his most famous *Night Watch* (1642, now at the Rijksmuseum, Amsterdam), reflect a dark palette. Artists generally paint in the colors of their surroundings. A quarter millennium later, his compatriot Vincent van Gogh used a similar bleak palette when he worked in Holland. Later, when van Gogh went to the sunny and colorful south of France, the colors begin to explode on his canvases. And, of course, there he painted flowers!

Van Gogh's *Vase with Fifteen Sunflowers*, painted in the south of France in 1889, and sold to a Japanese insurance executive for some $40 million in 1987, at the time the highest price ever paid for a single work of art. The Japanese are also big flower consumers, at about 110 stems per capita per year.

Conclusion

There are no villains among the hedonic compounds discussed here. Their positive health effects propounded historically have received very little scientific confirmation in modern times. Of course, part of their appeal historically has been envy – only rich people could enjoy the variety they provided life.

The sexiness might indeed be associated with the wealth signaled by their possession. But in the end, they all taste good, or at least interesting. Many are aromatic as well. And some add to the color of the dinner table, both in the food and in the vase. Enjoy!

Five

Coffee, etc.
Primary chemical ingredient: Caffeine, $C_8H_{10}N_4O_2$

Caffeine treats the symptoms, not the cause.

C. Grace Graham

How important is caffeine. In fact, the United States became a country because of it. The central catalyst of the Revolutionary War was the colonists' disaffection with the British Parliament's helter-skelter policies about the drug. In 1773 we have the Boston Tea Party. Taxes were related to the issue.[1] But more important was the matter of free trade. You can see the priorities of the colonists' complaints expressed in the *Declaration of Independence* three years later:

"For cutting off our Trade with all parts of the world: [read China]

For imposing Taxes on us without our Consent:"

The colonists wanted their tea unfettered by British merchants and ports and taxmen. You might even think of the Boston Tea Party as a drug protest, not unlike the marijuana machinations of today.

---

1 It's useful to note that the tax on tea was not the problem – the US Congress taxed tea from 1789-1872. Rather the issue beyond free trade was how tax laws were being passed in Parliament when Americans had no representation in that body.

96

Tea was the first delivery vehicle for caffeine to Americans, one that they would risk their lives for. Particularly after the second round with the British, the War of 1812, Americans' tastes turned to the more proximate and powerful product, coffee.

While tea, coffee, and chocolate come by their caffeine content naturally, today new interests in added caffeine are gaining market traction. Perhaps it is as horror writer Mira Grant says, "I just don't understand why anyone would want to get their caffeine in a less-efficient form."[1] I think she's referring to the long lines at Starbucks. In any case her idea is a scary one. Indeed, let's compare caffeine doses across products, appropriately starting with Monster in a can. Please see Exhibit 5.1.

Exhibit 5.1
How Do You Get Your Fix – Caffeine Content Compared

Product name	Common serving size	Mgs/serving	Mgs/ounce
Monster Energy	16 ounces	160	10
Red Bull	8.4 ounces	80	10
Redline Energy Drink	8 ounces	316	40
NoDoz Energy Shot	1.9 ounces	115	61
NoDoz OTC pill	1 caplet	200	200
Starbucks House Blend Coffee	12 ounces (Tall)	260	22
Nescafé Clasico	6 ounces water + 1 tsp.	65	11
Lipton Iced Tea	18.5 ounces	60	3
Black Tea brewed	8 ounces	30-80	4-10
Coca-Cola Classic	12 ounces	35	3
Diet Coke	12 ounces	47	4
Pepsi	12 ounces	38	3
7-Up	12 ounces	0	0
Baskin Robbins Jamoca ice cream	4 ounces	20	5
Hershey's Milk Chocolate bar	1.6 ounces	9	6
Hershey's Dark Chocolate bar	1.5 ounces	20	13

Source: Center for Science in the Public Interest, www.cspinet.org, accessed February 8, 2014.

1 Mira Grant, *Deadline* (New York: Orbit, 2011), 128.

As we will learn in the chapters to come there are ways to make drug delivery to the brain more efficient. Smoking or snorting delivers it almost directly to the blood stream, via the respiratory system – think nicotine or cocaine. Intravenous injection puts it directly into the blood, then brain – think heroine. Ingestion really slows things down. According to Ms. Grant's prescription (I hope in jest), best for caffeine would be the NoDoz caplet, then some of the new energy drinks, then a Starbucks House Blend tall. The last is what I order there, and I've got a pound or so of the stuff in my freezer for my French press. Out here in California you can get a coffee enema. Maybe that works faster than merely swallowing it. Never done that one myself.

Most of this chapter we will spend on the marketing of coffee. While some of the energy drinks offer more caffeine and we consume much more soda, coffee still delivers the most caffeine to American brains.

The chests of tea tossed into Boston Harbor contained the mild tasting ingredients for a popular hot drink, one that would have been particularly appropriate on that cold night in December 1773. It also contained an addictive hedonic compound – caffeine. The bitter, white crystalline alkaloid and psychoactive drug is found in varying quantities in a variety of plants around the world including the coffee plant, the tea bush, and the kola tree. The biologists believe the substance helps the plants in insect management – it paralyzes and kills those that would feed on the plants and yet attracts the good pollinators.

If humans were insects, we'd be in the latter category depending on the quantity we consume. The US Food and Drug Administration classifies caffeine as a GRAS (generally recognized as safe) drug because humans almost never consume ten grams of the stuff at a time. Ten grams would kill you. Fifty NoDoz caplets at a time would probably do the trick. But, as a suicide aid caffeine would be a bad choice – you might end up just paralyzed. In any case, most of us consume quantities in the milligrams (mgs) range – see Exhibit 5.1. We'll talk more about the consequences of consumption later in the chapter.

History

Tea. Our story about caffeine starts with my favorite legend ever. One meaning of the term Buddha is "*awakened* one." The Buddhist monk that brought the faith to China circa 1500 was one Bodhidharma. In Buddhist art he is generally portrayed as a *wide-eyed* [my italics], thickly bearded, ill-tempered Western barbarian (from either India or Persia). This appearance enhances the legend. So the story goes that Bodhidharma was meditating in front of a wall and accidentally fell asleep for nine years. He was so disgusted with himself when he woke up that he cut off his own eye lids. The lids fell to the ground, took root, and grew into the first tea bush.

Caffeine consumption actually began in China about one-thousand years earlier according to historical evidence. The earliest written account of its use is in a third century medical text claiming that "to drink bitter tea constantly makes one think better." By the time Bodhidharma was supposedly permanently peeling his eyes, tea drinking was widespread in China.

Production techniques and marketing strategies changed over time, evolving to operations like the Hangzhou Longjing Tea Planation – it's just a forty-five-minute bullet train ride (at more than 200 mph) from Shanghai. Advertising copy on their website is inviting:

> Longjing actually means, "Dragon Well", a place suitable for the planting of the famous green tea. Longjing Tea is one of China's best teas and is one reason for Hangzhou's international fame. The tea is grown in the Longjing mountain area of Hangzhou, southwest of the West Lake.
>
> The flat and smooth tea leaves (resembling pine needles with a yellow to dark green color) brew a tea with light to dark green color, a fragrant scent, and a refreshing taste. The place is frequently visited by those who come for a taste of the Longjing tea, well noted for its greenness, fragrance, mellow taste, and beauty of tea leaves... A trip to the village of Longjing is a drive along the verdant mountains. Tea terraces rise up on either side of the village and it's an interesting area to walk around and watch the locals at work.

Even better is their sales pitch. If you've been to the California wineries you know the routine. This is how we grow and process our tea (grapes). Now take a taste of our favorite leaves (vintages), and exit through gift store. Nice marketing borrowed from the West (or perhaps vice versa). Their home-grown marketing pitches of ancient times are reflected in the modern messages as tea as medicine – it doesn't just taste good, it's good for you as well.

"Watch the locals at work" indeed. Actually, the reason tea has almost always come from China is the inexpensive labor there. Producing tea has been resistant to mechanization. So, almost nobody can compete with their prices.

It is, of course, also grown in Japan. Seeds arrived there in 805, and green tea was for centuries a mainstay of Japanese culture. The Japanese tea ceremony (preparation) is a religious and societal icon. China's adjacent neighbors, Korea and Vietnam, adopted the brew even sooner. Tea was offered to another neighbor, the Russian Czar, in 1618.

Marco Polo reported about Chinese tea taxes in the thirteenth century. By the seventeenth century the drink had spread to Europe, first brought by Dutch traders. It was initially distributed in British coffee houses circa 1650 and spread to the colonies from there. Ultimately India proved both a wonderful producer and consumer of the product.

By the mid-1700s tea had become the national drink in Britain. Trade was controlled by two monopolists, the Chinese Hongs (trading companies) in Canton (modern Guangzhou) and the British East India Company. As full teacups drained British coffers, perhaps the second ugliest triangular trade was invented – manufactured goods to India, opium to China, and tea back to Britain. Indeed, the ugliest trade triangle – money and manufactured goods to West Africa, slaves to the West Indies, and sugar back to England – all came together in British teacups.

We'll get to the Opium Wars in chapter 8. But, we leave the topic of tea with it remaining the national "soft" drink of the United Kingdom even today. It is also the most popular drink world-wide today.

Coffee.

A morning without coffee is like sleep.

Anonymous

None of the legends about the discovery of coffee are nearly as funny as that about the wide-eyed Bodhidharma, so we'll just go with the documented history. Mocha, a Red Sea port of Yemen, is identified by historians as the 1400s birthplace of roasted and brewed coffee. In addition to fighting drowsiness, it was sold as helping a body in other ways. During the next century it spread from there around the Muslim world and then to Venice. Pope Clement VIII's blessing it as a Christian drink in 1600 boosted sales in Europe, and the first coffeehouse opened on the Continent in Italy in 1645. The Queen's Lane Coffee House (recently branded as QL) was opened in Oxford in 1654 and is still serving the brew today.

The British introduced coffee to their North American colonies, but sales really didn't take off (Americans loved their alcohol) until the British withheld tea during the Revolutionary War and the War of 1812. Coffee consumption then became a matter of politics for Americans. Also, the extra caffeine is sure to have gotten them over the more bitter taste. The French started coffee production in the West Indies, in what is now Haiti, and in 1788 it was exported to our new country. While coffee arrived in Brazil a bit earlier, its exports did not take off until after its independence from Portugal in 1822.

Rain forest destruction and cruel labor practices and exploitation were all part of the story of coffee's new popularity. The industry now supports some one-hundred million workers in developing countries around the world, particularly in equatorial Africa and Central America. The labor intensive production process includes cultivating the trees, picking the berries, drying or fermenting them, then roasting the beans for grinding.

The Civil War interrupted the growth of coffee sales in the United States – up from three pounds per capita in 1830 to eight pounds in 1859.

Congress collected a four-cent tax on imported beans and blockaded Southern ports. However, the Union army was a major purchaser thus teaching the soldiers to brew it in camps and by the side of the road during the arduous marches of the conflict. Soldiers preferred to carry the beans and a grinder to ensure freshness. From those Virginia campsites, coffee moved west with American pioneers and ranchers, and was transformed from hot quick energy to American lore. Mark Pendergrast quotes from the November 14, 1949 *New York Times* in his excellent book *Uncommon Grounds*:

> Over second and third cups flow matters of high finance, high state, common gossip and low comedy. [Coffee] is a social binder, a warmer of tongues, a soberer of minds, a stimulant of wit, a foiler of sleep if you want it so. From roadside mugs to the classic demi-tasse, it is the perfect democrat.[1]

Coffee consumption peaked in the United States in the 1940s at about twenty pounds per persons per year. That leads us to the topic of caffeine consumption.

Consumer Behavior

Caffeine enters the American body via a variety of vehicles. Mostly it arrives along with our morning coffee. Indeed, it is perfectly appropriate that the spice/hedonic molecule/drug is named for the coffee plant. We consume substantial quantities of the compound as part of coffee, tea, some soft drinks, chocolate bars, energy drinks, ice cream, over-the-counter pain relievers (such as Anacin and Excedrin), and its most concentrated form, NoDoz.

Throughout history caffeine has been consumed primarily as a medicine. The drug acts as a central nervous system and metabolic stimulant, reducing drowsiness and increasing alertness and focus. Global consumption of caffeine is in the neighborhood of 120,000 metric tons per year. This amounts to one

---

1 Mark Pendergrast, *Uncommon Grounds: The History of Coffee and How It Transformed Our World* (New York: Basic Books, 1999), 235.

serving of a caffeinated beverage for every person on the planet every day of the year, making it the most popular psychoactive substance of all.[1]

Caffeine consumption itself is not tracked directly, but must be calculated from industry statistics. The US Food and Drug Administration (FDA) tells us that "97 percent of the caffeine intake of teenagers and adults comes from beverages [coffee, tea, and soft drinks]…Any significant change in the caffeine intake of the US Population would depend on modification of coffee drinking practices, given that all other caffeine sources make up only a minor contribution to overall caffeine consumption."[2] The FDA's best estimate of average adult American caffeine consumption is about 300 mgs per day – a Starbucks House Blend Tall contains 260 mgs caffeine. We do have good data on coffee and tea consumption allowing the comparisons across countries you see in Exhibit 5.2.

Exhibit 5.2
Coffee and Tea Consumption in Selected Countries

Country	Per capita (pounds/year) Coffee	Tea
Finland	26.4	0.5
Netherlands	18.5	1.6
Sweden	18.0	0.9
Italy	13.0	0.2
Brazil	12.8	0
Germany	12.1	0.5
France	11.9	0.5
United States	9.2	0.7
Japan	7.3	2.2
United Kingdom	6.2	6.0
Saudi Arabia	3.5	1.6
United Arab Emirates	2.0	2.4
China	0	1.8
India	0	1.1

Sources: MarketLineonline.com, FaoStat.fao.org (Food and Agricultural Organization of the United Nations), ChartBin.com, fas.usda.gov/gats all accessed March 1, 2014.

1   See http://www.abc.net.au/quantum/poison/caffeine/caffeine.htm. Accessed March 1, 2014.
2   Lazlo P. Somogyi, *Caffeine Intake by the US Population* (Oakridge, TN: Oakridge National Laboratory, US Food and Drug Administration, 2010), 1.

With the exception of the United Kingdom, the Europeans are the big coffee drinkers. While coffee may be the national drink in the United States, in Finland it's a national fetish. They must not have beds there. If you've read or seen any of the *Girl with the Dragon Tattoo* books or movies you know the Swedes are nuts about their coffee. The high consumption of coffee in Brazil is no surprise – that's where the most coffee is grown. Coffee consumption in the Arab countries is surprisingly low given its origins in neighboring Yemen.

Judging by the statistics in column two, the British are the champion tea drinkers. And don't be fooled by the appearance that they are drinking more coffee than tea – the USDA estimates that one pound of tea leaves will yield nine gallons of tea while one pound of coffee beans yields 2.5 gallons of coffee. Perhaps the most surprising comparison in the lot is that between tea and coffee consumption in Japan. This represents a recent cultural shift that will be explained toward the end of the chapter.

Consumer surveys[1] indicate that 83 percent of American adults drink coffee, 60 percent say they take it daily. Of those who drink it daily, the average adult drinks about three cups/day. Most coffee is consumed at breakfast, about 65 percent, while 30 percent is consumed between meals and 5 percent at dinner or lunch. These quantities really haven't changed much during the last century. In fact, per capita consumption was 9.2 pounds both in 1910 and 2010. It peaked at 16.5 pounds per capita in 1946 – a lot of the World War II GIs picked up the habit on those long night watches and in foxholes around the world.

The National Coffee Association (NCA) 2013 survey noted a demographic bifurcation of coffee consumption – younger people (ages eighteen to thirty-nine) reported substantially lower consumption levels than last year, while older groups (over forty) reported higher. Daily consumption of gourmet coffees remained steady at 31 percent while traditional brands sales fell to 49 percent.[2] In most surveys women drink about 80 percent of the coffee that men do. Coffee consumption peaks in our fifties. The NCA also reports that 80 percent of coffee is consumed at home and the other 20 percent at

---

1 Harvard School of Public Health, see http://www.hsph.harvard.edu/news/multimedia-article/facts/, accessed March 1, 2014.

2 Marvin G. Perez, "Coffee Consumption Increases in US, Association Survey Shows," *Bloomber.*com, March 22, 2013, online.

work, traveling/commuting, and restaurants in that order. They also report that Hispanics and African Americans consume about 90 percent of what Caucasians do.

Mark Pendergrast in *Uncommon Grounds* tells the story of one Joe Bratney, a chef and owner of a restaurant in Staten Island, New York, who claimed to consume fifty cups of Joe a day. Fifty cups, wow! Joe said, "I feel like a changed person after my first cup every morning." One has to ask, if you get a good kick out of the first cup, how good can the next 49 be? Joe is off the scale when it comes to coffee drinking. We can get some indication of the variability of coffee consumption around the average 3.1 cups per day for daily coffee drinkers from recent Mayo Clinic study[1] that reports a relationship between high coffee consumption and early death. In the "Consequences of Consumption" section of this chapter we will discuss the health considerations. Here we are only interested in the variability issue. The sample studied included almost 44,000 healthy American adults with an average age of about forty-three. See Exhibit 5.3 below.

The study suggests that around 20 percent of Americans are coffee teetotalers,[2] so to speak. Sixty percent drink about two cups per day. Over 30 percent are in the range of four cups per day or more.

Exhibit 5.3
Variability in Coffee Consumption

Cups per week	% for men	% for women
0	19	21
1-7	20	29
8-14	21	15
15-21	5	3
22-28	22	26
>28	13	7

Source: Mayo Clinic Proceedings.

1 Junxiu Liu, Xuemei Sui, Carl J. Lavie, James R. Herbert, Conrad P. Earnest, Jiajia Zhang, and Steven N. Blair, "Association of Coffee Consumption with All-Cause and Cardiovascular Disease Mortality," *Mayo Clinic Proceedings 88(10), October 2013, 1066-1074.*
2 This nicely corresponds with the National Coffee Association surveys on non-drinkers.

We close this section with the macro consumption/production statistics for coffee and tea. The world production of coffee is about eight million metric tons per year. Brazil produces 33 percent, Vietnam 15 percent, Indonesia 6 percent, Colombia 6 percent and Ethiopia 5 percent. Over 4 million metric tons of tea are produced globally each year. China accounts for 37 percent of tea production, India 25 percent, Kenya 9 percent, Sri Lanka 8 percent, and Turkey 5 percent.

Marketing

As I've indicated throughout this chapter, the number of forms of caffeine delivery is impressive. The FDA estimates that in the United States 56 percent of the caffeine consumed comes from coffee, 17 percent from tea, 16 percent from soft drinks, 10 percent from other beverages, and less than 2 percent from food. Thus, marketing of coffee will be the focus here, with brief mention of the fastest growing segment, energy drinks.

Product. In the 1980s we in the marketing academic community believed we knew everything there was to know about marketing coffee. With the mountains of data created by grocery store scanners, coffee became the most studied product in history. Coffee became a commodity. Yes, there was instant (mostly Robusta beans harvested in Asia and Africa), ground (mostly Arabica beans harvested mostly in Latin America), and decaffeinated. But, American coffee was a weak brew vis-à-vis that consumed in other countries. Brazilians called it tea. The top brands were Maxwell House, Folgers, and Nescafé. The only thing that made the products distinctive was the ubiquitous television advertising.

Then came Starbucks. Twice the caffeine (read stronger) plus a new (read third) place to consume it, and a customer customized product (think Steve Martin's order in *LA Story*: "half double decaffeinated half caf, with a twist of lemon"). Virtually no mass-media advertising, simply word-of-mouth. Now, only two brands of coffee make the Interbrand Top 100 List for 2013: Nescafé, #37, valued at $11 billion and Starbucks, #91, $4 billion. Other caffeine peddlers also make that list: Coca-Cola fell to #3 at $79 billion, MacDonald's, #7 at $42 billion, and Pepsi, #22 at $18 billion.

The product line extensions are now dizzying (maybe it's the caffeine). Nescafé now offers 48 brand extensions with Nescafé Clasico leading the way on Safeway's shelves. And if you think that's a wonderful array of choices, at Starbucks your options are near infinite. The latest hot item is "single-cup brewing" (Keurig, and so on) – the NCA tells us that in-home ownership of the machines jumped from 10 percent to 12 percent just in the last year. At current growth rates single-cup products may equal the sales of the traditional roast and instant offerings by the end of the decade.

Then you have to throw in the explosion of energy drinks in the last decade, Red Bull and Monster Energy leading the way. Particularly troubling are the caffeine added products. Soft drinks often have added caffeine over and above that from ingredients such as kola nuts. Added caffeine is generated in the coffee decaffeination process and/or through chemical synthesis. Insecticide. Yummy. Three new products contain added caffeine – energy drinks, energy shots (Five-Hour Energy), and for a short while, caffeinated alcoholic beverages. This last disaster of a product was reformulated without caffeine in 2010 by Coors (brand name Spark) and Anheuser Busch (Tilt) after consumer and USDA complaints and states attorneys' general legal threats. Speaking of dizzying, imagine those corporate dopes trying to offer young people a mix of a stimulant and a depressant. Recall that more than a century ago the US Surgeon General banned sales of Coca-cola on military bases when it was revealed that both alcohol and caffeine were in the secret formula.

Place. Coffee is ubiquitous like its brethren sugar and salt. IBISWorld, a marketing research firm, estimates 159,892 companies will sell coffee in 293,523 establishments in the United States this year. More than 11,000 of the establishments will be either owned or licensed by Starbucks. Across all kinds of stores J.M. Smucker Co. (Folgers, and so on) sold the most coffee with a US market share of 22 percent. Starbucks followed with 18.7 percent, 7-Eleven at 3.9 percent, Dunkin' Brands at 1.5 percent, and Walmart at less than 1 percent. There are three major segments in the overall coffee market in the United States – packaged roasted beans, instant (soluble) coffee, and that RTD (ready-to-drink, that is, served in a cup or a bottle) in the stores.

Last year the three top selling brands in your grocery store were Folgers (owned by Smucker's) at $1.4 billion, Maxwell House (Kraft) at $700 million, and Starbucks at $335 million. Private labels sold $448 billion in grounds as well. Decaf sales follow a very similar pattern – Folgers $63 million, private label $47 million, Maxwell House $25 million, and Starbucks $21 million.

Nescafé brands (Nestlé) dominate instant sales in grocery stores, Tasters' Choice and Clasico were $133 million last year, followed by Folgers at $90 million, Maxwell Houses brands at $75 million.

Among the thousands of coffee chains around the country Starbucks stores dominate with a 33 percent market share and Dunkin' Donuts follows with a market share of 16 percent. Almost all stores and chains sell a variety of foods, and it is hard to separate the food versus coffee revenues. Besides grocery stores and coffee shops Starbucks also sells on airliners, in hotels, at companies, hospitals, universities, and so on. Starbucks top-line revenues for its US operations were almost $10 billion last year, and half that was just for coffee at $5.2 billion.[1]

Price. Global coffee prices have always been quite volatile because of the weather, politics in the countries of production, and changing consumer budgets and preferences. Toward the middle of the last century American consumers noticed when prices at the counter of their local diner jumped from a nickel to a dime a cup. But generally, Americans are price insensitive when it comes to coffee.

Since 1980 world prices have varied between a low of 60¢ a pound in 2002 to a high of $2.73 per pound in 2011. Bad weather in Indonesia was to blame for that dramatic price spike. The 2012 price was $1.88 and the 2013 was $1.60 per pound. Generally prices are headed upwards as coffee drinking becomes more popular in places such as Germany, Russia, and China.

At my Safeway a twelve-ounce package of Folgers roasted was $10.99 (assuming water, energy, and your time are free, that's about 6¢ a cup) and Nescafé Clasico (instant) was $7.29 for 7 ounces (about 7¢ a cup). At Starbuck's pound of House Blend costs around $12.00, but if you order it at the counter already brewed a twelve-ounce tall runs about $2.00. The most

---

1   This last estimate is from IBISWorld, see clients1.ibisworld.com.

expensive brand I found on Amazon (although ironically not from Brazil) was an Ethiopian one, Exotic Origins Coffee: 90 Point - Buna Hawisa Ceremonial Select at about $30.00 pound.

I also notice that this exotic is not "fair trade." Less than one percent of coffee sold around the world is classified as such. Consumers are increasingly willing to pay the higher price that goes along with assurances that the farmers and workers are not exploited – fair prices and reasonable working conditions are attested to by the certifying agency.

Finally, as in the previous chapters, I took he Safeway shelf prices for tea ($5.50 for eight ounces of Lipton) and coffee ($8.99 for twelve ounces of Nescafé Clasico) and multiplied them times the tonnage imported (201,000 metric tons, and 1,566,000 metric tons, respectively) to estimate the overall size of the market in the United States for the two beverages combined at $46 billion.

Promotion. Twenty years ago television advertising for coffee was prominent. Print and social media are now taking over, although the ongoing McCafé television campaign runs against that trend.

Among the one-hundred top global advertisers are three that focus on their caffeine products – Nestlé spent over $800 in the US market last year, McDonald's more than $1 billion, and Red Bull about $300 million. Both Nestlé and Red Bull have extensive sales forces that sell their caffeine products to a variety of retail and institutional buyers.

Certainly the emphasis of Red Bull promotion is through its ownership/ sponsorship of a broad variety of sports teams, athletes, events and even video games around the world. Many are involved in extreme sports. In the United States a soccer franchise, a NASCAR racing team, and NFL running back Reggie Bush are all on the payroll. The target market is young men.

Consequences of Consumption

This coffee falls into your stomach, and straightway there is a general commotion. Ideas begin to move like the battalions of the Grand Army of the battlefield, and the battle takes place. Things remembered arrive

*at full gallop, ensuing to the wind. The light cavalry of comparisons de-
liver a magnificent deploying charge, the artillery of logic hurry up with
their train and ammunition, the shafts of with start up like sharpshooters.
Similes arise, the paper is covered with ink; for the struggle commences
and is concluded with torrents of black water, just as a battle with powder.*

Honore de Balzac, "The Pleasures and Pains of Coffee."

Immediate Effects. De Balzac is talking about how coffee affects you as you
are drinking it. We understand these short-term effects pretty well. The long-
term effects we will discuss shortly, and we do not understand them well.

Caffeine stimulates both the nervous and metabolic systems. It is used ca-
sually and in medicines to reduce physical and mental fatigue. Alertness, faster
and clearer flow of thought, better mental focus and physical coordination all
follow consumption in under an hour and for some almost immediately upon
consumption. A moderate dose of caffeine usually wears off after five hours –
thus the brand 5-Hour Energy. Of course the effects vary according to dosage,
body size and tolerance. Sounds good.

The US National Institutes of Health (NIH) counter argues: "…caffeine
can make you restless, anxious, and irritable. It may also keep you from sleeping well and cause headaches, abnormal heart rhythms, or other problems."
Irritable and wide awake, that sounds like Tom Hank's description of Parker
Posey, his fiancée in *Got Mail*: "She makes coffee nervous." Parker Posey also
had a bit too much Starbucks in *Best in Show*.

It is possible to overdose on caffeine. Caffeine intoxication can result
from dosages over 500 mg at a time. Beyond the NIH list of symptoms
listed just above, throw in face flushing, increased urination, gastrointestinal problems, muscle twitching, rambling speech, mania, disorientation,
delusions, hallucinations, psychosis, and even death. This has been one of
the complaints about young people overdosing on energy drinks appearing often in the press. *Forbes*[1] reports that the official cause of death of a

---

1 Dan Munro, "Sugar Linked to $1 Trillion in US Healthcare Spending," *Forbes*, November 27,
2013, online.

fourteen-year-old girl in Maryland was "cardiac arrhythmia due to caffeine toxicity." She had consumed two 24-ounce Monster Energy drinks the day before. The FDA is investigating such deaths, and local governments in New York and California are pursuing new regulations against the high caffeine content and marketing to kids.

Addiction. The average American coffee drinker has about three cups a day. My favorite example of caffeine addiction also comes from Mark Pendergrast in *Uncommon Grounds*:

> Cathy Rossiter, who took part in a 1993 Johns Hopkins study on the effects of caffeine withdrawal… favors Mountain Dew, chugging the heavily caffeinated lemon-lime soft drink all day. Her need was so intense that she found herself standing in a supermarket line holding a Mountain Dew in either hand while she was in labor with her second child.
>
> For the study, Rossiter agreed to abstain from caffeine for two days. "It felt like a migraine, just right behind your eyes. It was like someone had a knife digging out your brains." She nearly threw up – not surprising, since caffeine withdrawal symptom include headaches, drowsiness, fatigue, decreased performance, and for extreme cases, nausea and vomiting. Rossiter made it through the two days but refused the offer to help her kick the habit permanently. With relief she went back to her Mountain Dew.[1]

Is addiction too strong a term? Certainly the tolerance, craving, and withdrawal are there. Binging can be, but not as with sugared products. Most experts say it takes a week for caffeine withdrawal to fade.

Recently researchers at American University and Johns Hopkins have officially labelled the addiction as "Caffeine Use Disorder." I say "officially" because for the first time the affliction is described as such in the *Fifth Edition of the Diagnostic and Statistical Manual of Mental Disorders* (DSM-5). One of the

---

1 *Uncommon Grounds*, 416.

researchers, Laura Juliano[1] at American, elaborates: "The negative effects of caffeine are often not recognized as such because it is a socially acceptable and widely consumed drug that is well integrated in our customs and routines… There is a misconception among professionals and lay people alike that caffeine is not difficult to give up. However in population–based studies, more than 50 percent of regular caffeine consumers report that they have difficulty quitting or reducing caffeine use."

The habitual user, like me and my half cup every morning, is really just treating symptoms of withdrawal for twenty-four hours. Water, cold on the face works as well as hot in the cup. The key is to sleep well. The three-cup-a-day user is simply treating his or her withdrawal symptoms. Had the previous day not started with that first cup, the mental and metabolic lows would be milder, perhaps not even noticeable. Recently researchers at Johns Hopkins Medical School report that performance increases due to caffeine consumption come mainly from drinkers experiencing a short-term reversal of withdrawal symptoms. By controlling for caffeine use in study participants, the researchers found that performance enhancements are absent without caffeine withdrawal.[2] In this sense coffee acts as does sugar, it makes your mental and physical energy levels more volatile.

Long-Term Effects. Coffee, caffeine, and health have been studied a lot. The findings about long-term consequences are all over the place. For example, a National Institute of Health/AARP study reported in 2012 that coffee consumption was associated with longer life.[3] That means our fifty-cups-a-day drinker in from Staten Island should live to 120! Last year a Mayo Clinic study reported that coffee consumption over twenty-eight cups per week to be associated with a shorter life. What should Joe Bratney believe?

---

1 "Caffeine use disorder: A widespread health problem that needs more attention," American University Press Release, January 28, 2014, contact basu@american.edu.

2 Travis Bradberry, "Caffeine: The Silent Killer of Emotional Intelligence," *Forbes*, August 21, 2012, online.

3 Neal D. Freedman, Yikyung Park, Christian C. Abnet, Albert R. Hollenbeck, and Rashmi Sinha, "Association of Coffee Drinking with Total and Cause-Specific Mortality," *New England Journal of Medicine*, 366(2), May 17, 2012, pages 1891-1904.

The most recent review of all this research well summarizes current thinking in the medical community:

> Coffee is a complex beverage containing hundreds of biologically active compounds, and the health effects of chronic coffee intake are wide ranging. From a cardiovascular (CV) standpoint, coffee consumption may reduce the risk of type 2 diabetes mellitus and hypertension, as well as other conditions associated with CV risk such as obesity and depression; but it may adversely affect lipid profiles depending on how the beverage is prepared. Regardless, a growing body of data suggests that habitual coffee consumption is neutral to beneficial regarding the risks of a variety of adverse CV outcomes including coronary heart disease, congestive heart failure, arrhythmias, and stroke. Moreover, large epidemiological studies suggest that regular coffee drinkers have reduced risks of mortality, both CV and all-cause. The potential benefits also include protection against neurodegenerative diseases, improved asthma control, and lower risk of select gastrointestinal diseases. **A daily intake of about 2 to 3 cups of coffee appears to be safe and is associated with neutral to beneficial effects for most of the studied health outcomes.** However, most of the data on coffee's health effects are based on observational data, with very few randomized, controlled studies, and association does not prove causation. Additionally, the possible advantages of regular coffee consumption have to be weighed against potential risks (which are mostly related to its high caffeine content) including anxiety, insomnia, tremulousness, and palpitations, as well as bone loss and possibly increased risk of fractures.[1]

It is really important to notice that the benefits are mostly related to *coffee* consumption while the risks are associated with *caffeine* consumption. The

---

1   James H. O'Keefe, Salman K. Bhatti, Harshal R. Patil, James J. DiNicolantonio, Sean C. Lucan, and Carl J. Lavie, "Effects of Habitual Coffee Consumption on Cardiometabolic Disease, Cardiovascular Health, and All-Cause Mortality," *Journal of the American College of Cardiology*, 62(12), 2013, pages 1043-1051.

literature on tea consumption is similar in this respect. Another important point is that all of the relationships discovered in the data are statistically significant, but most often practically weak. That is, any potential benefit of regular doses is small, as are the risks.

Ways to Reduce Consumption of Caffeine

Looking at the numbers one would have to conclude that human kind has become addicted to caffeine. The hedonic compound was not part of the diet for Paleolithic Man, and has only entered into our consciousness during the last five centuries. It's brain entertainment with little damage done, except to our pocketbooks, in moderate doses.

The US Food and Drug Administration (FDA) is at this writing girding its loins to regulate added caffeine. Michael R. Taylor, FDA deputy commissioner, responded to questions:[1]

Q: The announcement comes just as Wrigley's (a subsidiary of Mars) is promoting a new pack of gum with eight pieces, each containing as much caffeine as half a cup of coffee. Is the timing coincidental?

A: The gum is just one more unfortunate example of the trend to add caffeine to food. Our concern is about caffeine appearing in a range of new products, including ones that may be attractive and readily available to children and adolescents, without careful consideration of their cumulative impact.

One pack of this gum is like having four cups of coffee in your pocket. Caffeine is even being added to jelly beans, marshmallows, sunflower seeds and other snacks for its stimulant effect.

Meanwhile, "energy drinks" with caffeine are being aggressively marketed, including to young people. An instant oatmeal on the market boasts that one serving has as much caffeine as a cup of coffee, and

---

1   See this document and other FDA updates at their website. http://www.fda.gov/downloads/forconsumers/consumerupdates/ucm350740.pdf. Accessed March 5, 2014.

then there are similar products, such as a so-called "wired" waffle and "wired" syrup with added caffeine.

The proliferation of these products in the marketplace is very disturbing to us.

Q. What is your first step in this [regulation] process?

A. We have to address the fundamental question of the potential consequences of all these caffeinated products in the food supply to children and to some adults who may be at risk from excess caffeine consumption. We need to better understand caffeine consumption and use patterns and determine what is a safe level for total consumption of caffeine. Importantly, we need to address the types of products that are appropriate for the addition of caffeine, especially considering the potential for consumption by young children and adolescents.

We've already met with some companies to hear their rationale for adding caffeine to varied products and to express our concern. We've also reached out to the American Beverage Association, which represents the non-alcoholic beverage industry, and the Grocery Manufacturers Association, which represents food, beverage and consumer-products companies.

Q. What is currently considered a safe amount of daily caffeine?

A. For healthy adults FDA has cited 400 milligrams a day—that's about four or five cups of coffee—as an amount not generally associated with dangerous, negative effects. FDA has not set a level for children, but the American Academy of Pediatrics discourages the consumption of caffeine and other stimulants by children and adolescents. We need to continue to look at what are acceptable levels.

We're particularly concerned about children and adolescents and the responsibility FDA and the food industry have to protect public health and respect social norms that suggest we shouldn't be marketing stimulants, such as caffeine, to our children.

Q. What currently are FDA requirements concerning caffeine being added to foods?
A. Manufacturers can add it to products if they decide it meets the relevant safety standards, and if they include it on the ingredient list. While various uses may meet federal food safety standards, the only time FDA explicitly approved adding caffeine was for colas in the 1950s. Existing rules never anticipated the current proliferation of caffeinated products.

Q. Is it possible that FDA would set age restrictions for purchase?
A. We have to be practical; enforcing age restrictions would be challenging. For me, the more fundamental questions are whether it is appropriate to use foods that may be inherently attractive and accessible to children as the vehicles to deliver the stimulant caffeine, and whether we should place limits on the amount of caffeine in certain products.

Q. Have you taken any actions on other caffeinated products?
A. In 2010, we brought about the withdrawal from the market of caffeinated alcoholic beverages, primarily malt beverages, in part because of studies indicating that combined ingestion of caffeine and alcohol may lead to hazardous and life-threatening situations. Caffeine can mask some of the sensory cues that people might normally rely on to determine their level of intoxication.

Q. Don't new regulations take a lot of resources and time?
A. They do. But we believe that some in the food industry are on a dubious, potentially dangerous path. If necessary, and if the science indicates that it is warranted, we are prepared to go through the regulatory process to establish clear boundaries and conditions on caffeine use. We are also prepared to consider enforcement action against individual products as appropriate.

However, we hope this can be a turning point for all to prevent the irresponsible addition of caffeine to food and beverages. Together, we should be immediately looking at what voluntary restraint can be used by industry as FDA gets the right regulatory boundaries and conditions in place.

I'm hopeful that industry will step up.

We know from their behavior regarding other hedonic substances that the companies' executives won't do anything to hurt their profits voluntarily. Wrigley did take their caffeine-laden gum off the market. But, just wait for the next Republican president to be elected, then you may fire when ready, Wrigley. Here are a few things the government can do.

1. Tax caffeine content, and particularly added caffeine. Recall that the US government taxed tea *after* the Revolution. The Boston Tea Party was not a tax revolt. Read your history if you disagree. Better, read the Declaration of Independence. The Boston Tea Party was a protest against trade controls and taxes *without representation*. And, as I mentioned in previous chapters, I am against taxing consumers directly. Tax the food and beverage processors. Such an approach eliminates one of their best arguments about damage to competitiveness. It levels the corporate playing field. With effect, we already tax tobacco, alcohol, and most recently in some states, marijuana. Moreover, there's a political interest group that might be persuaded to support such a tax – the 50 percent of caffeine users say they would like to reduce their consumption.
2. Front-of-the-package labeling of caffeine content is a no-brainer requirement.
3. Ban mass-media advertising of all products containing added caffeine. If Starbucks has proven anything, word-of-mouth works just fine (although I notice that they have begun to advertise). Company websites, online group forums, and blog posts are becoming more important sources of information rather than "non-permission" mass-media advertising.

4. Short of a ban on advertising, it seems better policing of companies' marketing claims is in order. Consider just two quick examples from the Nescafe.com, click on "Coffee and Well-being":

> "Today, experts agree that moderate coffee consumption of up to 4-5 cups per day is not associated with detrimental effect on health…"

This is hogwash. I wonder how many experts they are talking about? Is it two, several, many, most, or what? In this area, experts agree on little. Please take look at the Mayo Clinic research cited just above. Or,

> "The intriguing complexity of coffee means it can deliver a whole range of emotional benefits that go beyond taste – from stimulation to relaxation to refreshment, and beyond."

I guess this is true if *beyond* means nervousness, anxiety, and the loss of emotional intelligence.[1]

Marketing Miscreant – Caffeine

I can think of five good candidates. First would be Wrigley's caffeine gum. Kids will love that one. Impossible to control. Nice. But, I just learned about that today.

Second would be Coors and Anheuser Busch for trying to sell drinks mixing caffeine and alcohol in their Spark and Tilt brands, respectively. Really? I do note that Kahlua's label lists both coffee and alcohol, but they claim on their website that the caffeine levels are miniscule.

I'm not too happy with Starbucks. It's really annoying that I am probably addicted to my favorite brand of coffee more for the high dosage of caffeine

---

1 Travis Bradberry, "Caffeine: The Silent Killer of Emotional Intelligence," *Forbes*, August 21, 2012, online.

than the "strong" flavor. Also, for about ten years my co-authors and I have lambasted the ethnocentricity and hubris of Starbucks in forcing the Chinese to put a Starbucks store in the center of the Forbidden City in Beijing. This would be akin to Chinese mini-auto-maker Cherry placing a showroom among the cherry trees across from the Jefferson Monument in Washington, DC. The Chinese protestors finally ousted the eyesore in 2007. We still have a picture of that marketing relic on page 359 of the seventeenth edition of *International Marketing.*[1]

Red Bull marketing practices are nasty – I almost went with Red Bull. Yes, let's encourage *Jackass* behavior globally at $283 million a year. But the most heinous aspect of their marketing is their reputed sales tactic of colluding with bartenders to sell more alcohol. Give them a Red Bull, that'll keep them drunk and alert and able to order another one.

But, Nestlé wins the DoubleM award in this chapter. Of course, Nestlé's behavior was egregious with respect to infant formula in the 1970s. We have a case on our *International Marketing* website about that, and now that I think about it, another on Starbucks as well.

On the face of it getting the Japanese tea drinkers hooked on coffee is an amazing marketing victory. You'll notice in Exhibit 5.2 above that Japanese consumed more coffee than tea circa 2013. The historic switch in preference took place in 1999. But let's open the Nescafé kimono regarding their "masterful" marketing.

Nothing gets my goat quicker than marketers taking advantage of children's innocence – it's the worst ethics. We take the story from a wonderful book by French psychologist Dr. Clotaire Rapaille, *The Culture Code.* In his words:

> My first meeting with Nestlé executives and their Japanese advertising agency was very instructive. Their strategy, which today seems absurdly wrong, but wasn't as obviously so in the 1970s, was to try to convince Japanese consumers to switch from tea to coffee. Having spent some time in Japan, I knew that tea meant a great deal to this culture, but I had no sense of what emotions they attached to coffee.

---

1   Philip R. Cateora, Mary C. Gilly, John L. Graham, and R. Bruce Money, *International Marketing* (New York: McGraw-Hill, 17th edition, 2016), 359.

I decided to gather several groups of people together to discover how they imprinted the beverage. I believed there was a message there that could open a door for Nestlé...

I designed this [market research] process to bring participants back to their first imprint of coffee and the emotion attached to it. In most cases, though, the journey led nowhere. What this signified for Nestlé was very clear. While the Japanese had an extremely strong emotional connection to tea (something I learned without asking in the first hour of the sessions), they had, at most, a very superficial imprint of coffee. Most, in fact, had no imprint of coffee at all.

Under these circumstances, Nestlé's strategy of getting these consumers to switch from tea to coffee could only fail. Coffee could not compete with tea in the Japanese culture if it had such weak emotional resonance. Instead, if Nestlé was going to have any success in the market at all, they needed to start at the beginning. They needed to give the product meaning in this culture. They needed to create an imprint for coffee for the Japanese.

Armed with this information, Nestlé devised a new strategy. Rather than selling instant coffee to a country dedicated to tea, they created desserts for children infused with the flavor of coffee but without the caffeine. The younger generation embraced these desserts. Their first imprint of coffee was a very positive one, one they would carry throughout their lives. Through this, Nestlé gained a meaningful foothold in the Japanese market.

Over the ensuing years coffee consumption has burgeoned as those kids grew up. Indeed, Starbucks might have thanked Nestlé for the help! Of course, Nescafé does quite well there, at last count a 66 percent share of the instant coffee market.

Six

Tobacco

Primary chemical ingredient: Nicotine, $C_{10}H_{14}N_2$

"If children don't like to be in a smoky room they'll leave." When asked by a shareholder about infants, who can't leave a smoky room, Harper stated, "At some point, they begin to crawl."

CHARLES HARPER, R.J. REYNOLDS CHAIRMAN

6097.

LEGACY TOBACCO DOCUMENTS LIBRARY, UCSF

I f you got the impression from the last chapter that tea was the most important hedonic compound in the foundation of the United States you'd be wrong. Hands down, tobacco was much more important. It delivered the English language and ultimately Adam Smith's philosophy, whose subsequent misinterpretation led to Harper's comments above. Let me explain.

As you know, the Spaniards and Portuguese were way ahead of the British on the whole colonization thing. Only after the British prevailed against the Spanish Armada in 1588 did their colonial ambitions begin to bear fruit. Sir Walter Raleigh, having been granted a royal patent from Queen Elizabeth I to explore Virginia, sponsored two ventures there. Both the 1584 and 1587 attempts failed. Indeed, the latter to Roanoke, Virginia was hampered when supply ships were ordered to stay in port to prepare for the Armada. By the time the supply ships arrived, there were no colonists left to supply. To this day their fate is an historical mystery.

A third attempt, supported by a broader group of British investors in the Virginia Company finally succeeded. The group arrived in 1607 at Jamestown, Virginia, preceding the Plymouth Rock expedition by eleven years. The first few years of the Jamestown colony were mostly a matter of survival. Only 61 of the original five-hundred survived disease and starvation to see the arrival of new supplies in 1610.

Investors were considering again to throw in the towel. A number of "industries" had been developed toward making the colony economically viable – making metal tools for the Native Americans, glassblowing, wine, olive oil, silk weaving, lumber, and mining. All foundered.

Aboard one the 1610 supply ships was one John Rolfe who had happened to nap a cache of tobacco seeds from Trinidad or Bermuda (sources disagree which), which had grown wild after a Spanish shipwreck there. Rolfe not only successfully harvested tobacco, he also harvested Pocahontas, daughter of the local chief. His new wife helped not only in production of the tobacco, but also in marketing it back in Britain. Sadly the germs associated with that international marketing adventure killed her before she could return.

King Tobacco had saved the venture and the British had a foothold in the New World. Thus, the primary language of the new country became English. While the Founding Fathers were writing the Declaration of Independence in 1776, they were also reading Adam Smith's *The Wealth of Nations* and his "invisible hand" that apparently Charles Harper thought would take that infant out of that smoky room.

Yes, tobacco saved the Jamestown and Virginia ventures and delivered the Anglo culture to the continent. But, now we are learning that tobacco killed some 100 million people around the world in the last century, and will kill one billion in the present century.

History[1]

The paleobotanists tell us that the tobacco plant, native to the Americas, was first cultivated in the Peruvian/Ecuadorean Andes circa 4000 BC. Its use spread across the Americas, including the Caribbean Islands, by the time Columbus landed in 1492. Given its ubiquitous use among Native Americans, it is surprising that the Norse explorers five-hundred years earlier didn't pick up the practice from their trade with the natives in Newfoundland.

Iain Gately in his wonderful book, *Tobacco*, describes the way Native Americans consumed tobacco products historically:

> Tobacco was sniffed, chewed, eaten, drunk, smeared over bodies, used in eye drops and enemas, and smoked. It was blown into warriors faces before battle, over fields before planting and over women before sex, it was offered to the gods, and accepted as their gift, and not least it served as a simple narcotic for daily use by men and women... Its mild analgesic and antiseptic properties rendered it ideal for treatment of minor ailments... for snake bites, fever, or cancer... Tobacco played a central role in the spiritual training of shamans.[2]

One of the early uses of tobacco was as an insecticide similar to caffeine. The Europeans justified its adoption primarily based on its medicinal uses. Indeed, I highly recommend you visit Plimoth Plantation in Plymouth, Massachusetts as well as Jamestown and Williamsburg, Virginia where actors play the roles of the early colonists. When we took the tours with our kids the in-character "colonist" talked about the "wonderful medicinal properties" of the tobacco she was tending, and at Williamsburg we heard the story of John Hancock's rum smuggling commerce before the Revolution.

---

1 Iain Gately's *Tobacco: A Cultural History of How an Exotic Plant Seduced Civilization* (New York: Grove Press, 2001) has been a wonder resource for the writing of this chapter.
2 *Tobacco: A Cultural History...*, 5-6.

Particularly the early British explorers couldn't market the tobacco solely based on its hedonic high. King James I, the witch killer crowned in 1603, equated smoking tobacco with alcoholism, addiction, and Satanism. This is the King James that commissioned the translation of the Bible into English for the Church of England. The first anti-tobacco advertising campaign may have been his royal pamphlet, *A Counterblaste to Tobacco*. The year he published the pamphlet he also raised taxes on tobacco by 4000 percent. Except for his burning four-hundred witches per annum, the King seems a pretty smart guy. The Virginia Company hid its early interests in the tobacco trade at the time. They didn't have e-mails to delete, they just didn't use the word in their written strategic plans. James's law making was so effective that in 1614 seven thousand tobacco shops opened in England [read with sarcasm]. As with the other spices, slavery shortly became essential for the trade.

Meanwhile in places like Brazil and the Caribbean Islands the natives were seen using snuff. The Spaniards soon established a monopoly for its manufacture in Seville. It quickly became the key delivery vehicle for nicotine in Europe through the 1700s, while North American colonists tended to favor the pipe. With its popularity came all kinds of restrictions on the Continent such as papal bans and Russian Czar Michael in 1643 promulgating a law requiring nose removal for snuff takers. This sounds a little like Bodhidharma's cure for sleeping too much from the last chapter. In England in 1761, John Hill reports for the first time a correlation between snuff consumption and nasal polyps – that is, cancer. In the East both the Turks and Chinese imposed death penalties for smoking circa 1634.

Aside from the first US tobacco tax passed to help finance the Civil War, the 1800s brought three big advances for the spice worldwide. It's not clear which of the three has killed more people since. First, the Treaty of Tianjin allowed cigarettes to be imported into China. Next, Philip Morris Esq. opened its first tobacco shop in London. Finally, James Bonsack received a patent for the first practical cigarette-making machine able to cough out [so to speak], 100,000 sticks per day. Production costs plummeted and consumption began a new, explosive growth.

Tobacco

The best summary of tobacco events in the twentieth century is Allan Brandt's *The Cigarette Century: The Rise, Fall, and Deadly Persistence of the Product That Defined America*.[1] Actually, the title itself is the most concise summary of all. I quote from the book jacket:

> From agriculture to big business, from medicine to politics, *The Cigarette Century* is the definitive account of how smoking came to be so deeply implicated in our culture, science, policy, and law. The invention of mass marketing led to cigarettes' being emblazoned in advertising and film, deeply tied to modern notions of glamour and sex appeal. It is hard to find a photo of Humphrey Bogart or Lauren Bacall without a cigarette. No product has been so heavily promoted or has become so deeply entrenched in American consciousness.

Yes, deeply implicated, deeply tied, deeply entrenched, tobacco – as all marketing folks know, repetition pesters, but often makes the point.

Early in the century, the tide rose with British American Tobacco's (BAT) cigarette advertising used films in China, Japan, and Korea. Philip Morris introduced the Marlboro brand as a women's cigarette in 1924. The US government broke up the American Tobacco monopoly and successfully prosecuted the companies for price fixing. In China the government became the monopolist, confiscating BAT assets and its biggest market.

The latter half of the century saw the introduction of both the Marlboro Man and Joe Camel. But, it also saw the beginning of the consumer/medical community/government full-on attack on tobacco. Indeed, just this last year we all witnessed the golden anniversary of the tipping point – the 1964 Surgeon General's report that affirmed that smoking causes cancer in males. It only took thirty-three more years for the Congress to pass a bill prohibiting the Departments of State, Justice, and Commerce from promoting the sale or export of tobacco, thus ending perhaps the greatest governmental hypocrisy in

---

1 Allan M. Brandt, *The Cigarette Century: The Rise, Fall, and Deadly Persistence of the Product That Defined America* (New York: Basic Books, 2007).

American history. Shockingly, the American Chamber of Commerce in 2016 still has no qualms about fighting smoking regulations in foreign countries. I hope soon the AmCham board members with a brain will put this heinous American practice to an end.

Consumer Behavior[1]

Different from the arguments about salt, sugar, and coffee, there is no argument about tobacco and its nicotine. It is an addictive drug that kills people, a lot of them.

The hint of good news in this part of the story is that American consumers have been cutting back. See Exhibit 6.1 for details. As you can see per capita cigarette consumption took off with modern manufacturing techniques, and exploded during World War II. Then came the new power of television advertising. Cancer studies began to have an impact on consumption in the 1950s after the Korean War. In 1963 per capita consumption peaked at about 4300 cigarettes per person per year. Scary numbers. With the publication of the Surgeon General's report in 1964 cigarette consumption has crashed to a level in 2016 just below 1000. This is remarkable progress. The graph also shows the government actions that coincided with the continuous declines in smoking – consumer information campaigns, a doubling of federal taxes in 1983, and a broadcast advertising ban in 1971.

---

1 The statistics in this section are gleaned from the following sources: the US Center for Disease Control, the US Census, the US Surgeon General, the 2012 Tobacco Atlas, Statisa Tobacco and Smoking Dossiers 2013, and IBISWorld.

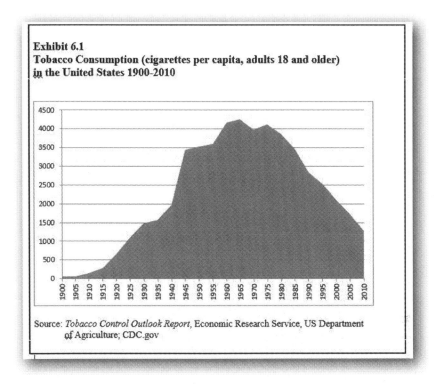

Exhibit 6.1
Tobacco Consumption (cigarettes per capita, adults 18 and older) in the United States 1900-2010

Source: *Tobacco Control Outlook Report*, Economic Research Service, US Department of Agriculture; CDC.gov

The careful reader will notice as odd the blip up in consumption following the TV advertising ban. But it coincides with the return of Vietnam veterans from that awful conflict. You can see the acceleration of demand associated with the major wars in Exhibit 6.1. And now we have new research that details how the stresses of military deployments stimulate smoking behavior: "Military deployment is associated with smoking initiation and, more strongly, with smoking recidivism, particularly among those with prolonged deployments, multiple deployments, or combat exposures. Prevention programs should focus on the prevention of smoking relapse during or after deployment."[1] Other than that anomaly, cigarette smoking has thankfully plummeted.

The bad news is that anyone still smokes at all. Circa 2016 about 16 percent of American adults still smoke (that is down from its peak in 1963 of over 40

---

1 B. Smith, M.A. Ryan, D.L. Wengard, T.L. Patterson, D.J. Slymen, C.A. Macera, "Cigarette Smoking and Military Deployment: A Prospective Evaluation," *American Journal of Preventative Medicine* 35(6), 2009, 539-46.

percent). That means about forty-two million Americans are doing almost all the cigarette smoking; and they are inhaling on average a pack a day. As in most health related statistics, females demonstrate their superior judgment – 17 percent of men and 13 percent of women are smokers. Smoking varies by age group: 18-44 years, 17.0 percent; 45-64, 16.9 percent; and 64+, 7.5 percent. Ethnicity makes a difference as well, 17.1 percent of whites are smokers, 18.1 percent of blacks, and 10.4 percent of Hispanics. Rates of smoking generally decline with higher education – 23 percent with a high school diploma and 9 percent with a college degree. Finally, smoking prevalence breaks at the poverty line – 28 percent below and 17 percent above.

The creepiest numbers are related to children. Twelve percent of American children are exposed to second hand smoke in the home. Almost 9 percent of thirteen- to fifteen-year-olds smoke. Ten percent have smoked an entire cigarette before the age of thirteen. For 83 percent of American smokers, consumption starts as a child. This last statistic is key – this means that the battle ground for reducing the consumption of cigarettes is with underage smokers. Apparently Big Tobacco sees it similarly. A *Washington Post* article exposed their targeting of children:

> One of the documents quotes from a Sept. 30, 1974, presentation to the Reynolds board of directors in Hilton Head, S.C., in which the company's marketing vice president, C.A. Tucker, addressed the looming decline in RJR's business and the need to reorient the company's entire marketing focus on young people.
>
> "They represent tomorrow's cigarette business," Tucker said. "As this 14-24 age group matures, they will account for a key share of the total cigarette volume for at least the next 25 years." Noting a surge in youth sales by competitor Philip Morris Co.'s Marlboro brand, Tucker added, "This suggests slow market share erosion for us in the years to come unless the situation is corrected. . . . Our strategy becomes clear for our established brands: 1. Direct advertising appeal to the younger smokers."[1]

1 John Mintz and Saundra Torry, "Internal R.J. Reynolds Documents Detail Cigarette Marketing Aimed at Children," *Washington Post*, January 15, 1998, A01.

Most experts argue that as disposable income increases so does demand for cigarettes. This view seems inconsistent with the previously mentioned poverty gap and observed behaviors during the 2008-09 recession when the percentage of smokers increased in the United States for the first time in fifteen years. Some argue that the increasing stresses of job and income losses caused consumers to relieve stress through tobacco use.

Cigarette consumption varies dramatically around the world. Exhibit 6.2 includes a sampling of countries. You might compare the numbers there to the 4,300 cigarettes per capita per year in the United States in 1963. The Serbians, Greeks, and Russians are the gold-, silver-, and bronze-medal winners of cigarette consumption. Americans had the biggest smoking problem in the 1960s. Now that health disaster has shifted to China. The Middle Kingdom residents smoked some 2.2 trillion cigarettes in 2009 – that's 38 percent of the total produced globally. The next four countries together – Russia, the United States, Indonesia, and Japan – consumed only half the Chinese amount. We will revisit how the Chinese are trying to manage their 281 million smokers in Chapter 13. The lowest levels in the world are in Africa. Tobacco is expensive there and in India as well.

Exhibit 6.2
Tobacco Consumption in Countries (cigarettes per capita)

Country	Cigarettes/year	Country	Cigarettes/year
Serbia	2861	Saudi Arabia	809
Greece	2795	Netherlands	801
Russia	2786	United Kingdom	750
Japan	1841	Sweden	715
China	1711	Finland	671
Italy	1475	UAE	583
United States	1028	Brazil	504
France	854	India	96

Source: Tobacco Atlas, 2012.

Of course, there are ways to consume tobacco other than cigarettes: Roll-your-own (RYO), *bidis* (wrapped in leaves, particularly popular in India and recently banned in the United States by the FDA), *kreteks* (containing cloves), pipe tobacco, hookah, cigars, chewing tobacco, moist snuff, dry snuff, dissolvable products (like throat lozenges), and, most recently, e-cigarettes. Presently, all these other options total less than 10 percent of total tobacco consumption globally. In the United States about 11 percent of the tobacco consumed is from cigars, chewing tobacco, and smokeless forms, with men doing most of the chewing, sucking, and puffing.

Governments and medical officials around the world are trying to catch up to the growing demand for e-cigarettes, especially as the delivery device is particularly attractive to teens. In the United States 3.3 percent of sixth to twelfth graders reported trying e-cigarettes in 2011. That number jumped to 6.8 percent in 2012. At this writing a bill has been introduced in the US Senate that bans sale of electronic cigarettes to children. The bill includes a definition: "…a battery operated-product designed to deliver nicotine, flavor, or other chemicals and that turns chemicals, such as nicotine, into an aerosol that is inhaled by the user." Kids are attracted to the colors and flavors the tobacco firms are offering. In addition to the lack of information about industry marketing practices of the tobacco companies, the health implications of e-cigarettes are uncertain.

The location of production is a key consideration. World tobacco production has stabilized above seven million metric tons per year over the last three decades. In 2011 China produced more than 3.1 million metric tons, India 1.0, Brazil 0.95, the United States 0.27, and Malawi 0.17 million metric tons. Of the six trillion cigarettes produced around the world most are consumed locally with about ten percent being imported. German exports are the greatest at 180 billion per year, the Netherlands about 115 billion, Poland 90 billion, the United States 60 billion, and Indonesia 57 billion.

Tobacco production in the United States is divided among North Carolina at 173,000 metric tons, Kentucky 89,000, Virginia 25,000, South Carolina 24,000, and Pennsylvania and Georgia about 19,000 metric tons each.

We close this section on consumer behavior with one dreary datum – in the United States 86 percent of smokers have tried to quit at least once. Worse still the US Food and Drug Administration discounts this fact in its policy making about the drug.[1]

Marketing

Here we focus on the marketing of manufactured cigarettes as they constitute about 90 percent of tobacco consumption in the United States.

Product. The form of cigarettes sold in the United States is unusually standardized. Variations on the twenty-stick pack, ten-pack carton are few. Of the $42 billion top-line revenues for the tobacco industry 62 percent is generated from nonmenthol cigarettes, 27 percent from menthol cigarettes, 7 percent from chewing and smokeless tobacco, and 3 percent from cigars. The remaining 1 percent of revenue is generated from such other products as pipe tobacco, *kreteks*, e-cigarettes, and tobacco extracts and essences.

There are a variety of sources other than tobacco for a nicotine fix – gums, patches, suckers, and nicotine infused water are prominent examples.

New product innovation in the industry is rather bleak with the exception of e-cigarettes during the last several years. The federal government has prohibited flavored cigarettes as they might appeal primarily to children. Here's a list of yummy-sounding choices: bacon, blueberry waffle, apple pie, banana split, cherry cheesecake, and Graham cracker. Obviously I find the last most objectionable. However, manufacturers can sell such flavored products as cigarillos and/or kreteks wrapped in brown tobacco leaves.

E-cigarettes are perceived as healthier than traditional cigarettes. Rather than delivering nicotine to the lungs via smoke, the vehicle is water chemical vapors, thus the new term "vaping." They are so far produced in a variety of flavors that appeal to younger smokers. And, at least so far, e-cigarettes have been subject only to sales taxes, not tobacco taxes. Some of the newer smokeless options, such as lozenges and snuffs are gaining traction because they avoid pervasive no-smoking regulations.

---

1 Anna V. Song, Paul Brown, and Stanton A. Glantz, "When Health Policy and Empirical Evidence Collide: The Case of Cigarette Package Warning Labels and Economic Consumer Surplus," *American Journal of Public Health*, December 12, 2013, online.

American tobacco farmers and cooperatives sell their production mainly to multinational tobacco companies. Altria Group (formerly known as Philip Morris) dominates the US industry with a 57 percent market share. Their flagship brands are Marlboro and Virginia Slims. Reynolds American holds about a 19 percent share of the market with Camels, Salems, and Winstons (my old college brand). Lorillard captures about 16 percent of the market with Newports and Kents.

All three major firms are spreading their portfolios of products to include smokeless brands, e-cigarette brands, and even smoking cessation brands via mergers and acquisitions.

Place. As a kid growing up in California in the 1960s cigarettes were easily available to teens in vending machines for about 50¢ a pack. Now their availability to children is much more, but not nearly enough, restricted by law. Retailers are required to post a license for sales directly to consumers. Most recently states have begun to restrict sales to those twenty-one and older.

Today most cigarettes are sold to consumers in supermarkets and convenience stores. The manufactures sell 69 percent of their produce to wholesalers that in turn sell to the markets and stores. Some of the larger chains and superstores buy directly from the manufacturers – they deliver 17 percent of their sales directly to supermarkets and 8 percent to convenience chains. In the 5 percent "other" category are tobacco product shops and other niche stores. Institutional buyers also are part of the other category, including hotels, bars, casinos, airports, and sports facilities. Online sales are a growing part of the other category as well. Amazon.com prohibits their sale, but a variety of online retailers allow it – their customers enjoy the convenience and potential for tax savings.

The most recent positive change in cigarette distribution is CVS Caremark pharmacy chain's policy to halt all sales of tobacco products: "We have about 26,000 pharmacists and nurse practitioners helping patients manage chronic problems like high cholesterol, high blood pressure and heart disease, all of which are linked to smoking," said Larry J. Merlo, chief executive of CVS. "We came to the decision that cigarettes and providing health care just don't go together in the same setting." The company estimates a $2 billion loss in sales revenues affecting other products such as gum and other incidental sales items. The early financial results show a decline in front-of-store sales for CVS, but pharmaceutical sales have more than made up for that revenue loss. A variety of local, state, and federal officials are exhorting other huge pharmaceutical retailers – Rite Aid, Walgreen, Kroger, Safeway, and Walmart – to follow suit.

Only 1.2 percent of American produced cigarettes are exported. During the 2008-09 recession, US exports fell below imports for the first time in history. Most of our exports go to Japan and our imports come from the Dominican Republic.

Price. Because of a complex set of government controls and subsidies the price of leaf tobacco to US manufacturers was relatively stable – at around $1.90 per pound – until 2005. The longstanding federal government price support system was thrown in the ash can as US exports collapsed in the face of global competition. The 2004 Fair and Equitable Tobacco Reform Act passed by Congress eliminated price supports, poundage quotas, acreage allotments, and geographic restrictions on production that had been in place for decades. All these subsidies and restrictions were passed decades ago in the name of saving jobs. A massive consolidation of tobacco farms ensued reducing the number of farms from 40,000 to 15,000 by 2007 Prices also crashed to about $1.50 per pound in 2005. They have since then climbed back to almost $2.00 per pound in most recent years as world prices have climbed.

In 2013 the topic of tobacco subsidies came up again in the Congress. Senator John McCain got a bit crankier when he learned that subsidies hadn't been completely eliminated by the 2004 legislation. "It turns out that Joe Camel's nose has been under the tent all this time in the form of hidden crop insurance subsidies," said McCain. Between 2008 and 2012 the federal government paid tobacco farmers almost one billion dollars in the form of premiums for crop insurance. But the Senate rejected the amendment to the 2013 Farm Bill that would have halted such payments. Thus your federal tax dollars are still used to make tobacco prices cheaper and cigarettes more attractive.

As annoying as all this federal support for tobacco is, it really affects the price of a pack of Marlboros very little. The 10¢ a pack that goes to the farmer is an insignificant cost relative to the manufacturing and marketing costs charged and the profits accrued by the tobacco companies and their distributors and the federal and state excise and sales taxes. The federal government taxes each pack in all states at $1.01.

The differential state taxes explain the huge variation in the per pack price around the country. In the latest survey by www.theawl.com, a pack of cigarettes will cost you about $5 in Kentucky, North Dakota, and West Virginia. The most expensive packs can be purchased in Hawaii at $9.68, Illinois at $11.59, and New York at $14.50. Given that the average price per pack in neighboring Pennsylvania is only $6.95, trunk loads of the stuff are heading north at a vigorous pace. The nine-dollar difference between Kentucky and New York is due to the latter's gold-medal excise tax on tobacco.

If we use an average retail price of $8 per pack that works out to an adult market value of about $112 billion in the US

In a bit we will take up the topic of the consequences of tobacco consumption. The critics of the industry suggest that the price of a pack of cigarettes that includes all the healthcare and lost labor costs would add up to something like $35 per pack.

Promotion. "Here's Johnny!" So went Ed McMahon's introduction of Johnny Carson on January 1, 1971. At 11:59 that night a Virginia Slims ad starring Veronica Hamel (later of *Hill Street Blues* fame) became the last cigarette ad on television in the United States. President Nixon had signed the bill that banned TV advertising of cigarettes in April 1970. The companies had the gumption to bargain for the ban taking effect after the New Year's Day college football games. It wasn't soon enough for Johnny. In 2005 Johnny died of emphysema. He was a life-long smoker.

Perhaps the most famous cigarette jingle every, "Winston tastes good like a cigarette should," affected me. As I mentioned earlier I smoked Winstons for a couple of my college years in the late sixties. Then the tobacco companies were among the biggest spenders in mass-media advertising, particularly television.

The first known advertisement in the United States was for the snuff and tobacco products of P. Lorillard and Company in a New York newspaper in

1789. Print has remained the principle mass media option of the big tobacco companies. Most recently $86 million went to magazine ads, $4 million to newspaper ads, and $2 million to Internet campaigns. My favorite Internet campaign is for Camel's "spit-free" Snus tobacco product line: see https:// snus.tobaccopleasure.com/modules/security/Login.aspx. There they explain, "High moisture + low salt content = no spitting." Nice.

Without the TV ad ban of 1970, the big tobacco firms would have continued spending like the big guys. Recall that P&G, General Motors, McDonald's, and Johnson & Johnson all spent more than a billion each in the United States last year. Imagine billion dollar advertising budgets for cigarettes.

Of course, it's hard to gauge the promotional value of all the smoking imagery appearing in movies and television over the years. In the early years Johnny Carson used to smoke on camera. It is also impossible to determine how much the industry has spent to encourage that footage. We do know that the imagery influences smoking behavior. And in 2012 the CDC reported an increase in on-screen smoking for the first time in five years.

In July 2015 I made my first visit to the bricks-and-mortar version of the Legacy Tobacco Documents Library at the University of California, San Francisco. Stanton Glantz and his colleagues have created a game-changing, yes even a culture-changing research tool for investigating and measuring the depths of tobacco-industry malfeasance. It includes some six million documents that were made public during the numerous federal and state tobacco hearings. Before a nice lunch at an Indian restaurant a couple of blocks down Parnassus, we sat in his office discussing tobacco and other hedonic-molecule matters. He gave me two wonderful gifts from his library – to be exact, two numbers. The first was 6097 – when you search on "Boddewyn" it produces that many hits. We'll discuss that at the end of the chapter. The other was $500,000. That's the amount Brown & Williamson Tobacco Corp. agreed to pay Sylvester Stallone for product placements in five of his films – *Rhinestone Cowboy, Godfather III, Rambo, 50/50,* and *Rocky IV.* The letter was dated June 14, 1983. It's just one jewel in that treasure trove of truth about tobacco.

Most recently his group published a report documenting Big Tobacco paying for such product placements in more than 750 films between the years 1978-1994.

Another heinous approach to promotion was the tobacco companies collaborating with the candy companies to market candy cigarettes. As I recall, when I was ten, I could buy a pack of Chesterfield (my dad's preferred brand) white candy sticks with red-dyed tips and pretend to be a grownup. They also marketed chocolate cigarettes wrapped in white paper.

Fast forward to February 19, 2014 and you might have viewed an e-cigarette ad on Jon Stewart's *The Daily Show*. Here's what the ad said: "For everything friends do for each other, return the favor. Friends don't let friends smoke. Give them the only electronic cigarette worth switching to, the Njoy King. Cigarettes, you've met you match." Actually I didn't see the e-cigarette verbiage during the first high-speed run through the ads on my DVR. But the image caught my eye. When I went back to it, I just about jumped out of my chair. Now state attorneys general are taking a hard look at such ads and their revival of all the old tobacco ad tactics of the past.

Hedonic compounds are often featured on *The Daily Show*, one of our favorites. That night five alcoholic beverages were advertised as well: Hennessey cognac, Captain Morgan white rum, Corona, Heineken, and Bud Light. A little Dunkin' Donuts coffee is pretty innocent, but Wrigley's 5 Gum (that "stimulates" your senses) bears a creepy resemblance to the 5-Hour Energy brand. Recently the big gum maker pulled its caffeinated gums off the market "to give the FDA time to formulate regulations" regarding their sale.

Perhaps one of the most important findings in recent years regarding advertising and children comes from Connie Pechmann and her associates.[1] They report that "Adolescents look up to and aspire to be like the young, attractive models in cigarette ads." Their work has shown that it is more effective to use young-looking adults in cigarette advertising than same-age peers as models for the teenage audience. It's a good bet that the cigarette companies

---

1 Cornelia Pechmann, Dante Pirouz, and Todd Pizzuti, "Symbolic Interaction and Adolescent Reactions to Cigarette Advertisements," a paper presented at the annual conference of the Association for Consumer Research, 2009, Pittsburg, Pa.

had figured that out some time ago, even as they argued, "see the adults in our advertising – our ads don't target teenagers." I'd guess that Andrew Puzder and the Carl's Jr. folks back in Chapter 3 cast their Jim Beam Bourbon Burger ad with this principle in mind.

Public Relations. While the other marketers of the legal hedonic compounds (salt, sugar, coffee, and alcohol) spend millions on public relations, the tobacco companies have been the champion customers of the PR industry. While British Petroleum and the auto-makers fight expensive PR battles with their critics, the tobacco companies have been engaged in a centuries-long war with consumer groups and potential regulators. Recall our story about King James I. There is no better book on this war in the last century than Allan Brandt's *The Cigarette Century*. He documents the weapons used by the American tobacco moguls – the PR expenditures, the political contributions, the "research" sponsored by the industry, and the lies.

The big tobacco firms' conviction of price fixing in 1941 made them wary of top-level meetings among the firms. But on December 14, 1953, they took the risk to meet at the Plaza Hotel in New York to consider strategies to manage the threat of the evolving cancer research. The next day they hired the largest PR firm in the country, Hill & Knowlton (HK). HK is still one of the largest PR firms, but its doings are now obscured by WPP's (the largest advertising, PR, and communications company in the world) corporate control. Professor Brandt best articulates what happened next:

> Hill [that is, John W. Hill,[1] HK's president] and his colleagues set to work to review a full range of approaches open to them. Dismissing as shortsighted the idea of mounting personal attacks on researchers or simply issuing blanket assurances of safety, they concluded instead that seizing control of the science of tobacco and health would be as important as seizing control of the media. It would be crucial to identify scientists who expressed skepticism about the link between cigarettes and cancer, those critical of statistical methods, and especially

---

1 As far as I can determine this John Hill is no relative of the John Hill that first reported an association with snuff and nose polyps in 1761 as discussed earlier in the chapter.

those who had offered alternative hypotheses for the cause of cancer. Hill set his staff to identify the most vocal and visible skeptics. These people would be central to the development of an industry scientific program in step with its larger public relations goals. Hill understood that simply *denying* the harms of smoking would alienate the public. His strategy for ending the "hysteria" was to insist that there were "two sides." ...so Hill would engineer "controversy." This strategy – invented by Hill in the context of his work for the tobacco industry – would ultimately become the cornerstone of a large range of efforts to distort scientific process in the second half of the twentieth century.[1]

Does all this sound familiar?

A story for another book is the huge power American industry exerts over government through campaign donations. While the US Constitution specifies that Congress is "To regulate Commerce with foreign Nations, and among the several States...", it often seems that the corporations are controlling the Congress. In 2010 Altria Group/Philip Morris USA spent over $10 million on its lobbying efforts in the United States. Big Tobacco spends at least $1 million on Democratic Party candidates in each two-year federal election cycle and in the last two decades has spent four times that on Republican candidates. In the 1996 campaign the tobacco interests donated $8.6 million to Republicans vs. $2.0 to Democrats. Earlier that year President Clinton had ordered huge restrictions on cigarette advertising directed at children.

Consequences of Consumption

Three stand out: (1) Over forty million Americans are addicted to an expensive drug – nicotine; (2) Smoking caused more than twenty million premature deaths in the United States during the last fifty years – the Centers for Disease Control (CDC) reckons the number was 480,000 last year (a new study adds

---

1 Allan M. Brandt, *The Cigarette Century* (New York: Basic Books, 2007), 167.

60,000 to that ugly statistic);[1] and (3) the economic costs of health care treatment for smokers and lost worker productivity are in the neighborhood of $300 billion each year. Anyone that derives part of their income from the sale of tobacco will disagree with these basic truths. Always ask about folks' biases, particularly the pecuniary ones.

Mark Twain quipped, "Giving up smoking is the easiest thing in the world. I know because I've done it thousands of times." Nicotine is a highly addictive drug. It is classified as such in the *Diagnostic and Statistical Manual of Mental Disorders* published by the American Psychological Association. Symptomatic of addiction and dependence are impaired control, preoccupation, denial, immediate gratification (short-term reward), deleterious effects, physiological dependence, craving, tolerance, and withdrawal. While these terms well describe a person's relationship to almost all the hedonic compounds discussed in this book, the relevance to tobacco and nicotine is perhaps most clear and most common.

The Surgeon General explains:

…smoking is not usually a choice. For most smokers, tobacco use is an addiction, and nicotine is the primary drug in tobacco that causes addiction. It only takes 10 seconds for the nicotine from one puff of smoke to reach the brain. And once it gets there, nicotine causes cells in the brain to release dopamine. One of the effects of dopamine release in the brain is to create a heightened sense of alertness and contentment. Over time, the brain cells of smokers are changed to expect regular bursts of extra dopamine that result from smoking. When a smoker tries to quit, these brain changes cause strong cravings for more nicotine.[2]

---

1   Denise Grady, "Smoking's Toll on Health Is Even Worse Than Previously Thought, a Study Finds," *New York Times*, February 12, 2015, page. A17.
2   US Department of Health and Human Services, *Let's Make the Next Generation Tobacco-Free, Your Guide to the 50th Anniversary Surgeon General's Report on Smoking and Health*, 2014.

R.J. Reynolds noticed the importance of nicotine in their own marketing research. They determined that Philip Morris was stealing their market share in the 1970s primarily due to Marlboro's increased nicotine content vis-à-vis their Winstons.

The medical community calculates that the more than forty million American smokers are shortening their lives by ten years, on average. The list of maladies smoking causes on the way toward the loss of those ten years are horrific: cancers of the larynx, esophagus, lung, stomach, liver, pancreas, kidney, ureter, cervix, bladder, and colon; stroke, blindness, birth defects, periodontitis, cardiovascular disease, diabetes, reduced fertility in women, male erectile dysfunction, ectopic pregnancy, hip fractures, and rheumatoid arthritis. Nobody quips about these.

And that $300 billion each year costs every American an average of $1,000. Their freedom to light up costs us all $1000 a year. Even the healthy smokers themselves have to add in the direct costs of their pack-a-day habit. In New York the addiction will cost you over $5000 per year.

Finally, back in 2001 Philip Morris apologized for a macabre report the company published in the Czech Republic that estimated the government there saved $1,277 every time a smoker died. Apparently, the company did not think through the public relations implications of this grisly bit of research. Where was Hill & Knowlton on that one?

Ways to Reduce/Control Consumption of Tobacco

The best news in this book was presented earlier in Exhibit 6.1. A 75 percent reduction in per capita consumption of tobacco during the last fifty years represents an unprecedented cultural shift. Reducing tobacco consumption is mostly a matter of managing marketing.

The standard pack of cigarettes hasn't changed much in that fifty years. Warning labels have helped. The proliferation of new products that appeal to children – flavored and colorful options – have been prevented.

The new e-cigarettes that potentially avoid some of the hazardous chemicals accompanying tobacco smoking may turn out to be a good thing or bad thing. While the innovation will certainly boost addiction rates, it may also reduce other health risks. As nicotine is derived from tobacco, the FDA intends to regulate e-cigarettes. We will all watch this issue unfold.

We have limited distribution, again with restrictions on sales to youths. Research on the hazards of second-hand smoke have led to broad limitations on where smoking can take place. But generally the same product is still conveniently available to all Americans.

Economic analyses have demonstrated that price increases have had perhaps the biggest impact on product trial and overall sales. Connie Pechmann and her colleagues report[1] that higher prices have worked in two ways. First, the addiction has literally become more expensive and therefore less attractive. Second, prices have been raised most dramatically via excise taxes that support counter advertising programs and cessation programs. But, we must remain careful with the tax tool – because a pack of cigarettes costs $13 in New York and $5 in Missouri 58 percent of consumption in the Big Apple is contraband.

Government actions related to promotional strategies have also made an important difference. It is quite clear that industry advertising has always stimulated demand for hedonic compounds in general, and tobacco in particular. The most recent meta-analysis published shows that advertising both influences trial and continued sales.[2] So banning mass-media advertising, particularly of image laden television ads has worked quite well. Additionally, research-based mass-media de-marketing campaigns have provided effective arguments against trial and usage. Both the medical research which provides the damaging evidence about tobacco usage and the marketing research that suggests the most effective messages and media to reach particularly youthful decision makers have been critical.

In 2009 the President signed into law the Family Smoking Prevention and Tobacco Control Act, giving the US Food and Drug Administration (FDA) comprehensive authority to regulate the manufacturing, marketing, and sale of tobacco products. Among the new restrictions are bans on outdoor advertising

---

1 David Glen Mick, Simone Pettigrew, Cornelia Pechmann, and Julie L. Ozanne, *Transformative Consumer Research* (New York: Routledge, 2012).

2 Michael L. Capella, Cynthia Webster, and Brian R. Kinard, "A Review of the Effect of Cigarette Advertising," *International Journal of Research in Marketing* 28(3), 2011, 269-279.

near schools, tobacco giveaways, sponsorship of events, vending machine sales outside of adult only facilities. Most recently The Centers for Disease Control provides a most comprehensive listing of the actions the federal, state, and local governments are taking to reduce smoking in the US.[1] Emphasized are "mass-reach health communication interventions and cessation inventions." The report includes funding targets of over $2 billion per year garnered from federal and state tobacco taxes.

Marketing Miscreant – Tobacco

Certainly John W. Hill of Hill & Knowlton would be a good candidate. But I can think of a deeper mole, that perhaps has even caused more damage to the public's health worldwide.

See Jean J. Boddewyn in action in his prime: https://archive.org/details/ tobacco_ypw27a00. The setting is Congressional hearings on HR 4972, a bill to curtail tobacco advertising. It's a stifling day on Capitol Hill in July 1986. But Professor Boddewyn is quite cool. He is a charismatic witness, self-assured and articulate. His arguments sound good, logical and fair. The bill ultimately goes down in defeat without a vote – it died in committee. Boddewyn wins again. Big Tobacco wins again.

Boddewyn is John Hill's archetype tool. His own academic work is big on words, thin on numbers. I'd call him a scholar, not a scientist. He's spent little time in the trenches of empiricism. This is the best kind of critic of science – no appreciation for the tedium of the trade. You can tell this by his obstinacy regarding the entire advertising- causes-consumption issue. Back in 1986, when he was making his case to Congress, this was perhaps debatable. Now, some thirty years later, the weight of the empirical evidence (in addition to the common sense) is clear: commercial advertising of tobacco products causes people to start smoking and to continue the dangerous behavior even when they want to quit. Perhaps he's changed his mind?

---

1   CDC, *Best Practices for Comprehensive Tobacco Control*, 2014.

Ideas and rhetoric do, of course, have value. Indeed, he has been widely lauded by his peers in the field we share, international business. Surprisingly I've never met the man except in the literature. Boddewyn is Professor Emeritus at Baruch College, City University of New York. He has received the Academy of International Business's highest honors, elected as its President (1992-94) and Dean of the Academy Fellows (2005-2008). His ideas and rhetoric were quite valuable to Big Tobacco. An honest critic would fess up to the degree of his bias. Professor Boddewyn, how much money did you make working for Big Tobacco?

The criticism of Boddewyn's biases is most strident at http://www. sciencecorruption.com/ATN166/00020.html. I wonder if Professor Boddewyn would like to deny their accusations? I excerpt their "stated opinions" here:

> While he systematically abused the public trust inherent in his position, he needed to retain the image of an independent consultant, and so was retained by the tobacco industry through an arm's length relationship via the industry's main Washington DC law firm which laundered payments and channeled industry project requests. When used as a witness in litigation, he was handled by Allen Purvis of the other main tobacco law firm. Later, he was paid via a private Belgium bank account or through his wife's company, Bodner Inc. in New York City.
>
> He provided services to the Tobacco Institute both as an expert on advertising (especially on the use of advertising to recruit teenage smokers) and also on economic matters. When his mantra of *"advertising has no effect on teenage smoking recruitment"* wore thin through constant repetition in the USA, he was handed over to Sharon Boyse at British-American Tobacco in London, who used his services at journalistic media conferences in Latin America, New Zealand, South America and the Indian and South-East Asian regions. It was a financially profitable relationship since he was also on a quarterly retainer from BAT.

Boddewyn was a Professor of Business at Baruch College, CUNY, but he was not really an economist. He specialized in the analysis of advertising and its effects on the recruitment of customers (particularly children). So he was both able to advise the cigarette companies as to how they could make smoking more attractive to teenagers, and simultaneously provided convoluted arguments to explain to Congress and the media why advertising had no effect on recruiting new smokers. Therefore, he maintained, advertising bans would serve no purpose. [And implicit in this claim was the corollary that advertising had no benefits for the tobacco industry!]

When required, he also performed many other services for the tobacco industry — appearing as a witness at Congressional hearings, writing op-eds, travelling the world to lecture at journalist briefings, advertising seminars, and so on. In return, the tobacco industry paid him generously and boosted his reputation as the preeminent 'independent academic' expert on advertising's effects on children.

While some might dismiss these accusations as leftist fluff, the authors' empirical evidence is impressive: "In November 1998, after many years of legal disputes, the representatives of the larger companies in the tobacco industry signed the Master Settlement Agreement (MSA) with 46 State Attorneys-General facilitated by the Clinton Administration. Under the MSA the major cigarette companies paid many hundreds of billions of dollars to compensate the states for Medicaid costs as a result of tobacco-induced health problems... As part of this agreement, six million documents (some hundreds of pages in length) were released for public scrutiny, and these have since been mounted on-line at the Legacy Tobacco Document Library at the University of California, San Francisco."

Recall that Boddewyn's name actually pops up 6097 in that data base. 6097!

Apparently Professor Boddewyn's signature was even for sale. Ronald M. Davis, who at the time was the President of the American Medical Association, published an article making the assertion that "British American Tobacco

Ghost-Wrote Reports on Tobacco Advertising Bans by the International Advertising Association and J.J. Boddewyn."[1] Part of the evidence Dr. Davis cites is interesting:

In the transcript of testimony by Michael Waterson (a tobacco industry consultant) in litigation over Canada's national tobacco control act of 1997,5 the following exchange occurs with Maurice Regnier, an attorney representing the Canadian Justice Department:

> *Question (Regnier):* "When we were reviewing the document by Infotab, which was not filed [in the court's public record], you mentioned that you had knowledge of a work by Boddewyn titled 'Tobacco Advertising Bans and Consumption in 16 Countries', that's correct?"
> *Answer (Waterson):* "I said I thought I had a memory of it, yes, that's correct."
> *Q:* "Did you know that this paper by Mr. Boddewyn was in fact ghost-written by Mr. Paul Bingham from British American Tobacco?"
> *A:* "I had no idea. I may have seen it.... I had no idea whether one person wrote it or another."
> *Q:* "I would like to show you, Sir, a document that has been filed through Mr. Jean-Paul Blais' discovery.... It was already filed in the record, My Lord. It is document ... ITL-124.... This document is signed by Mr. Paul Bingham. The third paragraph reads: You already have the IAA booklet by Boddewyn, which I ghost-wrote for him in nineteen eighty-six (1986). Although I cannot update this for you instantly, I gave you incidence of smoking numbers, as requested, for some of the countries that had bans."

---

1 Ronald M. Davis, "British American Tobacco Ghost-Wrote Reports on Tobacco Advertising Bans by the International Advertising Association and J.J. Boddewyn," *Tobacco Control*, 17, 211-214; see http://tobaccocontrol.bmj.com/content/17/3/211.abstract for more details.

Q: Do you have any knowledge, in view of this statement by Mr. Bingham, that Mr. Boddewyn's booklet was ghost-written by Mr. Bingham?"

A: "I have simply…no knowledge of this at all."

Ahhh, the witness's best friend, the memory lapse. You will also notice Boddewyn's memory lapses in his non-denial denial to Davis's article. In his response he complains about being "implicitly incriminated as being some sort of a 'paid hack' for the tobacco industry." This is a telling choice of words on his part. As Boddewyn's non-denial denial is interesting in its characteristic obfuscation I have included all three documents – Davis's article, Boddewyn's response, and Davis's rejoinder – on our website, www.Spiced.World. Paid hack? Marketing miscreant? You can be the judge of the truth in the matter.

Back to my own biases. Yes, I've been unhappy with Professor Boddewyn for about thirty years, ever since he gave unwarranted succor to the infant formula marketing folks including Nestlé. But much more important than that, Boddewyn's bluster is antagonistic to the fundamental argument of this book, that marketing causes consumption.

Finally, we know that millions in the United States and around the world died of cancers and other smoking related illnesses during the last four decades. Of the many millions of gallons of phlegm and blood they coughed up as they suffered, how much of it is a consequence of Dr. Boddewyn's eloquence? Doth I protest too much? No, not near enough.

An Ironic Epilogue. As I was wrapping up the manuscript for publication, I received an e-mail offer to submit a chapter for a book whose working title is *Consumer Perception of Product Risks and Benefits.* The author of the e-mail was one Gerard Emilien, MD, PhD, FRCP working in the Product Assessment Scientific Substantiation department of Philip Morris International R&D in Neuchatel, Switzerland. The penultimate sentence of his invitation was, "There is also a budget allocated for each chapter writing…I look forward to collaborating with you." Actually Dr. Emilien, you just have! Perhaps I should consult with Jean Boddewyn on how much I should ask for?

Seven

Primary chemical ingredient: Ethanol, C_2H_6O

*... I will not drink again of the fruit of the
vine until the kingdom of God comes.*

JESUS, LUKE 22:17

This is the pivotal chapter of the book. It is the last chapter on legal psychoactive substances. It is the first chapter on intoxicating compounds. And by some reckoning it covers the apex (or perhaps the nadir) of spices – the most harmful, alcohol.

The reckoning I'm referring to is by an eclectic group of about twenty European scientists led by a neuropsychopharmacologist and a management scientist. The group calls themselves the Independent Scientific Committee on Drugs. Meeting in a one-day interactive workshop to score twenty drugs on sixteen criteria they used multi-criteria decision analysis (MCDA) to derive the ranking of harm done by the drugs to others and to users presented in Exhibit 7.1. Its subsequent publication in *Lancet*, a top British medical journal attests to its excellence.

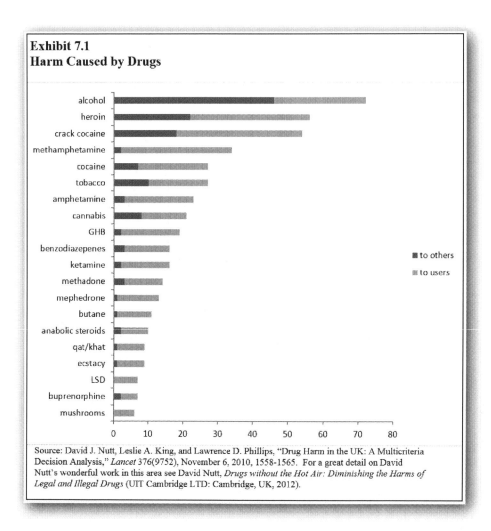

Exhibit 7.1
Harm Caused by Drugs

Source: David J. Nutt, Leslie A. King, and Lawrence D. Phillips, "Drug Harm in the UK: A Multicriteria Decision Analysis," *Lancet* 376(9752), November 6, 2010, 1558-1565. For a great detail on David Nutt's wonderful work in this area see David Nutt, *Drugs without the Hot Air: Diminishing the Harms of Legal and Illegal Drugs* (UIT Cambridge LTD: Cambridge, UK, 2012).

While I cannot argue with their methods and expertise, their analysis seems to have suffered a key mistake of omission: They didn't include sugar. Even so, their pooled opinions are quite valuable here. They identify alcohol as the worst, that is, the most harmful drug in the United Kingdom. We can assume this analysis well represents the case also here in the United States. One has to wonder what effect the pervasive advertising of the drug has on the public health here in the land of Jim Beam and Budweiser? We will revisit this compelling research in Chapters 11 and 12.

Sitting here today I would have to guess that my sugar addiction will kill me. But, as I mentioned in the Introduction, alcohol almost killed me more than once as a teenager. It also put me in jail a couple of times when I was nineteen. A fraternity brother and I worked on a $1.49 gallon of Red Mountain wine on the way to a dance my sophomore year at San Jose State. I found a convenient unlocked car out in the parking lot to pass out in. When the chagrined Chevy owner discovered a stranger sleeping in his own vomit *in his car* he called the cops. I woke up in a clean white jail jumpsuit lying on the floor of a fifteen-by-fifteen foot white padded drunk tank with six or seven other idiots. The tilted floor with the large drain in the middle handled our bodily fluids and allowed for a hose down at the end of the day. The brothers bailed me out and an alum lawyer had my record expunged.

That same year I was also thrown into the Candlestick Park jail for tossing seat cushions at security officers after a Giants game. The coffee and the two hours spent sobering up probably saved my life. I had driven that night. My date and friends weren't too happy waiting around for me.

By the way, as I was writing this chapter, my wife and I took a tour of Candlestick Park just before its 2014 destruction. The 49ers and Giants have moved on to new stadia. Ironically, on that tour, the first icon visited was the drunk tank. Our tour guide asked whether any of the twenty of us fans had spent time there. My wife raised my hand. Fortunately my wife was not my date that night. We saw Barry Bond's locker, reminding us of drug #15 above. Also we learned that the biggest drunk tank in an American stadium is, of course, the Philadelphia Eagles'. Apparently, there was some accuracy to *Silver Linings Playbook*! Considering the hooliganism at European soccer games, the facilities for drunks in the UK must dwarf the imagination.

History

Perhaps the first biotechnology of man was the fermentation of sugars into ethanol. There is good evidence that humans were drinking alcohol more than ten thousand years ago. Beer was probably first. Some early farmer, perhaps in China, stumbled across brewing by neglecting some grain and water in a jar or pot – with a little luck, a bit of yeast, and time, you have beer. Some even argue that beer and bread made for commerce and ultimately civilization. The records on wine are a bit newer, wine-stained pottery from Georgia circa 6000 BC.

While the Greeks in the first century AD recorded methods for distillation, the technology wasn't applied to making spirits for another millennium. Circa 1100 both the Italians and Chinese developed the technology. It's likely that the idea traveled along the Silk Road one way or another as did so many technologies of the time. One of the first distilled spirits mentioned in historical records is brandy, that is, distilled wine. And that brings us to Johnny Appleseed.

Back in the 1950s on Sunday nights American families gathered around their black-and-white televisions in the living room and watched Disneyland, hosted by Walt himself. At that point in time we only had one screen in the house. Only one! Much of those early shows were more than just entertainment, they were also educational. Davy Crockett at the Alamo, the zoology of *The Living Desert*, or Dr. Wernher von Braun teaching rocket science to us kids and adults. There was also a series on American legends – Pecos Bill, John Henry, Paul Bunyan, and Johnny Appleseed. The last was barefooted, wore a tin pot as a hat, and traveled around the frontier using seeds to plant apple trees. Johnny Appleseed was portrayed as a comical buffoon focused on providing food and flavor for frontier folk.

While Bill, John, and Paul were merely mythical, Johnny Appleseed was quite real. And he was nobody's fool. I highly recommend Michael Pollan's wonderful book, the *Botany of Desire*[1] on this topic and others. Pollan tells the stories of four of the planet's most successful plants – apples, tulips, marijuana, and potatoes – and their symbiotic relationship to Man and civilization. According to Pollan, one John Chapman (a.k.a. Appleseed) was really planting two other things along with his seeds and seedlings. The first was real estate. In the Northwest Territory in the 1830s one way to claim land was to plant an

---

1 Michael Pollan, *The Botany of Desire: A Plant's-Eye View of the World* (New York: Random House, 2002). Those of you that have read his book will recognize my imitation of his style, his personal touch.

orchard of at least fifty trees. He provided the settlers with the means to settle *and* own. Second, he provided the folks a source of alcoholic beverages.

Really. The apples you buy at the store today for their sweet and distinct flavors and textures are all grown through graftage, not seeds. If you take some of the seeds from your favorite Gala or Granny Smith and plant them, they are unlikely to produce what you bought at the grocery store. Rather than the sweetness you've become accustomed to, you may just get a "spitter." That is, it may be so sour that you spit out the first bite. The settlers didn't care if they grew spitters, because spitters made very fine hard cider. There were no liquor stores in 1850 – out West folks just made their own two gallons per person per year. You can see this fact reflected in Exhibit 7.2 below. Wine, and, yes, even beer were luxury items at that time. Hard cider was the Budweiser of the era. John Chapman, despite his quirky, barefooted, *Bible* toting character, was a very popular man in the Ohio Valley then.

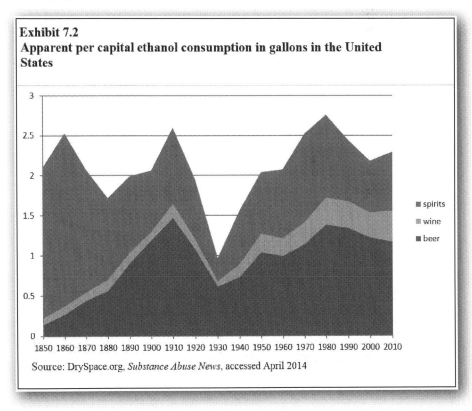

Exhibit 7.2
Apparent per capital ethanol consumption in gallons in the United States

Source: DrySpace.org, *Substance Abuse News*, accessed April 2014

This historical record of American consumption holds other important lessons as well. Prohibition did work, at least in the narrow sense. You can see spirits sales growing after resuming broadcast advertising in 1996. The growth in wine consumption during the 1980s is also evident. More soon on all these topics.

Finally, since I so much enjoyed relating the legend about Bodhidharma's eye lids and tea from Chapter 5, I have to add a rather modern myth about rum and American history. You may have run across this circulating as an email baton:

A LITTLE KNOWN TIDBIT OF NAVAL HISTORY - 1798.
The USS. Constitution (Old Iron Sides), as a combat vessel, carried 48,600 gallons of fresh water for her crew of 475 officers and men. This was sufficient to last six months of sustained operations at sea. She carried no evaporators (fresh water distillers).

However, let it be noted that according to her ship's log, "On July 27, 1798, the USS. Constitution sailed from Boston with a full complement of 475 officers and men, 48,600 gallons of fresh water, 7,400 cannon shot, 11,600 pounds of black powder and 79,400 gallons of rum." Her mission: "To destroy and harass English shipping."

Making Jamaica on 6 October, she took on 826 pounds of flour and 68,300 gallons of rum.

Then she headed for the Azores, arriving there 12 November. She provisioned with 550 pounds of beef and 64,300 gallons of Portuguese wine.

On 18 November, she set sail for England. In the ensuing days she defeated five British men-of-war and captured and scuttled 12 English merchant ships, salvaging only the rum aboard each.

By 26 January, her powder and shot were exhausted. Nevertheless, although unarmed she made a night raid up the Firth of Clyde in Scotland. Her landing party captured a whiskey distillery and transferred 40,000 gallons of single malt Scotch aboard by dawn. Then she headed home.

The USS. Constitution arrived in Boston on 20 February 1799, with no cannon shot, no food, no powder, no rum, no wine, no whiskey, and 38,600 gallons of water.

The truth of the matter is, of course, quite different despite the smoke screen of statistics. Gordon Calhoun's myth-busting blog sets the record straighter:

1. In 1799, the United States was at war with France, not England. The British were actually our unofficial allies in the "Quasi-War" with the French Republic.
2. The United States Navy moved away from using Jamaican rum as part of the grog ration and moved towards more home grown spirits such as Kentucky whisky. Captains also had a strict policy against public intoxication. A sailor found less than sober was often subject to flogging.
3. Speaking of Jamaica, the colony was a major British naval station. Why would it outfit an American warship during an alleged war with the British?
4. USS *Constitution* defeated four British warships (*Java, Guerriere, Levant,* and *Cyane)* ...in the War of 1812.
5. Having said that, *Constitution* never raided the home aisles. However, the brig USS *Argus* did (see the book *Fatal Cruise of the Argus*).
6. When a warship captured a merchant ship, the alcohol supply was the last thing on the captain's mind. Instead, he was looking for goods he could sell when the cruise was over. [1]

My favorite comment among the blog posts is from Christopher: "If you run the numbers provided – 209 days on cruise, 187,700 gallons of spirits, 475 men – you get [a consumption rate of] 1.89 gallons per man per day." That'd kill everybody on board!

The history lesson here: American culture says it's manly to get drunk. And it's fun to embellish the truth, particularly if you're too intoxicated to

---

1 http://hamptonroadsnavalmuseum.blogspot.com/2010/12/deleting-urban-legend-on-uss.html

remember it in the first place. Everybody laughs. But this topic is really not funny, historically or in the present.

Consumer Behavior

As you can see in Exhibit 7.2, the average American adult (18 years and over) consumes about 2.3 gallons of ethanol per year in the form of beer, wine, and/ or distilled spirits. Of course, there is no such thing as an average drinker. The CDC finds useful six categories of adult drinkers:

regular drinkers	52 percent	(12 or more drinks in the last year)
current infrequent drinkers	13 percent	(fewer than 12 drinks in last year)
former regular drinkers	6 percent	(no drinks in the last year)
former infrequent drinkers	8 percent	(no drinks in the last year)
lifetime abstainers	21 percent	(fewer than 12 drinks in lifetime)

This is a really poor way to determine consumption. These statistics are based on self-report measures, which we know are unreliable. Indeed, the most reliable way to measure alcohol consumption of a household is to go through the residents' trash. Comparing self-report to garbology studies have time and again shown that self-report measures understate actual observed consumption. And imagine asking a big drinker how many he's had – how accurate do you think his memory will be?

If we for a moment assume that the typical drink contains about 0.6 ounces of ethanol (the assumption made in the NIH statistics) that means the average American downs about 490 drinks per year. Not even close to the twelve the CDC asks about.

A division of the US National Institute of Health, the National Institute of Alcohol Abuse and Alcoholism[1] (NIHAAA) takes a more reasonable approach in

---

1 See www.niaaa.nih.gov for the wealth of information and statistics from which I have drawn for this chapter.

its surveys asking about consumption in the last month. They report that 88 percent of American adults have at least one drink in their life, 71 percent at least one drink in the last year, and 56 percent at least one drink in the last month. Twenty-five percent reported binge drinking in the last month (drinking five or more alcoholic beverages on the same occasion on at least one day in the past 30 days). Seven percent reported drinking heavily in the last month (binge drinking five or more times in the last month). This 7 percent also corresponds to the number of American adults displaying alcohol-use disorders (AUD) – a medical condition defined by a combination of alcoholism and harmful drinking that does not reach the level of dependence. That's about seventeen million with AUD.

NIAAA also delineates three levels of drinking with implied prescriptions:

1. Moderate drinking – for men, no more than four drinks on any single day AND no more than fourteen drinks per week. The numbers for women are three drinks in a day AND seven drinks per week. Actually these limits are more related to body weight than gender.
2. Heavy drinking – any consumption above #1. Do you have this problem?
3. Binge drinking – drinking so much in two hours that the blood alcohol concentration (BAC) is 0.08 grams per deciliter. For men that's about five drinks and four women four.
4. I've thrown in a fourth category. Competitive drinking, or getting drunk as fast as you can. This is a dangerous game we played frequently in my fraternity and in the Navy. I was quite disappointed and ashamed to recently learn that the San Diego State University chapter of my fraternity, ΔΣΦ, was booted from campus "for a pattern of policy violations that includes the harassment of a Take Back the Night March. Reinstatement requires a drug-and-alcohol free house. I do appreciate the National DSP office supporting the campus on this.

The CDC measures do help in comparisons across groups of consumers. For example, the CDC reports[1] that men drink more than women – 60 percent

---

1   US Center for Disease Control, *Vital and Health Statistics*, series 10, number 260, 2012, DHHS Publication No. (PHS) 2014-xxxx.

of men and 44 percent of women are regular drinkers. Ethnicity and culture influences consumption. Asian-Americans are most likely to be lifetime abstainers at 42 percent, followed by blacks and Latinos (31 percent), American Indians (23 percent), and whites (19 percent). Nineteen percent of married folks abstain compared to 16 percent of divorced or separated and 28 percent for never married. Finally, more drinking is done by higher income, more educated, and employed Americans.

The five states with the highest per capita consumption rates are: New Hampshire (4.4 liters per capita per year), District of Columbia (3.9), Nevada (3.3), Delaware (3.1), and North Dakota (3.0). It looks like drinking is associated with corruption and cold weather? The driest states are, guess what: Utah (1.3), West Virginia (1.8), Kentucky (1.9), Oklahoma (2.0), and Kansas (2.0). I would guess religion based temperance explains these dry five.

Some good news in the data regards kids. Like that of adults, their consumption of alcohol has declined steadily in the last few decades. In 1980 41 percent of high school seniors had consumed five or more drinks within the previous two weeks of the survey. By 2010 that percentage had dropped to 23.2 percent. The latter is still too large a bad number, but at least we can see things going in a positive direction.

The declines in consumption of beer recently observed may be explained by three trade-offs beer drinkers have been making. First is the trend for consumers to prefer lower calorie options across food categories. Beer delivers not only calories from the alcohol but also carbohydrate intake from the grains and such. The brewers have been trying to mitigate this problem during the last few years by introducing and advertising more, low-calorie beers. Now Bud Light, Coors Light, and Miller Lite outsell their full-calorie cousins by four to one.

Second, as can be seen in Exhibit 7.2, drinkers are more frequently choosing spirits over beer since the distillers began radio and television advertising in the 1996.

The third trade-off drinkers appear to be making is beer for marijuana. Researchers[1] reported in the peer-reviewed *Law and Economics Journal* in May

---

1   D. Mark Anderson, Benjamin Hansen, and Daniel I. Rees, "Medical Marijuana Laws, Traffic Fatalities, and Alcohol Consumption," *Journal of Law and Economics* 56(2), May 2013, 333-369.

2013: "The first full year after coming into effect, legalization [of medical marijuana] is associated with an 8-11 percent decrease in traffic fatalities… [and] sharp decreases in the price of marijuana and alcohol consumption, which suggests that marijuana and alcohol are substitutes." This is an important new line of research that may well argue for the more holistic understanding and policy making of the consumption of hedonic compounds that I advocate in this book.

Another new line of research on the genetic and epigenetic impacts on alcohol-use disorders (AUD) is important for similar reasons. NIHAAA has supported a stream of research on the gene/AUD link since 1989. They report that genes are responsible for about half of the risk for alcoholism. "For instance, some people of Asian descent carry a gene variant that alters their rate of alcohol metabolism, causing them to have symptoms like flushing, nausea, and rapid heartbeat when they drink. Many people who experience these effects avoid alcohol."[1] Indeed, a quick look at consumption across countries seems consistent with this new research. Obviously there may be treatment and policy implications of this work as well.

The World Health Organization (WHO) estimates that seventy-six million people on the planet suffer from alcohol-related disorders. Consumption of alcohol varies dramatically across countries. See Exhibit 7.3 for a quick comparison:

The US number is bit overstated compared to the CDC number of 2.3 gallons, 9.4 liters equals 2.5 gallons. You can see the impact of the US temperance movement in our relatively low consumption. This is also reflected in a surprisingly high abstinence rate of over 30 percent in the United States compared to 16 percent in Canada, 8 percent in Italy, 6 percent in the UK, and 4 percent in Germany.[2]

---

1   Genetics of Alcohol Use Disorders, see http://www.niaaa.nih.gov/alcohol-health/overview-alcohol-consumption/alcohol-use-disorders/genetics-alcohol-use-disorders, accessed April 8, 2014.
2   David J. Hanson, *Alcohol Problems and Solutions*, SUNY Postdam, online, accessed 2014.

Exhibit 7.3
Alcohol Consumption

country	liters/capita/year	country	liters/capita/year
Moldova	18.2	Italy	10.7
Russia	~18	Sweden	10.3
Czech Republic	16.5	Netherlands	10.1
S. Korea	14.8	United States	9.4
Ireland	14.4	Brazil	9.2
France	13.7	Japan	8.0
United Kingdom	13.4	China	5.9
Germany	12.8	India	0.8
Finland	12.5	United Arab Emirates	0.5
Serbia	11.9	Saudi Arabia	0.3
Greece	10.8		

Source: World Health Organization, online, accessed 2014.
http://www.who.int/substance_abuse/publications/global_alcohol_report/msbgsruprofiles.pdf

The Czechs are the big beer drinkers in the world at over ten liters per person per year. We'll see why in a bit. The overall consumption of France and Ireland is almost identical. But as you might guess, the French are drinking mostly wine, and the Irish their Guinness. In Asia spirits are more popular with the South Koreans consuming the greatest quantities. Mahatma Gandhi and Mohamad both preached abstinence thus explaining (along with low per capita incomes) the low rates of consumption in India and the Middle Eastern countries. Some might call the Russian number outdated, but the drastic three-year, 25 percent decline to 13.5 liters reported most recently by the Russian authorities begs skepticism.

The WHO's average adult consumption of ethanol estimate across countries is 6.13 liters per person per year. The WHO also estimates that in 2013 there were 5.4 billion adults (fifteen years and over) on the planet. Combining these estimates yields a rough estimate for the annual world production of ethanol for human consumption of thirty-three billion liters. We Americans consume about ten percent of that total, most of which is from domestic production.

We do import 588 million liters of ethanol. That arrives from abroad in the form of $3.7 billion worth of beer, $3.6 billion of wine, and $6.0 billion in spirits. Our five biggest supply countries are France (mostly wine), Mexico (beer), Italy (wine), the UK (spirits), and the Netherlands (mostly beer). Fortunately, we also export about 233 million liters of ethanol in the form of the $1.5 billion of beer, the $1.6 billion of wine, and the $2.0 billion we sell abroad. Our five best customers are, in order, Canada, China, Mexico, Japan, and the UK.[1]

Marketing

Product. Mankind's creativity is perhaps best displayed by the countless variations by which ethanol is produced and packaged for human consumption. Any carbohydrate (starch or sugar) you happen to have around can be converted into an alcoholic beverage. Cactus, potatoes, corn, barley, sugar, bananas, rice, grapes, cranberries, and apples are just the first ten that come to mind. Then there's the processing – aging, brewing, distilling, and such. Why be satisfied with just wine aged in fine wooden barrels when you can bump up its potency (and reduce its shipping costs) by distilling it into brandy? One of my son's favorite craft beers is aged in wine barrels. And then there's Palcohol, alcohol in the easiest-to-carry form, a powder. Great for hikers, but now it's banned in six states.[2]

We haven't even mixed it yet with anything edible such as spiked chocolates or other hedonic compounds. Kahlua, the original mix of coffee and rum, caffeine and ethanol – throw in a little vodka and cream and you have a White Russian. Wikipedia lists more 308 cocktails and 106 separate alcoholic beverages. Given that you can make any cocktail with any beverage – why not a Corpse Reviver with tequila instead of absinthe, for example – you might concoct at least 33,264 different ethanol delivery devices. And despite what we might think, Wikipedia doesn't know everything!

---

1 These calculations are based on import/export data from the Distilled Spirits Council of the United States. See www.discus.org.

2 Rachel Abrams, "Powdered Alcohol under Fire before It Even Goes on Sale," *New York Times*, April 4, 2015, page B1.

And none of this considers vanilla extract, chocolates laced with brandy, rum cake, or cooking with wine. Historically and today alcohol was and is often mixed with other medicines. Actually, now that I think about it, back in the 1960s, my sisters used to set their hair with Dad's beer.

The alcoholic beverage corporations all produce an array of products most recently adding flavors to traditional spirits brands such as Fluffed Marshmallow Vodka by Smirnoff (more on this wonderful product at the end of this chapter). Attempts were made to sell alcohol energy drinks, but producers were forced to clear the market after both consumer protests and government litigation threats.

During the last decade, small-scale craft breweries (independent firms with annual production of six million barrels or less) and more recently craft distillers have successfully penetrated the beverage markets. Their approach has been to generally mimic the marketing strategies of traditional vintners, as have the tea produces in Hangzhou, China as described in Chapter 5. Traditionally the ethanol content in a typical mass marketed twelve-ounce can of beer, a five-ounce glass of wine, and a 1.5-ounce shot of spirits has been about the same, 0.6 ounces. The percentage of ethanol has been 5 percent in beer, 12 percent in wine, and 40 percent (80 proof) in spirits. Now the craft breweries are eschewing many of the traditions and delivering higher percentages of ethanol in their products.

Place.[1] The brewers, vintners, and distillers use wholesalers and retailers to deliver their products into your glass. Following the demise of federal Prohibition in 1933, most states mandated this three-tier distribution system. Thus wholesalers are protected and vertical integration, that is, manufacturers selling directly to consumers, is prohibited.

In the United States. in 2013 there were 1938 wholesaling firms licensed to distribute beer with an aggregate sales revenues of $62 billion. About 5 percent of those sales are in kegs and barrels with the remaining 95 percent sold in bottles and cans. There were also 1526 firms licensed to distribute wine and spirits with aggregate revenues of $77 billion. Forty percent of those revenues came from wine sales (evenly split between white and red), 38 percent from

---

1 Many of these data are gleaned from a variety of reports from IBIS*World*.com.

spirits (rum 8 percent, whiskey 14 percent, and vodka 16 percent), and 18 percent from premixed alcoholic beverages. Revenues in wholesaling declined during the 2008-09 period but have recovered to slow stable growth due to population increases in the United States. Recall that per capita consumption has generally declined. Aggregating across both kinds of wholesalers 27 percent of sales went to retail liquor stores, 22 percent to grocery and convenience stores, 10 percent to hotels and motels, 27 percent to restaurants and bars, and 15 percent to others including casinos, pharmacies, and other wholesalers. Beer wholesalers employ seventy-one workers on average and wine and spirit retailers forty-eight – there is less liquid to move in the latter.

Despite even more complex and increasing legal constraints, the fastest growing element of alcoholic-beverage distribution is the Internet. In 2013 there were 2,500 firms averaging 2.4 employees each. Revenues generated from online sales were $2.7 billion in 2013, up from $1.5 billion in 2008. Sales of beer amounted to 36 percent, wine 34 percent, and spirits 21 percent. Online sales tend toward higher-end (quality and price) products, the fastest growing part of the industry. As with online purchases generally, greater rates are associated with younger buyers. Consumers 21-25 accounted for 27 percent of sales, the much larger 26-40 age group 41 percent. Ninety-five percent of sales are directly to consumers.

Price. It's time to get out your wallet. The highest prices ever paid for an ethanol fix are:

Beer – Samuel Adams Utopias, $900
Wine – Jeroboam of Château Mouton-Rothschild, 1945, $310,700
Spirits (scotch) – Macallan 64 Year Old in Lalique, $460,000

On the other hand, prices at my local Safeway are:

Beer – 12 ounce bottle of Budweiser, $1.00
Wine – 1.5 liters of E.J. Gallo's Barefoot merlot, $10.99 (a 5-ounce glass is $1.37)
Spirits (bourbon) – 0.75 liter of Jim Beam, $12.99 (a 1.5-ounce shot is 76¢)

So the cheapest 0.6-ounce of ethanol comes from that shot of Beam. You may remember the name from Chapter 2, the Jim Beam Bourbon Burger served up by Carl's Jr. along with Heidi Klum's thigh.

As the economy has stabilized since 2008 revenue growth in the industry has come from American consumers that are moving toward higher-priced beverages. At the top end of markets quality is measured more by rarity than any other criterion. In particular the craft beers and spirits are tapping into this product attribute. The US Department of Agriculture estimates the per capita expenditures on alcoholic beverages. In 2003 it was $490, in 2008 $528, and in 2013 it was $546. Using the 2013 figure, that translates into an average price paid per 0.6 ounces of ethanol (the amount in a typical drink) at $1.11, up from about $1.07 in 2008. As higher prices generally favor lower consumption, this is a good trend. By the way, that five-ounce glass of Mouton-Rothschild 1945 above would run you about $50,000. It must taste really, really, really good! Definitely not something you would chug.

When I checked the excise taxes on alcoholic beverages I was shocked. Seventy-four cents on a gallon of beer, $1.68 on a gallon of wine, and $16.67 on a gallon of spirit seems about right. But all these taxes charged by federal, state, and local governments have been heading steadily and dramatically downward. Twenty years ago the rates were $1.10, $2.39, and $24.08, respectively. This may save jobs and preserve shareholder value and executive salaries in the industries by keeping prices stable. But lower prices for alcohol multiply the misery the drug causes. This is an astonishing failure of our governments.

Finally, the USDA estimates total alcoholic beverages sales to consumers to be $170 billion in the United States. Sales are distributed as follows: consumed in the home ($43 billion sold in liquor stores, $23 billion in food stores) and consumed outside the home ($63 billion in restaurants and bars, and $5 billion in hotels and motels). The "other" categories are quite large at $36 billion.

Promotion. This morning my *New York Times*[1] featured a front-page ad for Bulleit Frontier Whiskey. I thought this an odd place for an apparent craft distiller – even a strange place for any ad, for that matter. Most of the craft

1 April 3, 2014.

beer and distillers depend on word-of-mouth promotion/advertising for their products. I checked the Bulleit website to learn more about the brand. I was faced immediately with the completely stupid, ineffective, and disingenuous "state your birthday" barrier to keep kids off the site. Ask any twelve-year-old whether that would dissuade him or her from fibbing and taking a look. Just this first page is marketing at its worst. A devilish dodge before I even got into the site. Then things got worse.

The website presents the brand as any mom-and-pop, red-blooded American, Kentucky frontier small business. Nothing is said on the website about Bulleit's London-based corporate parent Diageo. As one of the biggest corporations in the industry they can afford that front-page *New York Times* ad. Actually the word Diageo is used only once on the website – let's play "Where is Waldo" with Diageo. Let's see if you have the patience to find it. The location is listed at the end of this chapter (page 177). But both the ad and the website are pure Bulleit bullshit. Disgraceful marketing ethics.

Let's see if I can calm down now and accurately describe the industries' larger promotional practices. *Advertising Age* lists the Top 100 global advertising spenders circa 2012:[1]

Beer –	(#39) Anheuser-Busch InBev	$1.1 billion	Belgium and St. Louis
	(#54) SABMiller[2]	$0.7 billion	London
	(#71) Heineken	$0.5 billion	Amsterdam
Wine –	(#40) LVMH (Möet)	$1.0 billion	Paris
Spirits –	(#94) Diageo	$0.3 billion	London

All these companies are diversified, offering more than just beer, wine, or spirits. The letters LVMH correspond with Louis Vuitton, Möet, and Hennessy. That is, very expensive French purses, wines, and spirits (cognac). E. & J. Gallo with 22 percent of the US wine market is privately held, so statistics are

1 Most of the statistics in this section are from www.adage.com, accessed April 5, 2014.
2 As of the summer 2016 it appears SABMiller will be taken over by AB InBev.

scant. We do know that 43 percent of wine production in the States is from California. Diageo brands hold a 33 percent share of the spirits market in the US, followed by Beam Inc. brands at 18.5 percent. In early 2014 Suntory of Japan announced it was acquiring Beam. The bottom line on all this is that as with other hedonic molecules we have several multi-billion-dollar, profit-motivated companies each spending billions of dollars marketing their ethanol carrying products here in the United States. Five of the booze purveyors are among the top 100 Advertisers in the world. Powerful companies using powerful imagery in your family room, over and over and over again.

We focus here on #39, Anheuser-Busch InBev (AB) at $1.1 billion in media spending. Obviously these companies spend more on personal selling than mass-media advertising. In the AB annual report for 2012 they list $5.2 billion in "sales and marketing expenses." So about 20 percent of what they spend is on mass-media advertising. Let's drill down into their numbers for 2012:

Global revenues	$40 billion
North American revenues	$16 billion
Major brands	Budweiser, Corona, Stella Artois, Beck's, Michelob, Lowenbrau, Rolling Rock
Global "sales and marketing spending	$5.3 billion
Global media spending	$1.1 billion
Global spending on the Budweiser brand alone	$450 million
US advertising spending	$0.6 billion

- Magazines $53 million
- Newspapers $4 million
- Outdoor $27 million
- TV $461 million
- Radio $24 million
- Internet display $14 million

| Corporate tag line | "starting conversations **since 1366**" |

When I look back to how AB spent $0.5 billion in 2007, they have substantially shifted allocations from print to broadcast media. The most disturbing trend I can see across companies is Diageo moving $20 million from Internet advertising to broadcast media in the last five years. In contrast, the vintners and the craft brewers and distillers primarily use word-of-mouth and local sampling to promote their products. The fact that such strategies are yielding the fastest growth in the industry I see as a most positive trend. We will discuss further such media issues in some detail in Chapter 14.

Finally, that brings us to AB's public relations and legal expenses for protecting its brand name. The company has been in a decades-long battle over the Budweiser brand. The company launched a massive public relations program in the small Czech town of Ceské Budêjovice, where a local brewery produces Budweiser Budvar. Anheuser-Busch planted trees along main avenues, opened a new cultural center offering free English courses to citizens and management advice to budding entrepreneurs, and ran newspaper ads touting the possibilities of future cooperation. AB's goal was to win support for a minority stake in the Czech state-owned brewery, Budêjovicky Budvar N.P., when the government privatized it.

So why was AB interested in a brewery whose annual production of 500,000 barrels is the equivalent of two days' output for AB? Part ownership is critically important for two reasons. It is in search of new markets in Europe, and it wants to be able to market the Budweiser brand in Europe. AB doesn't have the rights to use the Budweiser brand in Europe because Budêjovicky Budvar NP owns it. Its public relations plan didn't work because many Czechs see Budvar as the "family silver."

Although the Czech prime minister asked publicly for American investors to put money into the Czech Republic, Czech Budweiser was not on the government's privatization list. "I believe in the strength of American investors, but I do not believe in the quality of American beer." Anheuser-Busch established the name Budweiser in the United States when German immigrants founded the St. Louis family brewery and began selling under the Budweiser brand in 1876, 19 years before the Czech brewery opened.

The Czechs claim they have been using the name since **1245**, before Columbus discovered the New World and that Budweiser refers to Budweis, the original name of the city where Budvar is located. That is the name commonly referred to beer brewed in that area hundreds of years before AB started brewing Budweiser.

AB markets Budweiser brand beer in North America, but in Europe, it markets Bud or Busch brands, because the Czechs have the legal rights to the use of the name Budweiser. Diplomacy and public relations didn't work, so what next? The parties have each other tied up in legal wrangling over who has the rights to the Budweiser name and to derivations of it, such as Bud. More than forty lawsuits and forty administrative cases are pending across Europe. Because US law protects AB's rights to the Budweiser label in the United States, the Czechs sell their beer as "Czechvar" here.

The Czech government petitioned the WTO to grant beer regions the same kind of labeling protection that it gives to wine regions. Just as sparkling wines made in the Champagne region of France are the only ones legally entitled to call themselves champagne, it would mean that only beers brewed in Ceske Budějovice could call themselves Budweiser and only those brewed in Pilzen, another Czech town, could claim to be pilsner. It seems unlikely that this request will win approval, because pilsner has become a generic designation for a style of beer, and unlike the grapes that come from Champagne, the malt and the hops that go into its beer do not come exclusively from Ceske Budějovice.

We all know that the proof of who's best is in the tasting, right? Both lagers have legions of fans. The US version lives up to its old slogan of "king of beers," at least as far as sales go: It's the top-selling beer in the world. The Czech version—nicknamed the "beer of kings" because it comes from a town that once brewed for royalty—has large followings in Germany and other parts of Europe. So the *St. Louis Post-Dispatch* hosted a blind taste test to determine which beer is better—Budvar won.

Recently the Europeans have won another battle: In 2009, Anheuser-Busch agreed to merge with InBev, with its global headquarters now in Leuven, Belgium.[1] 1245 still precedes even those conversations started in 1366. And, in the summer of 2016 AB-InBev was fooling American consumers again by replacing the iconic "Budweiser" label on its beer with "America." How patriotic, or is it European patronizing?

Consequences of Consumption

Let's start with the consequences for drinkers. The Mayo Clinic[2] describes the *possible* benefits of **moderate** levels of consumption (about a drink per day): Reduced risk of heart disease, stroke, and diabetes. But the evidence of the studies is not strong and the effects are small. Oh, I nearly forgot about "starting conversations since 1366." Hmm. I guess a Bud does take care of Dr. Raj Koothrappali's muteness around women on TV's *The Big Bang Theory*. Just one sip and he becomes a blabbermouth. If only that's all it did.

All the psychoactive substances discussed in the book, by definition, give pleasure. As a psychoactive drug, ethanol is believed by users to deliver relaxation, euphoria, artistic inspiration, good digestion, religious experiences, aphrodisia, and, of course, happiness. Its effects are biphasic meaning that its effects vary by how much is consumed. Certainly the initial sip delivers dopamine to the brain which causes euphoria and diminished inhibitions. Raj can talk to women. But in greater concentrations in the blood, the drug becomes a depressant. As that first sip wears off the sedative effect begins to take hold, often motivating the drinker to consume more to get back to the good feelings. Thus the slippery slope of alcoholic beverages – with greater

---

1 Al Stamborski, "Battle of the Buds: Taste Testers Say That Budvar Is Better," St. Louis Post-Dispatch, November 28, 1999, p. E1; "Prime Minister Says Budvar Will Stay Czech," Modern Brewery, March 2000; Gregory Cancelada, "Czech Brewery Retains Right to Use 'Budweiser' and 'Bud' Trademarks," St. Louis Post-Dispatch, February 17, 2003; Philip R. Cateora, Mary C. Gilly, John L. Graham, and R. Bruce Money, *International Marketing*, 17th edition (New York: McGraw-Hill, 2016), 200.

2 www.MayoClinic.org, accessed April 4, 2014. Circa 2016 more and more public health organizations are looking askance at such advice. See Justin Scheck and Tripp Mickle, "Drink Makers Battle Loss of ;Health Halo,'" *Wall Street Journal*, August 23, 2016, page A1, A8.

concentrations in the blood most humans get on the path of happy, talkative, boastful to impaired movement, slurred speech to nausea, vomiting to hypo- or hyperthermia, anesthesia to coma and once in a while to death. After some- one passes out from excessive consumption, blood alcohol levels can continue to increase. This is most dangerous. It's a medical emergency if arousal is dif- ficult. From happy to dead in one drinking session!

In the longer, run alcohol-use disorders and alcoholism loom. According to NIHAAA more than seventeen million Americans have an alcohol use prob- lem – either alcohol dependence/alcoholism or alcohol abuse. Alcoholism, the more serious of the two, is defined as a disease by the American Medical Association, and includes four symptoms we have talked about previously: craving, loss of control of quantity consumed, dependence (withdrawal symp- toms include nausea, sweating, shakiness, and negative emotional states), and tolerance (the need to drink greater quantities to feel the same effects). The good news from NIHAAA is recent research findings that "70 percent of peo- ple who develop alcohol dependence have [just] a single episode that lasts on average three to four years…many people who seek formal treatment are able to remain alcohol free, and many others recover without formal treatment."

Long-term alcohol abuse can damage the **brain** (interfere with commu- nication pathways, mood, behavior, facial-expression reading, physical and mental coordination), **heart** (cardiomyopathy, irregular heartbeat, stroke, high blood pressure), **liver** (cirrhosis, fibrosis, hepatitis, or fatty liver), **pan- creas, cancers** (mouth, esophagus, throat, liver, breast), the **immune system,** and **testosterone production**. This is not a happy list.

But what makes alcohol the most harmful drug is its effects on those most often innocent people around us:[1]

1.   In the United States 80,000 people die prematurely annually
2.   17,000 of those are killed by drunk drivers
3.   More than 10 percent of American children live with a parent with an alcohol problem

---

1   This list is gleaned from www.NIHAAA.nih.gov, www.CDC.gov, and www.about-alcohol- abuse.com, all accessed April 5, 2014.

4. Annually more than 600,000 college students are assaulted by drunk students

5. Annually 97,000 college students are victims of alcohol-related sexual assault or date rape

6. Pregnant drinkers cause Fetal Alcohol Syndrome (FSA) cases in the United States at about 5 per 100,000 births

7. 50 percent of US homicides are alcohol related

8. 50 percent of US domestic homicides are alcohol related

9. 32 percent of suicides are alcohol related

10. Over 20 percent of US assaults are alcohol related

11. As much as 50 percent of police work is spent addressing alcohol related problems

One study estimated the cost of alcohol consumption for American society in 2006. The researchers added up the direct and indirect costs of premature death, increases in diseases and injuries, property damage from fire and motor car crashes, alcohol-related crime, and lost productivity at work. The final bill was $224 billion[1] for 2006, the year we consumed $137 billion dollars on alcoholic beverages. Adjusting for our $170 billion consumption level last year, that suggests that the damage done then was some $279 billion. Beyond the price of the actual booze, the mayhem associated with its consumption costs every man, woman, and child in America about $885 each.

Ways to Control/Reduce Consumption of Alcohol

As was the case in the last chapter on tobacco, there are important lessons for policy makers in the history of alcohol control efforts. So we'll spend a little time on that topic, then turn to my own prescriptions.

The first fight over alcohol in the US was a matter of taxes, not health or civil order. In 1794 President George Washington raised an army of thirteen

---

1   E.E. Bouchery, H.J. Harwood, J.J. Sacks, C.J. Simon and R.D. Brewer, "Economic Costs of Excessive Alcohol Consumption in the US, 2006," *American Journal of Preventative Medicine* 41, 2011, 516-524.

thousand to quell the first threat to the new country. The causes of the so-called Whiskey Rebellion are well described by Iain Gately in his excellent book, *Drink: A Cultural History of Alcohol*:

> ...settlers in western Pennsylvania formed a rebel band named the Whiskey Boys and commenced an insurrection against the federal government. Their cause was an excise tax on domestic spirits, which had been imposed in 1791 and which was considered on the western edge of the United States to be unequal, immoral, and "dangerous to liberty."...A high percentage of these settlers were Scottish Irish, to whom free land and no taxes seemed a recipe for paradise, and the inconvenient presence of a few murderous indigenous tribes no worse than what they left behind [in Britain]...The art of distilling the water of life was part of the heritage of the Scotch Irish, and this ancestral solace was prepared wherever they settled. In emergencies, a Scotch Irish could make whiskey using only corn, water, fire, a kettle, and a wet towel.[1]

A few shots were fired and two of the Boys died. Then five thousand marched on Pittsburgh and the tax authorities. The excisemen immediately surrendered. But when the thirteen thousand federal troops showed up, the Whiskey Boys traded their protests for amnesty, and agreed to pay the 9¢ per gallon tax. The rebellion ended quietly.

Prohibition. Almost four thousand years ago the Chinese emperor of the time prohibited alcohol in his realm. As soon as he died, the law was repealed by his son. In the first half of the twentieth century prohibition laws were enacted in several European countries: Russia and the USSR, Iceland, Norway, Hungary, and Finland. The average duration of the law was about ten years. In Hungary it lasted from March 21 to August 1 in 1919.

Here, toward the end of 1917 Congress passed the Eighteenth Amendment to the US Constitution and the thirty-sixth state ratified it on January 16, 1919. The Amendment in part stated:

---

1 Iain Gately, *Drink: A Cultural History of Alcohol* (New York: Gotham Press, 2008), 215-218.

After one year from the ratification of this article the manufacture, sale, or transportation of intoxicating liquors within, the importation thereof into, or the exportation thereof from the United States and all the territory subject to the jurisdiction thereof for beverage purposes is hereby prohibited.

The protests leading up to the federal prohibition began almost a hundred years earlier. The Women's Christian Temperance Union and Protestant churches led the federal fight. Alcohol-related violence was their most persuasive complaint. The Eighteenth Amendment, implemented on January 17. 1920, was repealed on December 5, 1933 with the ratification of the Twenty-first Amendment, which granted rights of prohibition to the states.

As I mentioned earlier, Prohibition worked in the sense that, by most estimates, alcohol consumption declined by 50-60 percent. But government resources allocated to enforcement by the Volstead Act were inadequate to combat the underground and organized criminal activity around the distribution of foreign produced booze. Canada, Mexico, and Caribbean countries were ready to quench alcoholic-beverage demands of the thousands of speakeasies across the country. Violent crime rates were higher during Prohibition than before it. Also, the voices of personal freedom had remained numerous throughout the period.

State Regulation. You can get a glimpse of the state laws passed since prohibition by a sampling of a 2006 audit of Minnesota's provisions:

- Minnesota restricts retail competition in the liquor business more than most states. Minnesota prohibits most grocery, convenience, drug, and general merchandise stores from selling strong beer, wine, and spirits for off-premises consumption. In addition, most of the 226 cities with city-owned liquor stores have an off-sale monopoly on these products within their city boundaries.
- Minnesota's laws for beer and wine wholesalers are similar to those in other states. A retailer is generally able to purchase a manufacturer's brands from only one wholesaler.

- Adjusted for differences in taxes and dram shop insurance costs, off-sale beer prices are 7 to 9 percent higher in Minnesota compared with Wisconsin, where there are few state restrictions on retail competition.
- Similarly, adjusted wine prices are 5 to 7 percent higher in Minnesota than Wisconsin.
- However, adjusted prices for distilled spirits are 8 to 10 percent lower in Minnesota despite the state's more restrictive retail environment. The state's prohibition on the use of exclusive territories for the wholesale distribution of spirits is most likely responsible for Minnesota's lower off-sale retail prices.
- Overall, adopting less restrictive retail laws like those in Wisconsin could save Minnesota consumers about $100 million annually. But such law changes would negatively impact existing private liquor stores and jeopardize the $16 million in annual profits that municipal liquor stores currently provide for city services.
- In addition, some research suggests that adopting Wisconsin's retail laws might increase problems with alcohol abuse. But allowing grocery stores to sell wine would probably have significantly smaller economic and social impacts.

Recent Federal Regulation. The production of spirits is still regulated at the national level including licensing and taxes for home distilleries. Also, in 1984 a national minimum purchase age of twenty-one was signed into law by President Reagan with the following comments:

Some may feel that my decision is at odds with my philosophical viewpoint that state problems should involve state solutions and it isn't up to a big and overwhelming government in Washington to tell the states what to do. And you're partly right...[It's] a national tragedy involving transit across state borders. Beyond that, there are some special cases in which overwhelming need can be dealt with by prudent and limited federal action. And in a case like this, where the problem is so clear-cut, then I have no misgivings about a judicious use of federal inducements to encourage the states to get moving, raise the drinking age, and save precious lives.[1]

I have to wonder if the following note I received from an Orange County ER doctor would qualify under Reagan's "national tragedy" criterion?

By the way, I am a social drinker myself. I'm also an ER physician that is sick and tired of seeing the ER filled up with car accident victims, stabbing victims, beaten women, and abused children – all caused by alcohol abuse. I think the sellers of these products need to be assessed more of the social cost. Current taxes are not covering the bills and aren't even allocated to solve the problem or ameliorate its effects.

Then we have the infamous Super Bowl XXI ad with Spuds McKenzie surrounded by three babes and Bud Light. Senator Strom Thurmond and the Center for Science in the Public Interest, along with Mothers against Drunk Driving, complained that the campaign targeted children. Congress passed federal labeling laws regarding drunk driving and pregnant women. Larger restrictions on alcoholic beverages advertising were narrowly avoided with a Republican administration in place. Most recently, we have in the middle of the campus-alcohol-date rape controversy,[2] Anheuser-Busch putting a label on Bud Light with the message, "The perfect beer for removing 'no' from our vocabulary for the night #UpForWhatever." Really?

Industry Self-Regulation. In 1996 a very bad thing happened. The spirits makers ended long-standing self-imposed bans on broadcast media advertising. Radio ads had been banned since 1936 and television since 1948. Justifications by industry executives for ending the self-imposed ban are telling:

---

1 Steven R. Weisman, "Reagan Calls for Drinking Age of 21," *New York Times*, June 21, 1984, online.

2 Beth McMurtrie, "Why Colleges Haven't Stopped Binge Drinking," *Chronicle of Higher Education*, December 2, 2014, online; and Steve Kolowich, "Can Dartmouth Rehabilitate Itself?" Chronicle of Higher Education, February 20, 2015, online.

"There's no basis for letting two forms of alcohol advertising, beer and wine, on television and radio and discriminating against another form," said Fred A. Meister, president and chief executive of [the Distilled Spirits Council of the United States] DISCUS in Washington…

Liquor marketers have long sought to use television and radio to add motion, sound and other appealing stimuli to their ads. [What about information?] Mr. Meister said that for four years DISCUS had talked – and conducted research with consumers – about the possibility of lifting the ban. [1]

"We vie for market share with beer and wine and yet we're being discriminated against," Ms. [Judy] Blatman [a spokeswoman for DISCUS]. "All forms of beverage alcohol should be judged by the same criteria. There's no such thing as soft and hard alcohol – alcohol is alcohol."[2]

Variety reports that spirits industry TV advertising has now risen to more $243 million in recent years.[3] According to *Advertising Age*,[4] Beam allocated 43 percent of its ad spending to TV in 2012, up from 28 percent a year earlier. Diageo has been the biggest spender among the spirits makers, $17 million in 2012 on Captain Morgan and Skinnygirl, a lower-calorie, ready-to-serve cocktail line targeting women. More to come on this.

There is also a growing trend for product placement in broadcast programing that the spirits-industry guidelines ignore. For example, MillerCoors has formed a partnership with Time Warner's Turner to weave its beers and logos into shows such as *Sullivan & Son* and *Rescue Me*.

The self-regulation mandated by DISCUS still includes airing ads only on programs that have audiences with at least 71.6 percent over 21 years of age, no cartoon figures that are attractive to kids, no targeting of underage drinkers,

1 Stuart Elliott, "Liquor Industry Ends Its Ban in Broadcasting," *New York Times*, November 8, 1996, online.

2 Patricia Winters Lauro, "Media: Advertising; Cocktail Hour Returns to TV," *New York Times*, December 7, 2000, online.

3 Brian Steinberg, "Spirit Makers Are Spending More on TV Ads – And They're Stirring Themselves in as Part of the Show," *Variety*, October 10, 2013, online.

4 *Advertising Age*, "Hard Time: Liquor Advertising Pours into TV Looser Restrictions, Raft of Launches Lead More Booze Brands to the Tube," May 13, 2012, online.

and no claims of sexual prowess associated with consumption. Obviously, networks and programs can reject such ads. But particularly as advertising industry revenues declined during the 2008-09 recession the networks have relaxed their previous appropriateness standards.

For me the most distressing examples are the outdoor spirits advertising I see at family-friendly Angel's baseball stadium in Anaheim – neon signs advertising "Adult Chocolate Milk" and a blimp hawking Hangar Vodka. Outrageous!

My Own Prescriptions. If the failure of Prohibition taught us one lesson, it is that banning the manufacture and distribution of alcoholic beverages does not work. Much of the booze still got through, and the associated crime was worse. We can also learn from the tobacco experiences. Taxes and advertising limits do work. Both should be implemented in the case of alcoholic beverages, the most harmful drug of all, depending on how you count the damage done by its cousin, sugar. Both tools keep the competitive playing field level across beer, wine, and spirits and across the largest global marketers and the growing craft industries. These latter topics will be discussed in more detail and in a more comprehensive context in Chapter 14.

Also, I would be in favor of all college campuses banning social fraternities. Sorry, boys.

Marketing Miscreant – Alcohol

97,000 college students between the ages of 18 and 24 are victims of alcohol-related sexual assault or date rape.

NIHAAA

The darkest places in hell are reserved for those who maintain their neutrality in times of moral crisis.

DANTE ALIGHIERI

I don't think Jon Stewart is going to hell. Or, if he were, he could probably joke and snicker his way out. I loved the guy and the show. I was a religious viewer of his *Daily Show* on Comedy Central.

But his record on hedonic molecules was spotty. Bad Jon popped up with the 2/29/14 NJoy e-cigarette ad I mentioned in the last chapter. Good Jon surrounded it with other anti-smoking ads during that week. On his 3/31/14 show he demonstrated contrition for having fast food (salt and sugar) maker Taco Bell as an advertiser/sponsor. Good Jon.

He and his staff were quite creative with potential cultural memes. For his 9/17/14 show Good Jon came up with catchy phrases like "bumper brain" and "beer pressure." Both lambasted the NFL (1) for their brain damage epidemic and (2) for allowing Coors to pressure them into stronger penalties for their players' criminal behaviors. Ironically, Jon was also a victim of "beer pressure."

One of his funniest long-running routines had to do with "Jimmy Dean Pancake & Sausage on a Stick" (JDPSS) products. First airing on the 11/19/06 show, the product appeared more often than Dennis Leary. He didn't advertise the product, rather his sketches skewered it with ridicule for its incredibly bad nutritional value, something that can be only "technically defined as food." The only corporation he was harder on was Arby's. For one of the bits he even dipped the chocolate chip version of JDPSS into a jar of Baconnaise (a bacon-laced mayonnaise product) to increase the level of "malnutrition." Then, with his audience and staff egging him on, he took a bite, then gagged on it. Really funny stuff, Jon. A humorous approach to teaching good eating habits. Good Jon.

Jon Stewart gets the Marketing Miscreant award for this chapter for the grand hypocrisy of advertising Smirnoff's Fluffed Marshmallow flavored vodka on his 8/31/12 show. That was the episode with Clint Eastwood talking to the empty chair. This is a product designed for college men to buy/bring for their coed dates. Awful stuff – I bought a bottle and had a shot. The miniature marshmallows on the label make it seem like candy. What better way to take advantage of May West's advice on the matter, "One more drink and I'll be under the host." All this may seem kind of funny, even a silly criticism. That is, until you juxtapose it with the NIHAAA statistic above. I'll repeat it here for Bad Jon, "97,000 college students between the ages of 18 and 24 are victims of alcohol-related assault or date rape." Diageo (Smirnoff is in their brand stable), please show us your marketing research on his harmful product and prove me wrong.

Most recently (3/31/15), Jon aired a segment on fraternity date rape, and a documentary entitled *The Hunting Ground*. In the interview, Jon asked some tough questions. But, I assume because of "beer pressure," no one uttered the word "alcohol" during the entire segment. Bad Jon.

———————

Answer to question on page 163: Diageo is mentioned once on the Bulleit website on the Terms & Conditions page, the button is at the very bottom of the home page. You will find "copyright@diageo.com" as the 3418th word of 3748 on the Terms & Conditions page.[1]

---

1 See www.Bulleit.com. Accessed April 3, 2014.

Eight

Opium
Primary chemical ingredient: Morphine, $C_{17}H_{19}NO_3$

Poppy tears.

A poppy by any other name inebriates the same. Some call it "hop," "midnight oil," "tar," "dope," and "Big O." At www.noslang.com you can find hundreds of street terms for opium and its derivatives (mainly morphine and heroin) from "antifreeze" to "zero." The Greek *ópion* and the Latin *opium* both mean juice. The scientific name, *Lachryma papaveris* is Latin for poppy tears.

Three sorts of tears are associated with this ancient spice. First, the traditional production of opium involves the scoring or scratching the immature poppy seedpod which produces tear-like droplets of latex that, when dried, become the drug. The second connection to tears is the use of the drug as a powerful analgesic (painkiller), thus reducing tears. The third kind of opium tears are those of addiction, so often seen at funerals of the young.

History

Opium use is older than civilization. Evidence of its cultivation in Europe dates back to 4200 BC. The Sumerians, Babylonians, and Egyptians recorded its use in religious ceremonies, healing, and, euthanasia. The Phoenicians traded opium all around the Mediterranean more than four thousand years ago. Opium was a key part of surgical procedures among Islamic healers into the 1500s AD. Arab traders introduced the spice to China circa 1200. In Western civilization opium's medicinal uses as a sedative and painkiller was common beginning in the tenth century. Its use during the American Civil War was prolific. Indeed, that lovely war delivered not only its historic proliferation of hand guns (think O.K. Corral), but also its addiction to opium as a remedy for the wounds they caused.

In the 1800s British traders became the biggest drug cartel in human history. We will go into more detail about them in the Marketing Miscreant section of this chapter. Suffice it here to say that the British introduced its hedonic consumption into China, and the Chinese and Indian diasporas of the time helped spread the affliction around the world. The Chinese opium den was a cultural icon of the largest American and European cities of the time.

The city of San Francisco banned opium dens in 1875. The state of California made it a crime to sell opium without a prescription in 1907. Two years later the state criminalized both possession of the drug and the ubiquitous opium pipes. Ironically, my mother displayed an opium pipe as part of the "oriental" décor of our living room in the 1960s. As a teenager I always wondered what kind of tobacco might fit into that tiny bowl at the end of the long flute-like pipe stem.

While the US Constitution at the time disallowed arbitrary prohibitions, it did allow arbitrary taxation. Thus, beginning in 1889 a tariff on opium imports of up to $300 per pound was levied. In 1909 the federal government banned imports of the drug all together. Other taxes and restrictions on the distribution of opiates yielded a de facto prohibition of the drug in the United States in 1914. Now, of course, opium is regulated by the Drug Enforcement Administration (DEA) under the Controlled Substance Act.

In the last few decades the global pharmaceutical industry has produced a plethora of synthetic compounds that closely imitate effects of opiates. Raw opium, morphine (the primary active compound in opium), heroin (concentrated opium), and codeine (another active compound found in opium) are all properly called *opiates*. Opiates and all their synthetic sisters (such as Vicodin, OxyContin, and fentanyl) are subsumed under the more general term *opioids*.

Consumer Behavior

There are three primary purposes of the consumption of opium and its derivatives (both natural and synthetic) – pain relief, pleasure, and euthanasia/suicide. The latter are illegal, but not uncommon, in the United States.

Medicinal (Licit) Consumption. The nausea turned to stomach pain for me at about eleven that night. I spent about an hour sweating in bed, debating whether it was food poisoning or appendicitis, and whether I should wake my wife. The pain was definitely right-sided. By the time I realized I needed to go to the ER, I could barely get dressed and walk to get into the car. Once at the lightly crowded midnight emergency room I had to lie on the floor in a fetal position to await a bed and diagnosis.

How could it be that a grain-of-sand-sized calcium stone could make a grown man cry? My debilitating pain was caused by the stone passing down my ureter from my right kidney to my bladder. Women say kidney stones are worse than childbirth. Obviously, I cannot attest to that. What I can attest to is the benefits of morphine. That opium derivative relieved the pain. I don't remember ever feeling good in that ER bed, just not horribly bad.

All the medicinal forms of opium (we'll go into the list in detail in the Product section of the chapter below) are controlled by doctors' prescriptions in the United States. Doctors are to manage the efficacy, quantities, and continuation of these pharmaceuticals, particularly with concern for their addictive qualities.

When the morphine hit my brain via intravenous injection, it blocked the signals of pain (at what the neurologists call opioid receptors) coming from my stressed/injured ureter. The pointy little stone was still doing damage, but the sensations of pain were no longer delivered to my brain.

Illicit Consumption. Opium and almost all of its derivatives are listed under Schedule II of the US Controlled Substances Act of 1970. The law specifies three findings to qualify for this classification:

1. The drug or other substance has a high potential for abuse.
2. The drug or other substance has a currently accepted medical use in treatment in the United States or a currently accepted medical use with severe restrictions.
3. Abuse of the drug or other substances may lead to severe psychological or physical dependence.

Doctors' prescriptions are required for possession of these pharmaceutical products.

Two opium derivatives listed under Schedule I are heroin, with about twice the potency of morphine, and etorphine, a semi-synthetic opioid with a potency of 1000-3000 times that of morphine. Schedule I drugs are not available even with a prescription, and there are no acceptable medical uses of the substances. We do note that heroin is allowed for medical purposes in some European countries.

Hedonic Consumption. It's early on a summer evening, and the hollow white shaft of an old Bic pen is clamped between Heather's teeth. In one trembling hand she holds a yellow disposable lighter, and in the other, a small sheet of foil, four inches by six, sprinkled with heroin. The bright white powder shimmers in the muted light coming through her office window.

Without relaxing her jaw, Heather takes a verbal inventory: "OK. Pen, lighter, tin foil." The lighter flares. As she moves the fame under the foil plate, the powder dissolves into a greasy ribbon of smoke that rises heavily into the air. It smells like a chemical fire. Heather sucks noisily on the pen-straw, and the twisted plume doubles back and disappears up the shaft. She vacuums the air until she has captured every smoky molecule and there is no space left in her lungs for more. Junkies call this "chasing the dragon." All that's left on the foil is a yellow blemish.

The wonderful writing by David France[1] puts me closer than I ever want to get to the stuff. Oddly, his article, "Heather Does Heroin," appeared in *Glamour* in 1998. What I can't tell you is how I came across this little gem back when I first started collecting material for this book. My wife is a subscriber, perhaps she gave it to me? In any case, Heather's little act was not glamourous at all – that is, unless you really like heroin. That is, unless you are addicted to heroin.

Opium and its derivatives have been hedonically consumed in an impressive array of ways over the centuries and particularly in modern times. Smoking an opium pipe is different than a tobacco pipe in that the opium is actually heated, vaporized (not burned), and then inhaled. However, a heroin-tobacco mix can be smoked. Intravenous injection is most often used with heroin, and all forms can be snorted or taken orally as pills or mixed with food. There are a number of tricks to achieve a faster high, many of which are more dangerous to the user.

Of course, opium and its derivatives cause both psychological and physical dependence – that is, addictive consumption.

The National Institute of Drug Abuse defines the "rush" that hedonic consumers find so attractive:

> Once heroin enters the brain, it is converted to morphine and binds rapidly to opioid receptors. Abusers typically report feeling a surge of pleasurable sensation—a "rush." The intensity of the rush is a function of how much drug is taken and how rapidly the drug enters the brain and binds to the opioid receptors. …Heroin binds to and activates specific receptors in the brain called mu-opioid receptors (MORs).

---

1 David France, "Heather Does Heroin," *Glamour,* September 1998, pages 320-330.

Our bodies contain naturally occurring chemicals called neurotransmitters that bind to these receptors throughout the brain and body to regulate pain, hormone release, and feelings of well-being. When MORs are activated in the reward center of the brain, they stimulate the release of the neurotransmitter dopamine, causing a sensation of pleasure…With heroin, the rush is usually accompanied by a warm flushing of the skin, dry mouth, and a heavy feeling in the extremities, which may be accompanied by nausea, vomiting, and severe itching. After the initial effects, users usually will be drowsy for several hours; mental function is clouded; heart function slows; and breathing is also severely slowed, sometimes enough to be life-threatening.

- Opioids can depress breathing by changing neurochemical activity in the brain stem, where automatic body functions such as breathing and heart rate are controlled.
- Opioids can increase feelings of pleasure by altering activity in the limbic system, which controls emotions.
- Opioids can block pain messages transmitted through the spinal cord from the body.[1]

Finally, tolerance and horrific withdrawal symptoms are both penalties of hedonic consumption of heroin.

A final note here about controversies regarding the supply of the heroin antidote, naloxone, made by Amphastar Pharmaceuticals: It comes in both injectable form and as a nasal spray. In some locations around the country, the price per dose charged to emergency agencies trying to prevent heroin-overdose deaths was doubled in 2014. The agencies around the country complained. Most recently the New York attorney general reached an agreement with Amphastar to curb its prices.[2] Thanks to the company for a useful prod-

---

1 National Institute (of Health, NIH) on Drug Abuse, www.drugabuse.gov, accessed July 22, 2014.

2 David Goodman, "State Attorney General Strike Deal with Drug Company to Curb Price of Heroin Antidote," *New York Times*, February 5, 2015, page A21.

uct, but not the high prices. Amphastar is not Jonas Salk nor Nils Ivar Bohlin. You will meet Mr. Bohlin in Chapter 13.

Euthanasia/Suicide. Every day in the United States opioids are used illegally for this purpose. The laws are quite clear, but the ethics and the efficacy of different methods are continuously debated here in the United States and abroad. The night before I wrote this paragraph the editors of the *Economist* magazine[1] argued for passage of an assisted suicide law in the UK. Assisted suicide is permitted in California, Oregon, Washington, and Vermont. Several other states are considering legislation in this area. Most medical professionals working in the palliative and hospice care fields are loathe to discuss the topic. This is the case, even while the CDC reports that in 2012, of the 41,340 drug overdose deaths in the United States, 5298 (12.8 percent) were of suicidal intent.

These changes in views about suicide are coinciding with an uptick in the death rate in the United States in 2015. Three causes are often mentioned for the unusual increase in death rates: suicide, opioid overdose, and Alzheimer's disease. Indeed, in some cases the three potential causes of death are becoming harder to disambiguate.

Heroin Gets the Headlines. When I began the research to support this chapter my impression was that heroin was the big villain. It's certainly powerfully bad stuff. It certainly is one of the foci of movies about drugs and DEA drug-bust publicity. For the last twenty years or so I have been gathering articles from the *New York Times* and other media about the various spices on my list. The stack regarding marijuana is by far the tallest. In the last year e-cigarettes has really taken off. Philip Seymour Hoffman's heroin related demise in February 2014 gave a surprising boost to press attention to heroin.

But heroin is by no means the most dangerous opioid. The worst are the prescription drugs already in your medicine cabinet. Please take a look at Exhibit 8.1 for perspective. We will discuss prescription opioid pain relievers in the next section of the chapter.

---

1 "Easeful Death," *Economist*, July 19, 2014, page 12.

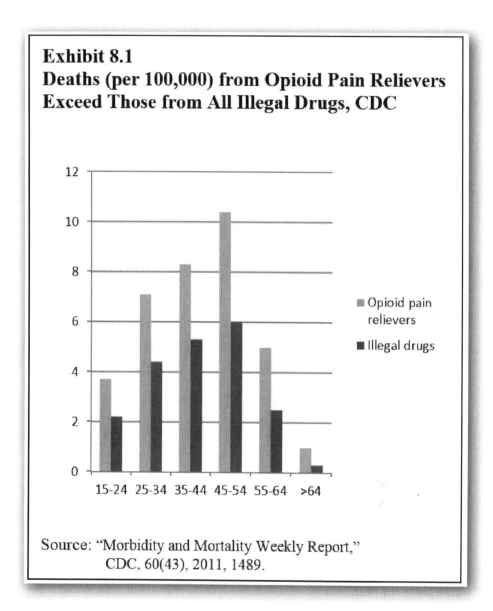

Exhibit 8.1
Deaths (per 100,000) from Opioid Pain Relievers Exceed Those from All Illegal Drugs, CDC

Source: "Morbidity and Mortality Weekly Report," CDC, 60(43), 2011, 1489.

Earlier I related the immediate (some attractive, some not) effects of heroin consumption as reported by the NIH. There's nothing attractive about the long-term effects of heroin consumption:

Repeated heroin use changes the physical structure and physiology of the brain, creating long-term imbalances in neuronal and hormonal systems that are not easily reversed. Heroin also produces profound degrees of tolerance and physical dependence. Tolerance occurs when more and more of the drug is required to achieve the same effects. With physical dependence, the body adapts to the presence of the drug and withdrawal symptoms occur if use is reduced abruptly. Withdrawal may occur within a few hours after the last time the drug is taken. Symptoms of withdrawal include restlessness, muscle and bone pain, insomnia, diarrhea, vomiting, cold flashes with goose bumps ("cold turkey"), and leg movements. Major withdrawal symptoms peak between 24–48 hours after the last dose of heroin and subside after about a week. However, some people have shown persistent withdrawal signs for many months. Finally, repeated heroin use often results in addiction—a chronic relapsing disease that goes beyond physical dependence and is characterized by uncontrollable drug-seeking no matter the consequences. Heroin is extremely addictive no matter how it is administered, although routes of administration that allow it to reach the brain the fastest (i.e., injection and smoking) increase the risk of addiction. Once a person becomes addicted to heroin, seeking and using the drug becomes their primary purpose in life.[1]

Really, really bad stuff!

The less than awful news? It seems that 99 percent of Americans know about this, and younger people are staying away in greater numbers. In 2011 4.2 million Americans aged twelve or older (or 1.6 percent) had used heroin at least once in their lives. NIH estimates that 23 percent of those who try it become addicted. The United Nations Office on Drugs and Crime (UNODC) reports the annual prevalence of opiates usage at 1.4 million or 0.5 percent in North America. These numbers have remained stable during this century.

The least bad news comes from the most recent NIH survey[2] of American twelfth graders: In 2010 1.6 percent of high school seniors reported ever try-

---

1 Ibid, National Institute of Drug Abuse.
2 Ibid, National Institute of Drug Abuse.

ing heroin, and 0.4 percent said they used it in the last month. Those numbers declined to 1.0 percent and 0.3 percent, respectively, in the 2013 replication.

Death and Addiction Lurking in Your Medicine Cabinet. Consider for a moment what prescription medications are in your home (or, for that matter, your kids' friends' homes). The pharmaceutical companies assure us that their products are safe as long as taken as prescribed. We do note that these assurances seem to be frequently reversed based on law suits, FDA disapprovals, and such. Prescription medications are abused in three ways: taking a drug prescribed for someone else; taking a drug in a greater quantity than prescribed (crushing and snorting a pill, for example); or taking a drug for another purpose (getting high, increasing test performance).

Just a sampling of the pertinent statistics: Of the 2.5 million ER visits for drug overdoses in 2011, 1.4 million were related to pharmaceuticals. Of the 41,340 overdose deaths reported in that year, 22,810 (55 percent) were related to pharmaceuticals, and 16,917 (41 percent) involved opioid analgesics specifically. After marijuana at 36.4 percent, the past-year prevalence of abuse among American twelfth graders of opioids such as Vicodin (7.5 percent) and OxyContin (4.3 percent) exceed the use of the illicit drugs such as ecstasy (3.8 percent), inhalants (2.9 percent), cocaine in any form (2.7 percent), and heroin (less than 0.6 percent).[1]

And this part of the consumption story gets worse. Prescription opioid abuse appears to be an important first step in the direction of heroin use. Nearly half of the young people who inject heroin surveyed in three recent studies reported abusing prescription opioids before starting to use heroin. Some individuals reported taking up heroin because it was cheaper and easier to get than prescription opioids. Many also reported crushing opioid pills to snort or inject the powder provided their initiation into these methods of consumption.[2] Yikes!

Even the doctors that two decades ago proselytized to revive production of opioids for pain relief have recanted. Dr. Russell Portenoy now complains: "Did I teach about pain management, specifically about opioid therapy, in a

---

1 University of Michigan, "2012 Monitoring the Future Study," cited at National Institute of Drug Abuse.

2 Ibid, National Institute of Drug Abuse.

way that reflects misinformation [de-emphasizing the risks]? Well, against the standards of 2012, I guess I did. We didn't know then what we know now."[1]

The Global Consumption and Supply. Geography, culture, and economics clearly influence the consumption and availability of opioids, both natural and synthetic. See Exhibit 8.2 for a glimmer of the differences around the world. The outstanding datum is the legal use of opioids in North America, mostly the United States supplied by the pharmaceutical industry. Congressional testimony has suggested that 80 percent of the global supply of pain pills is consumed in the United States.

Exhibit 8.2
Consumption of Opioids by Country

Countries	Opioids* (mg/capita)	Illegal Opiates** (% prevalence of use in year)
Canada	812.2	0.4
United States	749.8	0.6
Germany	395.6	0.3
Netherlands	264.0	0.3
UK	252.9	0.9
France	210.8	0.4
Sweden	190.7	0.1
Italy	169.4	0.8
Finland	159.8	0.1
Iran	78.2	2.3
Japan	24.3	0.1
China	6.4	0.2
Brazil	6.2	0.6
Saudi Arabia	4.3	0.01
UAE	3.4	0.02
Russia	2.0	1.6
Afghanistan	0.4	2.7
India	0.3	0.4
Global average	61.1	

* This statistic sums consumption of fentanyl, hydromorphone, methadone, morphine, oxycodone, pethidine as reported by the International Narcotics Control Board. See the University of Wisconsin, Madison Pain & Policy Studies Group, www.painpolicy.wisc.edu.
** The percentage of "youths and adults" that report using opiates in the last year from 2006 and 2011 *World Drug Reports* published by the UNODC.

---

1 Thomas Catan and Evan Perez, "A Pain-Drug Champion Has Second Thoughts," *Wall Street Journal*, December 15-16, 2012, page A1.

In this context, the mission statement of University of Wisconsin, Madison Pain & Policy Group is interesting: "The PPSG mission is to improve global pain relief by achieving balanced access to opioids in an effort to enhance the quality of life of people living with cancer and other painful diseases." They maintain that their opioids consumption numbers are an indicator of palliative care. It's not clear to me that dollars spent coincides with quality of elder care. Please see another of my books, *All in the Family* for details.[1] I do appreciate their good intentions on this. Moreover, it is certainly clear that while Americans and Canadians suffer from the abundance of opioids, people in less developed countries suffer from their scarcity.

Afghanistan and its neighboring Russia and Iran are the big consumers of illegal opiates. The United States and UK are both high on that list as well.

The global supply of licit opium and its associated opiates is tightly controlled in part by the United Nations Single Convention on Narcotic Drugs, at about two thousand tons per year.[2] Almost all this production is from four countries – Australia (Tasmania), India, Spain, and Turkey.

Today Afghanistan dominates the illicit production of opium at about four thousand tons per year which is in the neighborhood of 85 percent of the world total. It is interesting to note that after the Taliban banned the production of opium, it fell steeply to about eighty tons per year. After the American/British invasion and removal of Taliban control, production has burgeoned again. Mexico and Myanmar (Burma) are the next biggest suppliers of illegal opium. The illegal production uses the traditional backbreaking handwork approach of scoring and scraping off the dried latex.

As baby boomers around the world digress toward decrepitude the global forecasts for painkillers burgeon. Consequently, initiatives are being undertaken internationally to expand the licit production of opium to include Afghanistan and other countries. For example, GlaxoSmithKline and Johnson & Johnson, two multinational firms that control the highly mechanized

---

1 Sharon Graham Niederhaus and John L. Graham, *All in the Family: A Practical Guide to Successful Multigenerational Living* (Lanham, MA: Taylor Trade, 2013).

2 This number was incredibly difficult to find. I googled for two hours. The best source I could locate was the DEAMuseum.org. Even the agency responsible for setting the quotas – UNDOC – does not report them to the public as far as I can determine.

production in Tasmania are urging farmers there to alter the genome of the opium to provide better yields and more potent plants. They are also concerned about spreading their production portfolio in case of weather and other environmental threats.[1]

And it seems new competition is on the horizon in the form of local sources of supply. According to Professor Kenneth A. Oye at MIT, "All the elements are in place, but the whole pathway needs to be integrated before a one-pot glucose-to-morphine stream is ready to roll."[2] He's talking about producing morphine without poppies, via brewing methods using yeast genetically modified to turn sugar into morphine. Look out Afghanistan and Tasmania.

Marketing

Product. The army of licit opioids produced by the creativity of the pharmaceutical companies is astonishing. More than 100 are listed on Wikipedia. Here's what WebMD.com has under Opioid Pain Relievers:

Generic Name	Brand Name
fentanyl	Duragesic
hydrocodone	Norco, Vicodin
hydromorphone	Dilaudid, Exalgo
morphine	Astramorph, Avinza
oxycodone	OxyContin, Percocet

Opioids are available in pills, liquids, or suckers to take by mouth, and in shot, skin patch, and suppository form. Some of the manufacturers try to limit use by making the pills hard to chew and/or inject. Purdue Pharma likens its OxyContin abuse-deterrent features to a "seat belt" for the illicit use epidemic. More exageration by the company that knows how?[3]

---

1 Keith Bardsher, "Shake-Up on Opium Island," *New York Times*, July 20, 2014.
2 Donald McNeil Jr., "Makings of New Heroin," *New York Times*, May 19, 2015, pages D1, D2.
3 Alan Schwarz, "Painkillers Resist Abuse, But Experts Still Worry," *New York Times*, June 7, 2015, page A17.

During my study for this chapter I also came across several mentions of fentanyl, a Schedule II drug 50-100 times more potent than morphine. Since Prince's untimely death by fentanyl overdose in 2016, the pharmaceutical has gained new prominence. A growing value chain for its production starts with illegal shipments of ingredients from China going to Mexican cartels for production, and then delivery to US customers. Most recently, at least in one jurisdiction, fentanyl overdose deaths outpaced those caused by heroin.[1] Given that heroin is only 2.2 times the strength of morphine makes me wonder why heroin resides as a Schedule I drug? Of course, many aspects of our drug policies make no sense. Why should I be surprised about this?

The illicit list is shorter. Because heroin is about 1/10th the weight/volume of opium and 2.2 times the strength of morphine, the most available form of opium is heroin. Heroin is lighter and smaller to ship and easier to hide. A variety of chemical and mechanical means can be used to purify opium into heroin. It is usually available in four grades: No. 4 is its purest form, a white powder or salt, easily dissolved and injected; No. 3 is "brown sugar" for smoking, and Nos. 1 and 2 are raw forms of differing strengths. Black tar heroin is even a cruder form produced usually in Latin America.

Actually heroin was once a licit drug. Bayer had trademarked the drug and named it for the German "*heroisch*," which means "'heroic" or "strong." The company was stripped of the trademark in 1917 as a consequence of The Great War. The trademark on aspirin was also lost then. And, as we know from *Breaking Bad*, illicit narcotics are often branded. I recommend Elizabeth Barber's "cautionary tale" on the topic in the *Christian Science Monitor*, February 4, 2014. She mentions brand names such as "Ace of Spades," "Twilight," "Lady Gaga," and "Obama Care." The problem with these brands is that dead guys can't sue, no matter how dangerous the product.

Place. The legal restrictions on opioids in some cases prohibit their production – the obvious case is heroin. For the rest of the opioids the strongest restrictions regard distribution. The prime example is Vicodin, once called "the celebrity drug" or "the drug for teenagers," and it was the drug of choice

---

1 Katherine Q. Seelye, "Heroin Yields Ground to Fentanyl, Its More Potent Killer Cousin," *New York Times*, March 26, 2016, page A1, A14.

for Dr. House on that popular Fox television show still in syndication around the world.

I loved the headline: "One Nation, on Vicodin: Narcotic Painkillers Are Most-Used US Drugs." On April 20, 2011 CBS News reported:

America is a nation on painkillers, according to new statistics from IMS Health, the pharmaceutical data giant. About 131.2 million prescriptions were written for generic **Vicodin** (a hydrocodone/acetominophen combo), more than any other drug last year, IMS reported. The next most-prescribed drug was generic **Zocor** (simvastatin) for cholesterol...

Taken together, doctors wrote 244.3 million narcotic painkiller prescriptions last year, the majority of which have an addiction risk. The US population is 307 million -- so statistically, enough scrips were written for 80 percent of all Americans, including children. Middle America is being ravaged by oxycodone addiction. The FDA is seeking tougher controls on drugs like **OxyContin**.

OxyContin generated the biggest revenues at almost $3 billion, while Vicodin was a $170 million drug for Abbott Laboratories in 2012. At the request of the DEA, in 2013 an FDA advisory panel voted to place tougher restrictions on Vicodin, moving it from Schedule III to Schedule II. Schedule III classification had allowed phoned-in, lengthy prescriptions making abuse more likely. Under the threat of the reclassification, Abbott Labs' stock crashed from a high of $66 to a low of $33 between December 4, 2012 and January 14, 2013. The company lost half its value that monstrous month when its distribution was handcuffed by the FDA.

While the doctor may give you a sample, most prescription medications are purchased through the seventy thousand or so pharmacies in the United States – either the bricks-and-mortar sort or increasingly online and through the mail. Of course, the debates about cheaper drugs from Canada, and smuggling and such, rage on. Google has been under continuous attack for not doing a better job of suppressing the illicit pharmacies that lurk among its electrons. These will be topics for later chapters.

For heroin, we don't talk about distribution. Instead, we use the appropriate pejorative "drug trafficking." It is smuggled into the States from Afghanistan via Europe, from Mexico across the border by the drug cartels, and from Myanmar by ship and air. Domestic drug dealers/gangs cut (dilute), bag, and brand the product, and then traffic it to consumers through personal selling networks of teenagers[1] and other third parties. The distribution system is so efficient that now you can buy heroin at just about any high school in the country. The prohibition of heroin clearly has not worked.

Price. According to UNODC *2013 World Drug Report*, the price for a *kilo*gram of opium at the farm gate in Afghanistan last year was about $200. Add in the costs of shipping, personal selling, and other transaction costs, and that translates into a retail/street price of about $400 per *gram* for the best heroin in the United States. The retail prices are pretty stable, but the farm-gate numbers can be quite volatile depending on weather, wars, and interdiction efforts. The Internet is full of pricing information, but frankly I'm not interested enough to try to sort out all the marketing hype, purity issues, and so on. They also list the wholesale price for Colombian heroin at only $10,000 per kilogram. That suggests the cost of trafficking is quite high.

Finding estimates of the size of the illicit heroin business in the United States is tough. My best estimate is approximately $12 billion per year.[2] This coincides pretty well with the independent estimate of the folks at www. Progressive-Economy.org at $11 billion.

Sales of licit opioids are easier to track. The *New York Times*[3] refers to the "Opioid Economy" and reports that sales more than doubled in the last

---

1 Sudhir Venkatesh's *Gang Leader for Day* (New York: Penguin, 2008) I highly recommend for a detailed description of how drug dealing gangs work.

2 I started with global illicit opium production of 5000 tons, that when converted into morphine yields about 500 tons, and when converted into heroin (at 2.2:1) yields a global heroin production of 227 tons. North America has 1.4 million heroin users, of which 1.1 million are in the US That is 6.7 percent of the world's total users (16,490). US consumption then is 33.3 tons of heroin. At a street price of $400/gram, that's about $12 billion. Someone please check my assumptions and math and email me what you think.

3 Barry Meier, "Profiting from Pain," *New York Times*, June 22, 2013, online.

decade, from almost $4 billion in 2001 to over $8.3 billion in 2012. In twenty states doctors are allowed to sell drugs – the pharmacy price in Illinois is 53¢ while the doctors charge $1.44. A convenience for patients becomes a conflict of interest for their doctors. The opioid economy doesn't seem economic at all. Indeed, the CDC has termed the opioid-abuse "epidemic" as the fastest growing among all drug problems in the United States.

Promotion. The main tool of promotion for opioids is personal selling, whether we are talking about heroin or the vast array of Schedule II opioids. It might be the teenager on a West Oakland street corner passing a packet through a car window to a Piedmont customer while talking up the next shipment. Or, maybe it's a coat-and-tied "detail man" calling at a doctor's office and leaving copious samples. The sales pitches in form are often the same. "I know you've used xxx in the past, but the new and improved version is even better."

The classic case in the latter field is presented in the *Journal of Public Health* by Dr. Art Van Zee.[1] For its rich and instructive detail we mightily admire his description of Purdue Pharma's $200-million-per-year promotional campaign and we excerpt his article heavily here:

> From 1996 to 2001, Purdue conducted more than 40 national pain-management and speaker-training conferences at resorts in Florida, Arizona, and California. More than 5000 physicians, pharmacists, and nurses attended these all-expenses-paid symposia, where they were recruited and trained for Purdue's national speaker bureau. It is well documented that this type of pharmaceutical company symposium influences physicians' prescribing, even though the physicians who attend such symposia believe that such enticements do not alter their prescribing patterns.
>
> One of the cornerstones of Purdue's marketing plan was the use of sophisticated marketing data to influence physicians' prescribing. Drug companies compile prescriber profiles on individual

---

1 Art Van Zee, "The Promotion and Marketing of OxyContin: Commercial Triumph, Public Health Tragedy," *Journal of Public Health* 99(2), February 2009, pages 221-227.

physicians—detailing the prescribing patterns of physicians nation-wide—in an effort to influence doctors' prescribing habits. Through these profiles, a drug company can identify the highest and lowest prescribers of particular drugs in a single zip code, county, state, or the entire country. One of the critical foundations of Purdue's marketing plan for OxyContin was to target the physicians who were the highest prescribers for opioids across the country. The resulting database would help identify physicians with large numbers of chronic-pain patients. Unfortunately, this same database would also identify which physicians were simply the most frequent prescribers of opioids and, in some cases, the least discriminate prescribers.

A lucrative bonus system encouraged sales representatives to increase sales of OxyContin in their territories, resulting in a large number of visits to physicians with high rates of opioid prescriptions, as well as a multifaceted information campaign aimed at them. In 2001, in addition to the average sales representative's annual salary of $55,000, annual bonuses averaged $71,500, with a range of $15,000 to nearly $240,000. Purdue paid $40 million in sales incentive bonuses to its sales representatives that year.

From 1996 to 2000, Purdue increased its internal sales force from 318 sales representatives to 671, and its total physician call list from approximately 33,400 to 44,500 to approximately 70,500 to 94,000 physicians. Through the sales representatives, Purdue used a patient starter coupon program for OxyContin that provided patients with a free limited-time prescription for a 7- to 30-day supply. By 2001, when the program was ended, approximately 34,000 coupons had been redeemed nationally.

The distribution to health care professionals of branded promotional items such as OxyContin fishing hats, stuffed plush toys, and music compact discs ("Get in the Swing with OxyContin") was unprecedented for a schedule II opioid, according to the Drug Enforcement Administration.

Purdue promoted among primary care physicians a more liberal use of opioids, particularly sustained-release opioids. Primary care physicians began to use more of the increasingly popular OxyContin; by 2003, nearly half of all physicians prescribing OxyContin were primary care physicians. Some experts were concerned that primary care physicians were not sufficiently trained in pain management or addiction issues. Primary care physicians, particularly in a managed care environment of time constraints, also had the least amount of time for evaluation and follow-up of patients with complicated chronic pain.

Purdue "aggressively" promoted the use of opioids for use in the "non-malignant pain market." A much larger market than that for cancer-related pain, the non–cancer-related pain market constituted 86 percent of the total opioid market in 1999. Purdue's promotion of OxyContin for the treatment of non–cancer-related pain contributed to a nearly tenfold increase in OxyContin prescriptions for this type of pain, from about 670,000 in 1997 to about 6.2 million in 2002, whereas prescriptions for cancer-related pain increased about fourfold during that same period...

A consistent feature in the promotion and marketing of OxyContin was a systematic effort to minimize the risk of addiction in the use of opioids for the treatment of chronic non–cancer-related pain. One of the most critical issues regarding the use of opioids in the treatment of chronic non–cancer-related pain is the potential of iatrogenic addiction. The lifetime prevalence of addictive disorders has been estimated at 3 percent to 16 percent of the general population...

In much of its promotional campaign—in literature and audiotapes for physicians, brochures and videotapes for patients, and its "Partners against Pain" Web site—Purdue claimed that the risk of addiction from OxyContin was extremely small.

Purdue trained its sales representatives to carry the message that the risk of addiction was "less than one percent." ...Misrepresenting the risk of addiction proved costly for Purdue. On May 10, 2007, Purdue Frederick Company Inc, an affiliate of Purdue Pharma, along with 3 company executives, pled guilty to criminal charges of misbranding OxyContin by claiming that it was less addictive and less subject to abuse and diversion than other opioids, and will pay $634 million in fines.

Although research demonstrated that OxyContin was comparable in efficacy and safety to other available opioids, marketing catapulted OxyContin to blockbuster drug status. Sales escalated from $44 million (316,000 prescriptions dispensed) in 1996 to a 2001 and 2002 combined sales of nearly $3 billion (over 14 million prescriptions).

The remarkable commercial success of OxyContin, however, was stained by increasing rates of abuse and addiction. Drug abusers learned how to simply crush the controlled-release tablet and swallow, inhale, or inject the high-potency opioid for an intense morphinelike high...

Thanks again, Dr. Van Zee! I note that Purdue's miscreant behavior continues in 2016. New Jersey Attorney General Joseph Foster said about a current investigation of the firm's marketing practices, "On the one hand, they tell us they have nothing to hide and they are doing everything appropriately, but then why are they fighting so hard not to turn over this information?"[1] We will revisit the consequences of Purdue's marketing wizardry at the end of the chapter.

One of Purdue's marketing tricks was the development of a "prescribers" data base. This is a good idea, so good that the federal government now uses a similar approach to identify law-breaking doctors. Such doctors are often paid by pharmaceutical companies such as Insys Therapeutics, maker of Subsys, an addictive painkiller. Dr. Gavin Awerbuch, a Michigan neurologist that received $56,000 from Insys, "was arrested this spring after federal prosecutors said he defrauded Medicare of $7 million and improperly prescribed Subsys to patients who did not need it."[2]

Finally, mass-media advertising of opioids is not uncommon in the United States. It is prohibited internationally by the United Nations Convention on Psychotropic Substances, 1971: Article 10.2 states, "Each Party shall, with due regard to its constitutional provisions, prohibit the advertisement of such substances

---

1 Harriet Ryan, Purdue Pharma Resists Data Request," *Los Angeles Times*, August 27, 2016, page A1, A8.

2 Katie Thomas, "Drug Company Enlists Doctors under Scrutiny," New York Times, November 28, 2014, page A1, A4.

to the general public." The United States remains a signatory to that international treaty along with 175 other countries. However, in 2001 drug maker Celltech ran a print ad campaign in a dozen American women's magazines for Metadate, a Schedule II controlled treatment for ADHD. The DEA almost immediately delivered a cease and desist order which the company ignored. The newly elected Bush administration chose not to pursue the issue. Thus, a treaty-abrogating-door was opened through which other pharmaceutical firms have dashed through.[1]

The multinational pharmaceutical companies do have great resources to spend on such advertising. They are listed in Exhibit 8.3 below. These statistics are from 2015-16 – and they provide some perspective for the $200 million promotional investment Abbott Labs made in Vicodin more than a decade earlier. All these companies listed will be spending at least as much again on their armies of salespeople beyond these advertising dollars. The spending here in the States is mostly on television and magazine placements, with TV being about double print.

Exhibit 8.3
Top Ten Pharmaceutical Advertisers Globally 2014

Company Spending (top 100 global rank)	Headquarters	Global Spending (millions $s)	U.S. (millions $s)
Johnson & Johnson (16)	New Jersey	2107	1088
Pfizer (18)	New York	1984	817
GlaxoSmithKline (31)	UK	1364	453
Bayer (40)	Germany	1161	707
Astellas Pharma (70)	Tokyo	558	31
Novartis (74)	Switzerland	552	91
Takeda Pharma (87)	Osaka, Japan	442	3
Allergan (88)	California	431	389
Walgreens Boots Alliance (91)	Illinois	403	289
Merck & Co. (92)	New Jersey	396	352

*Source: *Advertising Age*, 2016

---

1 Karen Thomas, "Back to School for ADHD Drugs," *USA Today*, August 28, 2001, online; and www.bonkersinstitute.org/medshow/kidmetadate.html.

Consequences of Consumption

We've already mentioned the overdose ER visit and death statistics caused by opioid abuse. See Exhibit 8.2 for a quick reminder. The addiction rates are quite high – 23 percent for those who try heroin, and 3-16 percent for the legal opioids. There are a plethora of other risks and tragedies associated with abuse and addiction.

Used hypodermic needles deliver HIV and hepatitis C (HCV).

Perhaps the ugliest consequences of heroin abuse are for the unborn. Spontaneous abortion, low-birth-weight babies, other birth defects, and heroin addicted newborns are all part of the package that plagues pregnant abusers. The symptoms of the last, neonatal abstinence syndrome (NAS), include crying, fever, irritability, seizures, slow weight gain, tremors, diarrhea, vomiting, and possibly death. The incidence of NAS across drug abusers of all sorts is about forty per ten thousand live births.

More than half of federal prisoners are serving time for drug offenses, 8.8 percent of those for heroin related crimes. About 4 percent of homicides in the United States include narcotics-related circumstances. About half of all homicides in urban areas involve gangs active in the illicit-drug trade.

The drug screening industry is a $2 billion business in the United States. ER visits just for opioids other than heroin have tripled since in the last decade to over 900,000. There are now over 300,000 Americans in treatment programs for opioid addiction.

The bottom line? Of course, you cannot count the cost of premature deaths and human suffering. The National Institute on Drug Abuse reports the costs related to "crime, lost work productivity, and health care" amount to $193 billion for all illicit drugs. My comprehensive look across all the costs by major illicit drug types (cocaine, cannabis, amphetamines, and opiates) leads to an estimate of 20 percent (or about $40 billion) for heroin alone. The costs of licit-opioid abuse in our country is perhaps eight times that, at some $320 billion (see Exhibit 8.1 for one of the bases of this sad calculus). The CDC estimated the total costs in 2007 to $55.7 billion. Given that opioid sales have more than quadrupled since, another reasonable estimate for 2014 would be $250 billion. And this latter problem is still burgeoning.

Ways to Reduce Opioid Consumption

The budget for the DEA for 2014 was $2.87 billion. In their words, "The mission of the Drug Enforcement Administration (DEA) is to enforce the controlled substances laws and regulations of the United States and bring to the criminal and civil justice system of the United States, or any other competent jurisdiction, those organizations and principal members of organizations, involved in the growing, manufacture, or distribution of controlled substances appearing in or destined for illicit traffic in the United States; and to recommend and support non-enforcement programs aimed at reducing the availability of illicit controlled substances on the domestic and international markets."

The key terms here are "enforce" and "availability." These are not the problems we face. The problem is consumption, consumption, consumption! Their mission statement is mute on this crucial issue. Prohibition and interdiction have not worked. I repeat, you can still buy heroin at most US high schools.

The part I do appreciate about the DEA's efforts has more to do with the 2001 cease-and-desist letter sent to Celltech for advertising opioids in the *Ladies' Home Journal*. But then you have to compare the potential efficacy of the DEA's $2.87 billion versus the advertising budgets of Big Pharma represented in Exhibit 8.3.

It is critical to make policy on opioids in the context of understanding the relationship between illicit heroin and her licit sisters. Neil Osterweil[1] reported on Medscape.com:

> The CDC, DEA, and other agencies are working with state governments to address 3 key drivers of the prescription drug overdose problem: increased opioid prescribing; specific providers accounting for most of the inappropriate prescribing; and high-risk patients who engage in abuse and drug diversion and who fly under the radar of the vast majority of scrupulous prescribers.

---

1 Neil Osterweil, "Prescrption Drug Deaths Rise with Opioid Sales," www.Medscape.com, November 12, 2013, online.

Dr. Jones [a CDC expert] cautioned, however, that stricter controls to prevent the inappropriate use of opioids could drive abusers to other illegal options, such as heroin. "If someone is addicted to opioid analgesics, taking away their opioid doesn't take away their addiction," he said.

State-level prescription drug monitoring programs are a powerful tool that clinicians can use to identify prescription-drug shoppers, said Michael Zemaitis, PhD, from the University of Pittsburgh School of Pharmacy.

"Prescription monitoring, which is available in most states, gives you at least a window into what has been going on for the past couple of weeks," he told *Medscape Medical News.* "If you look up the person and see that he has been to 2 doctors, 3 emergency rooms, and 4 other pharmacies, you have pretty good idea that there might be something going on," he explained.

Dr. Jones's insight is key – all opioids are related, and attractive to consumers in the same way. Thus, we might control consumption using methods such as described by Dr. Zemaitis. Indeed, most recently the state of Florida has tightened prescription regulations and enforcement with an astounding drop in overdose deaths by 23 percent between 2010 and 2012.[1] This apparent success demands our continuing attention. Doctors are receiving new mandates and training as directed by state and federal agencies. The CDC issued new standards for prescriptions for painkillers in March 2016, and Congress approved a bill that includes provisions for new prevention, treatment, and recovery efforts later that year.[2] Local jurisdictions are joining the control efforts regarding the pharmaceutical firms' marketing practices via lawsuits in a way reminiscent of the tobacco fight in the 1990s.

My advice about heroin? Medicalization is the first step. Control its distribution. Tax the crap out of it. Control its promotion. Treat its victims.

---

1 Sabrina Tavernise, "Prescription Overdose Deaths in Florida Plunge after Tougher Measures, Report Says," *New York Times,* July 2, 2014, page A12.

2 I must also note that Congress and the President have acted to weaken the DEA earlier in the year. See Harrieth Ryan and Kim Christensen, "Amid Opioid Epedemic, Drugmakers Get a Break, *Los Angeles Times*, July 28, 2016, page A1, All.

Currently the marketing (product, place, price, and promotion) are all still out of control. Medicalizing heroin will allow the appropriate government and medical actors to monitor and limit distribution, raise the price via taxing, and control both personal selling and mass-media advertising. The last will allow anti-consumption advertising campaigns. Medicalizing the drug can reduce consumption.

Marketing Miscreant

I had no idea how much a street gang's structure mirrored the structure of just about any other business in America.

SUDHIR VENKATESH[1]

This choice was the easiest. There were other candidates. I might have railed Simon Cartmell – he was the CEO of Celltech who would have ignored the DEA's cease and desist letter for advertising prescription drugs directly to consumers in 2001. In a sense this dastardly pioneer helped deliver to your television screen all the annoying ads and their unintelligible disclaimers for prescription drugs like Viagra and Cialis. Really, a four hour erection?

Much worse though, were the producers of Purdue Pharma's OxyContin marketing campaign described above. The company paid $600 million in fines and other payments to resolve the criminal charge of "misbranding" the product and maisleading doctors and patients when it claimed the drug was less likely to be abused than other traditional narcotics. CEO Michael Friedman, Howard R. Udell, its top attorney, and Dr. ("do no harm") Paul D. Goldenheim, its medical director, all pleaded guilty to associated charges, paid some $34 million in fines, and have been disbarred from work in any government-related health care program for twelve years.

---

1 Ibid. *Gang Leader for a Day*, pages 34-35. The *Wall Street Journal* agrees: Tom Wainwright, "Nasty drug cartels face the same dilemmas as ordinary firms." February 20, 2016, page C3.

But there's worse still. Ever read James Clavell's *Nobel House*? A really good book inspired by Hong Kong's Jardine-Matheson Trading Company. If you go to their website (www.Jardines.com), you can glimpse their corporate head-quarters with the odd round windows that harken back to the portholes of their 1800s clipper ships. I loved that building with its seafaring roots the first time I traveled to the Crown Colony with MBA students some twenty years ago. International trade is both my career and passion.

Also at the company website, you can click on "History". The first thing that pops up is this:

> The history of the Jardine Matheson Group begins in the early 1830's although its origins can be traced back even further. Since its founda-tion Jardines has been one of Asia's most dynamic trading compa-nies, often having to reinvent itself in order to survive and prosper. Reflective of the times in which it traded, the Group has led the way in many businesses and has helped bring prosperity to the region.
>
> The historical chapters outline key events and, while not exhaus-tive, will provide a flavour of what is a very unique company.

There has never been a greater understatement made than their "while not exhaustive" caveat. The official company history ignores the fact that Jardine-Matheson was once the biggest drug cartel in world history. The drug-gang wars in American streets today are violent, tragic, and ugly things. But, the Opium Wars started by William Jardine involved entire armies and coalitions of countries fighting with muskets, swords, ships, and cannon.

During the early 1800s, the British taste for tea was creating a huge trade deficit with China. Silver bullion was flowing fast in an easterly direction. Of course, other goods were being traded, too. Exports from China also included sugar, silk, mother-of-pearl, paper, camphor, cassia, copper and alum, lacquer ware, rhubarb, various oils, bamboo, and porcelain. The British "barbarians" returned cotton and woolen textiles, iron, tin, lead, carnelian, diamonds, pep-per, betel nuts, pearls, watches and clocks, coral and amber beads, birds' nests and sharks' fins, and foodstuffs such as fish and rice. But the tea-for-silver swap dominated the equation.[1]

Then came the English East India Company epiphany. Opium. Easy to ship, high value to volume and weight, addicting to customers – what a great product! At the time the best opium came from British India, and once the full flow began, the tea-caused trade deficit disappeared fast. The Emperor of China complained and issued edicts, but the opium trade burgeoned.

In 1836 some high-ranking Chinese officials advocated legalizing opium. The foreign suppliers boosted production and shipments in anticipation of exploding sales. Then the emperor went in the opposite direction and ordered the destruction of the inventories in Guangzhou. By 1839 the trade was dead. Jardine sailed to England to sue the British Foreign Minister, Lord Palmerston, to wage war on China. He provided a detailed plan for war including maps, battle strategies with numbers of ships and troops required, and negotiation strategies upon victory. The British adhered to his plan by sinking junks in the Pearl River and blockading all Chinese ports.

The "magically accurate" British cannon pointed at Nanjing yielded negotiations there in 1842. The Chinese ceded Hong Kong and $21 million pounds to the British. Ports at Xiamen, Fuzhou, Ningbo, and Shanghai were opened to trade and settlement by foreigners. Hong Kong thus became the gateway to a xenophobic China, particularly for the last fifty years. Perhaps most importantly, China recognized for the first time its loss of great power status. The Celestial Empire came down to earth.

Ultimately, the Opium War was over foreign access to Chinese trade, and the treaty of Nanjing really didn't settle the issue. A second opium war was fought between 1857 and 1860. In that imbroglio the British and French forces combined to destroy the Summer Palace in Beijing. Such new humiliations yielded more freedoms for foreign traders, and notably the

---

1 Much of this material is taken from N. Mark Lam and John L. Graham, *China Now: Doing Business in the World's Most Dynamic Market* (New York: McGraw-Hill, 2007).

treaty specifically included provisions allowing the opium trade. All this for the sake of the spice!

We should also note that the British abolished slavery in the Empire in 1833, this the most horrible institution also created for the sake of spice.

Nine

MARIJUANA/CANNABIS
Primary chemical ingredient: Tetrahydrocannabinol (THC), $C_{21}H_{30}O_2$

*The actual and potential harm of use of the drug is
not great enough to justify intrusion by the criminal
law into private behavior, a step which our society
takes only with the greatest reluctance.*

RAYMOND P. SHAFER

Ray Shafer was a prominent Republican leader known for his moderate views. He served as the thirty-ninth Governor of Pennsylvania from 1967 to 1971. At the 1968 Republican Convention he gave the nomination speech for Nelson Rockefeller. Perhaps as a "reward" for that adversarial nomination speech, President Richard Nixon appointed him as chairman of the bipartisan National Commission on Marijuana and Drug Abuse in 1972. The Shafer Commission included an impressive array of medical and legal experts and members of Congress:

- Dana L. Farnsworth, MD, Vice Chairman
- Henry Brill, MD
- The Honorable Tim Lee Carter, US Representative, Kentucky (R)

- Mrs. Joan Ganz Cooney (founder of the Children's Television Network)
- Charles O. Galvin, SJD
- John A. Howard, PhD
- The Honorable Harold E. Hughes, US Senator, Iowa (D)
- The Honorable Jacob K. Javits, US Senator, New York (R)
- The Honorable Paul G. Rogers, US Representative, Florida (D)
- Maurice H. Seevers, MD, Ph.D
- J. Thomas Ungerleider, MD
- Mitchell Ware, JD

The Commission proceedings were supported by a staff of seventy-six and 3,700 pages of technical reports.

President Nixon warned Commissioner Shafer during their deliberations: "You're enough of a pro to know that for you to come out with something that would run counter to what the Congress feels and what the country feels, and what we're planning to do, would make your commission just look bad as hell."

The unanimous findings of the Commission, echoed by Shafer's Congressional testimony above, did look "bad as hell" to the conservatives in Congress. They still look bad to conservatives, unless you count the Libertarians as conservatives. Of course, at the time they were ignored. Four decades of experience later and they seem prescient as hell. We will return to aspects of the Commission's report in the final section of the chapter.

History

The weed grows everywhere. I can remember as a ten-year-old hiking through a slight arroyo on my uncle's farm in Nebraska, the seven-foot weeds towering over my head. It was a pint-sized forest, a fun place for us to play cowboys and hide-and-seek. My older cousin pointed out it was marijuana, but that didn't mean anything to me at the time. It was just a tall weed, nothing as curious as marijuana or the more formal Latin, *Cannabis*.

Adults around the world have recognized the usefulness of the weed for thousands of years. Ropes made of the fibers of the cannabis plant – that is, hemp – are still ubiquitous today. The first evidence of the hedonic consumption of the plant comes from Romania circa 3000 BC. The plant is indigenous to South and Central Asia and has been associated with spiritual ceremonies in ancient China, India, Egypt, and among the Aryans, Scythians, Thracians, Dacians, Mamluks, and Muslims. There's even an argument that Shakespeare enjoyed the stuff.

While the archeological evidence suggests opium use is older, given that you can get a high just from chewing a few leaves of hemp suggests prehistoric man probably appreciated cannabis first. Certainly its ease of production and use are what make it the most popular illicit hedonic compound globally.

Regulation of cannabis began only early in the last century in many English speaking countries. The 1937 Marihuana Tax Act prohibited production of hemp and cannabis in the United States, much to the delight of hemp fiber competitors of the time, Mellon, Hearst, Du Pont, and Scripps.[1] Of course, it is listed as a Schedule I drug under the US Controlled Substances Act of 1970.

Consumer Behavior

Despite the federal ban of marijuana in the United States circa 2016, it is legal for medical uses in several states and recreational uses (that is, hedonic consumption) in Washington, Colorado, Oregon, Alaska, the District of Columbia, and most recently, California, Massachusetts, and Nevada.

Medical Uses. The arguments over the medical uses of cannabis have swirled for decades. I started collecting information on the topic late last century, and the amount of information, particularly in the popular press, has increased faster than that on any other psychoactive substance discussed in this book. Part of the problem is the federal prohibition of the compound has virtually eliminated the scientific study of its effects on consumers and

---

1 Martin Booth, *Cannabis, A History* (New York: Picador, 2003).

consumption. So as I am writing these words, they are becoming obsolete. Not only are opinions changing fast, but so are the facts.

Cannabis is used as an herbal medicine to reduce nausea and vomiting of people in chemotherapy or with AIDS and to relieve pain and muscle spasticity. The American Society of Addiction Medicine and the FDA both criticize the several negative side effects of the herbal forms. No studies have shown marijuana to be an effective treatment for glaucoma.

Hedonic Consumption. The primary appeal of marijuana has always been its hedonic qualities. It increases dopamine release, produces euphoria, and affects brain function more generally. Michael Pollan in his excellent book, *The Botany of Desire*[1], elaborates the attractiveness of THC, the main ingredient in cannabis. His key sentence among his many paragraphs I take to be: "...it is the relentless moment-by-moment forgetting, this draining of the pool of sense impression almost as quickly as it fills, that gives the experience of consciousness under marijuana its peculiar texture." The user is focused on the immediate present, forgetting the constraints, inhibitions, and pains of the past and future. Funny is funnier, tastes are better, senses are heightened.

There are four main ways to consume marijuana – smoking, vaporizing, cannabis tea, and eating it as an ingredient in other foods – think brownies and candy bars. The edibles are particularly a problem related to unintended consumption by children, and even some adults. And potency labeling has often been found to be wrong – one study in California found 23 percent overstated and 60 percent understated the levels of THC content.[2] Sniffing and hash oil rubs (topical application) are also used. Maureen Dowd in a *New York Times* OPED[3] describes her first experience with marijuana, one perhaps not so hedonic after all:

> Sitting in my hotel room in Denver, I nibbled off the end [of the candy bar] and then, when nothing happened, nibbled some more. I figured if I was reporting on the social revolution rocking Colorado in

---

1   Michael Pollan, *The Botany of Desire* (New York: Random House, 2002), page 162.

2   Catherine Saint Louis, "Edible Marijuana Labels Often Have Potency Wrong, Study Says," *New York Times*, June 24, 2015, page A12.

3   Maureen Dowd, "Don't Harsh Our Mellow, Dude," *New York Times*, June 4, 2014, page A21.

January, the giddy culmination of pot Prohibition, I should try a taste of legal, edible pot from a local shop.

What could go wrong with a bite or two? Everything, as it turned out.

Not at first. For an hour, I felt nothing. I figured I'd order dinner from room service and return to my more mundane drugs of choice, chardonnay and mediocre-movies-on-demand.

But then I felt a scary shudder go through my body and brain. I barely made it from the desk to the bed, where I lay curled up in a hallucinatory state for the next eight hours. I was thirsty but couldn't move to get water. Or even turn off the lights. I was panting and paranoid, sure that when the room-service waiter knocked and I didn't answer, he'd call the police and have me arrested for being unable to handle my candy.

I strained to remember where I was or even what I was wearing, touching my green corduroy jeans and staring at the exposed-brick wall. As my paranoia deepened, I became convinced that I had died and no one was telling me.

It took all night before it began to wear off, distressingly slowly...

Consumption seems to be influenced by race, gender, and region of the United States. In a study[1] of US college students at a Midwestern university, which nicely controls for educational level, 45.6 percent of male Hispanic students reported consuming marijuana during the last year, compared to 41.5 percent for white male students, 36.0 percent for African-Americans, and 28.3 percent for Asian-Americans. The pattern is similar for women college students with African-Americans having a slightly lower prevalence than Asian Americans. The prevalence of male college students was higher than female students across the four ethnic groups, with the greatest difference between African-Americas and the smallest between whites.

---

1 Seam Esteban McCabe, Michele Morales, James A. Cranford, Joge Delva, Melnee D. McPherson, and Carol J. Boyd, "Race/Etnicity and Gender Differences in Drug Use and Abuse among College Students," *Journal of Ethnicity and Substance Abuse*, 6(2), 2007, pages 75-95.

As can be seen in Exhibit 9.1 consumption seems to be greater on the West Coast where prices are lower and supplies of innovative strains are closer. The exception, of course, is Utah, where the influence of religious (Mormon) prohibition is obvious. Also, greater consumption appears correlated with more liberal legal environments. Obviously the causality is unclear. Finally, age is a factor as well. Among the three age groups 12-17, 18-25, and 25+ the totals across the fifty states show the prevalence rates for the 18-25 year-olds to be double both their younger and older counterparts. For example, prevalence rates for Californians are 12-17, 8.8 percent; 18-25, 21.7 percent, and 25+, 6.7 percent.

Exhibit 9.1
Marijuana Consumption and Street Prices

State or Province	Marijuana Consumption* (% prevalence of use in last <u>month</u>)	Retail Prices** ($/ounce, for high quality, August 2014)
Alaska[R]	13.0	$290
Oregon[R]	12.2	$208
District of Columbia[R]	10.5	$346
Colorado[R]	10.4	$238
Washington[R]	10.2	$232
California[M]	9.1	$245
New York[M]	8.2	$346
Hawaii[M]	7.6	$310
Illinois[M]	7.0	$355
Florida	6.7	$303
North Dakota	5.2	$405
Texas	5.1	$337
Utah	4.4	$287
Quebec		$191 (U.S. dollars)
British Columbia		$189

[M] = medical marijuana legal
[R] = recreational use legal

* National Survey on Drug Abuse and Health, see
http://www.samhsa.gov/data/NSDUH/2k12State/NSDUHsae2012/Index.aspx.
**www.priceofweed.com, August 2014.

The Global Consumption and Supply. The 2014 World Drug Report lists the prevalence of consumption of cannabis globally as 3.8 percent. That amounts to some 180 million folks reporting having used marijuana in the last year. As indicated in Exhibit 9.2 below, Nigeria and the United States report the highest prevalence data among big countries around the world. Of note among the other counties listed is the relatively low numbers in The Netherlands despite their reputation and liberal enforcement of their prohibition. Given that in Singapore they have a death penalty for marijuana smuggling, their prevalence rate is perhaps understandable – they list among their airport arrival forms the extremely rare capital punishment penalties.

The supply of marijuana is by far the most difficult to estimate because production is mostly small in scale and local. Indeed, author Michael Pollan reported growing his own as part of his research for *The Botany of Desire*. Prominent in the exporting estimates are Morocco, Afghanistan, India, Lebanon, and Pakistan in descending order. Other countries are now relaxing their laws on production – Colombia is an important example.

Exhibit 9.2
Consumption of Cannabis by Country

Countries	Marijuana Consumption* (% prevalence of use in year)	Retail Prices* ($/ounce, for high quality, August 2014)
Nigeria	14.3	
United States	13.7	~$300
Canada^D	12.6	$221
Spain^D	10.6	$170
France	8.6	$156
United Kingdom	6.8	$231
Netherlands^D	5.4	
UAE	5.4	
Germany^T	4.8	$222
Afghanistan	4.3	
Iran	4.2	
Russia^D	3.5	
India	3.2	
Finland	3.1	
Brazil^T	2.6	
Sweden	1.2	
Saudi Arabia	0.3	
Japan	0.1	
Singapore	0.0004	
Globally	3.9	

^{D} = decriminalized***
^{T} = tolerated
*World Drug Reports 2013.
**www.priceofweed.com, August 19, 2014.
*** As compiled and reported by Wikipedia.org, "Legality of Cannabis by Country", August 2014.

In the US in 2010 thirty-five thousand outdoor farms were destroyed that contained some seven million plants. Thus, the average outdoor farming operation included about two hundred plants. Of course the 4,600 indoor operations eradicated were smaller, averaging less than a hundred plants. After looking at several articles on the topic, my own estimate at the success rate of the DEA in its eradication efforts is at best 10 percent.

Therefore, *successful* US production is up to around sixty-three million plants. Estimates of ounces of marijuana per plant vary around five to fifteen ounces depending on growing conditions (indoor and out). We'll assume ten ounces per plant. We also know that Mexico and Canada in recent years have been ramping up their exports to the United States to about 50 percent of US production. So ninety-five million plants seems a reasonable estimate for total US supply for the thirty million users in the country. That's a consumption level of about one to two pounds of marijuana per year per American user, and some 30,000 tons for the country.

The reader will note that all these numbers are best estimates. One advantage of the legalizations in Washington, Colorado, and so on is that better data will soon be available to develop better estimates of the metrics of the marijuana market.

Marketing
Product.
Traditionally three main types of marijuana/*Cannabis* plants have been cultivated: *sativa* (origins in Europe, the tall plant from my uncle's Nebraska farm in the 1950s), *indica* (India), and *ruderalis* (Russia). *Indica* generally contains more THC, the primary active compound. All three traditional types are highly susceptible to horticultural modifications/hybridizations in just a few generations.

In addition to THC, there are more than 400 other compounds included in a cannabis plant that yield weaker, but unstudied effects. Prominent among those are CBD, CBN, and THCV. There won't be a test on these, but you should know that they are there.

Spiced

The potencies of the three main forms of cannabis differ substantially: flowers (THC at 5 percent), resins (at 20 percent), and hash oil (60 percent). Seven preparations are often mentioned: dried flowers, kief (a powder), hashish, tincture, hash oil, infusion (often into dairy butter), and pipe resin.

Twenty-first century horticulture now delivers an incredible new array of more potent weed to the pot shops in Washington and Colorado. Michael Pollan attributes the better high to breakthroughs In the 1980s:

> …enterprising growers soon discovered that by crossing the new species [*indica*] with *Cannabis sativa*, it was possible to produce vigorous hybrids that would combine the most desirable traits of each plant while downplaying its worst…In a wave of innovative breeding performed around 1980, most of it by amateurs working in California and the Pacific Northwest, the modern American marijuana plant was born. Even today *sativa* x *indica* hybrids developed during this period – the Northern Lights, Skunk #1, Big Bud, and California Orange – are regarded as the benchmarks of modern marijuana breeding; they remain the principal genetic line with which most subsequent breeders have worked.[1]

Notice the branding. Also recognize that the illicit nature of the business allowed for innovations unfettered by an intellectual property regime such as our current patent system. Legalization would have slowed down these "product improvements."

Just one example of a new product offering among many: www.weedist.com lists "SAGE n SOUR, *sativa* dominant, THC 16 percent/CBG .7 percent, sandalwood tasting euphoric high…." And, the product innovations will just keep coming from so-called technology accelerators opening in California, mixes of psychoactive substances such as coffee and cannabis, new techniques for concentrating THC into extracts, and hard-science approaches producing 3-D images of marijuana strains, as well as new medicines derived from cannabis.

---

1 Ibid. *The Botany of Desire*, page 132.

Place. The distribution system for marijuana in the United States is in a complete state of flux. We have a full-scale mashup of farming, entrepreneurship, horticulture, technology, finance, real estate, federal and local regulations, spotty enforcement, corruption, violence, morals, misinformation, and a political establishment afraid to touch, even talk about any of it. Yikes! Going into more detail on how things work now is simply folly.

Indeed, one indication of the mess I just described is the recent demise of the US National Drug Intelligence Center (NDIC). The federal agency was established in 1993 and unceremoniously, even quietly shutdown with the following online announcement:

On June 15, 2012, the National Drug Intelligence Center (NDIC) closed. To provide access to historical materials, an archived version of the NDIC website is available at http://www.justice.gov/archive/ndic/. This website is no longer maintained and may contain dated information.

According to Dave Gibson[1] at *Examiner.com*, the NDIC reported a 60 percent one-year decline in Mexican drug cartel distribution in American cities, from 2,500 cities in 2010 to 1,500 in 2011. If the data are correct, this is astonishingly good news for law- enforcement efforts? Or perhaps it's an indication of the power of the movement for legalization of marijuana – local medical marijuana dispensaries putting the drug gang cartels out of business?[2] Or perhaps the data themselves are bad, and the agency that produced them is worse than a waste of money? Or perhaps the Obama administration didn't appreciate the political implications of their information? Personally, I like best the second explanation, the legalization caused demise of the cartels story. We will return to this broader issue in Chapter 14.

---

1 Dave Gibson, "Why Did Obama Close the National Drug Intelligence Center?" *Examiner. com*, September 29, 2012, online.

2 This is a theory I have only seen suggested by Mary Emily O'Hara, "Legal Pot in the US is Crippling Mexican Cartels," *news.vice.com*, Mary 8, 2014.

At this point I will bail out of this mess by betting on the future.[1] Indeed, between the burgeoning of both research activities and free-enterprise, the half-life of facts[2] in this area is by far the shortest in the book. By the mid-2020s you will be able to order the best product in the world by voice over your lapel iPin and a FEDEX drone will deliver the package in an hour if you're willing to pay the price. No more street-corner drug dealers. No more violent Mexican drug cartels, just big, high-brand-equity, tax-paying marketing companies that operate more like Nike or Apple than Al Capone. Enforcement of regulations of marijuana sales to minors will carry triple Singaporean-style penalties, although not death itself. Each product will be marked at the molecular level and tracked with RFID/GPS innovations. More on this in Chapter 15.

Price. Want to spend an annoying day? Try to find historical records on prices of marijuana. I can find good, current, crowd-sourced information on street prices at www.priceofweed.com, by state and some countries. The best information about historical prices comes from DEA reports archived at the NDIC website. There you can also glean information about the prices of domestic versus imported product circa 2001, for example:

Marijuana is readily available throughout the Central District. The Los Angeles HIDTA reports that the THC content for Mexican marijuana ranges between 4 and 6 percent, while domestic marijuana's THC content reaches levels as high as 26 percent. The DEA Los Angeles Field Division reports that marijuana of Canadian origin, with a potency of up to 28 percent, is readily available in Los Angeles.

The wholesale prices of low-grade Mexican marijuana and high-grade domestic marijuana have remained stable. Mexican marijuana typically sells for between $330 and $500 per pound. The price of domestically produced marijuana ranges between $2,550 and $6,000

---

1 Two worthwhile reads on this topic are Bruce Barcott, *Weed the People: The Future of Legal Marijuana in America* (Time Books: New York, 2015); and Mike Power, *Drugs Unlimited: The Web Revolution that Changing How the World Gets High* (St. Martin's Press: New York, 2013).

2 Samuel Arbesman, *The Half-Life of Facts: Why Everything Know Has an Expiration Date* (Current: New York, 2012).

per pound. BC Bud, a hybrid type of cannabis grown in British Columbia, Canada, sells for approximately $6,000 per pound.

At the street level, the retail price for Mexican marijuana in the Los Angeles HIDTA ranges between $60 and $80 per ounce; the price for domestic midgrade marijuana (4-10 percent THC) ranges between $200 and $250 per ounce; and the price of domestic marijuana ranges between $400 and $600 per ounce. The DEA Los Angeles Field Division reports the same prices.[1]

If you compare these prices with those currently reported by priceofweed.com listed in Exhibit 9.2, you can see that prices have remained about the same or declined some on US streets during the last decade or so.

You can also see the rather large differences in retail prices around the country and in a few other foreign countries (see Exhibit 9.2 above). Prices are lower out West, nearer the more innovative production locations. Prices are also lower in the European countries, where demand is not so great. We should all be watching closely as state and local taxes begin to affect prices and demand in Washington and Colorado.

Finally, if we multiply the an average US retail price of $300/ounce by the demand estimates for the country of 30,000 tons I reported earlier, that yields a $285 billion estimate for the overall size of the market.

Promotion. In the immediate past, personal selling dominated the promotional expenditures of marijuana distributors. If you wanted to buy an ounce of marijuana, you were talking to a teenager on the street or perhaps an upscale supplier, a guy like the drug-dealer character John Goodman played in the recent Denzel Washington movie, *Flight*. (As an aside, consider how many roles Denzel has played where illicit drugs were a key part of the plot? Scary.) The same guys that were selling you heroin in the previous chapter probably had a line of marijuana to peddle as well. Certainly, in that circumstance, that makes marijuana a gateway drug. "You should try this other stuff – the high is even better," so the pitch goes.

---

1 National Drug Intelligence Center, *California - Southern District Drug Threat Assessment,* December 2001 see http://www.justice.gov/archive/ndic/pubs0/668/marijuan.htm.

As legalization of marijuana continues beyond the Washington and Colorado experiments and the medical marijuana states, personal selling moves into the stores. Now you're talking to a retail clerk with an array of only marijuana products on display.

The onslaught of mass-media advertising has begun. Billboards, Internet ads galore, and on March 4, 2014 the first television ad for marijuana? So the popular press reported. Actually the television ad for medical marijuana never appeared. But, you can get a glimpse of the press garnered at places such as the *NBC Nightly News* and *Time* magazine even on the mention of a television campaign. See http://time.com/12390/marijuana-commercial-first-tv-ad/. Legalization advocates have been using mass-media advertising – the Oregon $2.3 million campaign is a case in point. See http://impact. oregonlive.com/mapes/print.html?entry=/2014/08/oregon_marijuana_le-galization_4.html. I also recommend an interesting piece on marijuana mass-media advertising by Michael Wolff in *USA Today*[1] describing a fundamental self-interest operating:

> The coming legalization of marijuana, advocated last week by *The New York Times* in perhaps the most noted editorial in its history, will create a consumer product as sought after as cigarettes (in their day) and booze. Hence, legalized marijuana, among its other lucrative effects — including closing gaps in state budgets with certain heavy taxes — offers a gold mine for the media business.
>
> Media have, in many ways, never recovered from the loss of cigarette advertising, one of the all-time great revenue generators for newspapers, magazines, television, radio and advertising agencies. Marijuana could be as big a market as cigarettes and, as pot brands try to establish and distinguish themselves, as prodigious as advertisers.
>
> On Sunday, the *Times* ran a full-page ad for a company called Leafly, which describes itself as "the world's largest information resource about cannabis" and "the Yelp of cannabis."

---

1 Michael Wolff, "Wolff: The Marijuana Media Miracle," *USA Tody*, August 3, 2014, online.

> Legalizing pot means, at least on some level, legalizing its marketing, too. It would seem churlish and merely part of a continuing governmental grudge to forbid pot manufactures from advertising — and counterproductive once pot starts generating major tax revenue…Pot, as the great leveler and unifying cultural principle, could change that.

In 2014 the mass-media outlets (print, radio, and TV) in Colorado were just beginning to advertise marijuana. Green Mile Collective advertises its medical marijuana in the OC Weekly in Orange County, CA. The only thing "medical" in its flyers is the phrase, "First Time Patient Specials." In the ad they offer "Wheel Wednesday, Free Joint Friday, and Happy Hour ALL Day Sunday." I have to wonder if they'll take the same approach to advertising their "pharmaceuticals" on the TV news when they get around to it? You can now find magazines on the stands with titles like *Cannabis Now*. And please recall from Chapter 1 that I identified the American Marketing Association as the arbiter of marketing ethics in the filed. Even the AMA has jumped on board with a *Marketing News* thirty-two-page cover story entitled "High Times." Rather than a *high* one, this is a very difficult time for policymakers around the country.

Most recently the trade shows have begun in earnest. In June 2015 the Cannabis World Congress and Business Exposition was held at the Jacob K. Javits Convention Center in New York City. Their website mentions a dozen exhibitors and three dozen partners. The attendance was estimated to be two thousand, or "thousands" as the one organizer put it. Really small at this writing. I have to wonder if the organizers appreciated the irony of holding it at the Javits Center – you may recall he was an important member of the Shafer Commission in 1972.

Consequences of Consumption

Effects on Users. The immediate consequences of marijuana consumption are the euphoria described earlier, and a series of other physical and mental effects: reddening eyes, dry mouth, skin sensations of heat or cold, increased heart rate, relaxation, impaired motor skills, and decrease in short-term memory. Not death.

Michael Pollan also eloquently argues the case that marijuana leads to creative thinking. However, eloquence is not evidence, and I believe the jury is still out on that immediate effect.[1] At least when sober you can actually remember the great ideas you just had! And who knows what other things smokers might have produced, but for the highs that took up their time. We already mentioned the theory about Shakespeare. Pollan reports a longer list of creatives getting high: the ancient Scythians, Plato, Aristotle, Socrates, Euripides, Keats, other "poets and theorists," Fitz Hugh Ludlow, jazz and rock musicians, Allen Ginsberg, Cezanne, Carl Sagan, Aldous Huxley (on mescaline), and even himself. He reports,[2] "The notion that drugs might function as cultural mutagens occurred to me while reading *The Selfish Gene* while high on marijuana..."

There are some that argue that the eight-hour paranoia that Ms. Dowd reported following her cannabis candy bar consumption can lead to longer-term mental health problems such as schizophrenia. New research at Northwestern University[3] provides evidence that long-term use (three years) by young adults can change brain structure and function and hurt memory, with effects that last at least a few years beyond cessation of regular consumption. These really creepy findings are accompanied with a call for further research. I couldn't agree more! There is good news here. President Obama is moving to lift federal barriers to much needed systematic research on the long-term consequences of cannabis consumption. Most recently, even the DEA has approved research on the benefits of medical marijuana for the treatment of Post Traumatic Stress Disorder (PTSD) in veterans.

---

1 Almost all studies use self-report measures of the drug's effects. See Mitch Earlywine, *Understanding Marijuana: A New Look at the Scientific Evidence* (Oxford: Oxford University Press, 2002).

2 Ibid. *The Botany of Desire*, page 150.

3 Jodi M. Gilman, John K. Kuster, Sang Lee, Myung Joo Lee, Byoung Woo Kim, Nikos Makris, Andre Van Der Kouwe, Anne J. Blood and Hans C. Breiter, **"Cannabis Use is Quantitatively Associated with Nucleus Accumbens and Amygdala Abnormalities in Young Adult Recreational Users,"** *Journal of Neuroscience*, April 16, 2014 (in press).

The best concise summary of the societal and longer-term personal consequences of marijuana consumption is the *New York Times'* so-called "most noted editorial in its history" appearing July 31, 2014 and written by Philip Boffey.[1] Rather than reinventing that material, I excerpt it here:

For Michele Leonhart, the administrator of the Drug Enforcement Administration, there is no difference between the health effects of marijuana and those of any other illegal drug. "All illegal drugs are bad for people," she told Congress in 2012, refusing to say whether crack, methamphetamines or prescription painkillers are more addictive or physically harmful than marijuana.

Her testimony neatly illustrates the vast gap between antiquated federal law enforcement policies and the clear consensus of science that marijuana is far less harmful to human health than most other banned drugs and is less dangerous than the highly addictive but perfectly legal substances known as alcohol and tobacco. Marijuana cannot lead to a fatal overdose. There is little evidence that it causes cancer. Its addictive properties, while present, are low, and the myth that it leads users to more powerful drugs has long since been disproved.

Marijuana's negative health effects are arguments for the same strong regulation that has been effective in curbing abuse of legal substances. Science and government have learned a great deal, for example, about how to keep alcohol out of the hands of minors. Mandatory underage drinking laws and effective marketing campaigns have reduced underage alcohol use to 24.8 percent in 2011, compared with 33.4 percent in 1991. Cigarette use among high school students is at its lowest point ever, largely thanks to tobacco taxes and growing municipal smoking limits. There is already some early evidence that regulation would also help combat teen marijuana use, which fell after Colorado began broadly regulating medical marijuana in 2010.

---

1   Philip M. Boffey, "What Science Says about Marijuana," *New York Times*, July 31, 2014, page A20.

As with other recreational substances, marijuana's health effects depend on the frequency of use, the potency and amount of marijuana consumed, and the age of the consumer. Casual use by adults poses little or no risk for healthy people. Its effects are mostly euphoric and mild, whereas alcohol turns some drinkers into barroom brawlers, domestic abusers or maniacs behind the wheel...

Federal scientists say that the damage caused by alcohol and tobacco is higher because they are legally available; if marijuana were legally and easily obtainable, they say, the number of people suffering harm would rise. However, a 1995 study for the World Health Organization concluded that even if usage of marijuana increased to the levels of alcohol and tobacco, it would be unlikely to produce public health effects approaching those of alcohol and tobacco in Western societies.

Most of the risks of marijuana use are "small to moderate in size," the study said. "In aggregate, they are unlikely to produce public health problems comparable in scale to those currently produced by alcohol and tobacco."

While tobacco causes cancer, and alcohol abuse can lead to cirrhosis, no clear causal connection between marijuana and a deadly disease has been made. Experts at the National Institute on Drug Abuse, the scientific arm of the federal anti-drug campaign, published a review of the adverse health effects of marijuana in June that pointed to a few disease risks but was remarkably frank in acknowledging widespread uncertainties. Though the authors believed that legalization would expose more people to health hazards, they said the link to lung cancer is "unclear," and that it is lower than the risk of smoking tobacco...

Marijuana isn't addictive in the same sense as heroin, from which withdrawal is an agonizing, physical ordeal. But it can interact with pleasure centers in the brain and can create a strong sense of psychological dependence that addiction experts say can be very difficult to break. Heavy users may find they need to take larger and larger doses to get the effects they want. When they try to stop, some get withdrawal symptoms such as irritability, sleeping difficulties and anxiety that are usually described as relatively mild...

Nonetheless, that health problem is far less significant than for other substances, legal and illegal... [see data included in the article as Exhibit 9.3 below]

Exhibit 9.3
U.S. Dependency Rates of Various Psychoactive substances

Compounds	% of General population who had ever used	Of those users, % who became dependent on drug
Tobacco	76	32
Heroin	2	23
Cocaine	16	17
Alcohol	92	15
Anti-anxiety drugs	13	9
Marijuana	46	9

Source: U.S. Institute of Medicine, 1999.

"Although few marijuana users develop dependence, some do," according to the study. "But they appear to be less likely to do so than users of other drugs (including alcohol and nicotine), and marijuana dependence appears to be less severe than dependence on other drugs."

There's no need to ban a substance that has less than a third of the addictive potential of cigarettes, but state governments can discourage heavy use through taxes and education campaigns and help provide treatment for those who wish to quit...

Marijuana "does not appear to be a gateway drug to the extent that it is the cause or even that it is the most significant predictor of serious drug abuse," the Institute of Medicine study said. The real gateway drugs are tobacco and alcohol, which young people turn to first before trying marijuana.

It's clear, though, that marijuana is now far too easy for minors to obtain, which remains a significant problem... Although marijuana use had been declining among high school students for more than a decade, in recent years it has started to climb, in contrast to continuing declines in cigarette smoking and alcohol use... Nearly 70 percent of the teenagers in residential substance-abuse programs run by Phoenix House, which operates drug and alcohol treatment centers in 10 states, listed marijuana as their primary problem.

Those are challenges for regulators in any state that chooses to legalize marijuana. But they are familiar challenges, and they will become easier for governments to deal with once more of them bring legal marijuana under tight regulation.

The last point made by the *Times* is perhaps the most important. By legalizing marijuana we can more effectively and efficiently control it. I also appreciate the comments about "taxes and educational campaigns" as useful tools to discourage consumption. But I am not impressed with the reduction to "just" 24.8 percent for underage drinking the *Times* proclaims above.

Societal Effects. Not considered in this particular *Times* article are two other personal and societal consequences marijuana consumption – jail time for users and a general disrespect for the rule of law and an associated lawlessness.

Prison Population. What is wrong with us? Nobody jails people like we do. Cuba, Rwanda, and Russia are the closest to our rates, but still way behind. See Exhibit 9.4 below. We should be ashamed to suffer these numbers in the so-called "Land of the Free."

Exhibit 9.4
Incarceration Rates for Selected Countries

Country	Prisoners/100,000 population
United States	707
Cuba	510
Rwanda	492
Russia	470
Canada	118
Mexico	211
China	172
Germany	78
Japan	51
Singapore	233

Source: World Prison Brief, International Centre for Prison Studies, 2014.

According to the US Bureau of Justice Statistics, the latest figures here in the states show 196,575 sentenced prisoners under federal jurisdiction. The state and local number totals are 1.3 million. Fifty-one percent of federal prisoners are serving time for drug offenses. Seventeen percent of state and local prisoners are incarcerated because of drug offenses. In both federal and state/local prisons, about 12.5 percent of residents are there on marijuana charges.

From here on I'm taking an ethnocentric perspective on the incarceration statistics because I am hoping to influence our Governor Jerry Brown on the marijuana matter. The California state prison population has been shrinking of late, from a high of 173,000 in 2007 to 112,000 in 2015. That is good news. This means less than 15,000 are serving time in California prisons for marijuana violations now. Each of those prisoners costs about $50,000 per year, for a total outlay of about $750 million per year in California. With the vote for legalization comes an opportunity to pardon those 15,000 mostly male California prisoners. Using the same calculus, a federal vote for legalization and pardons for all marijuana convicts would save about $1.25 billion per year.

Lawlessness. The foothills of the Sierras in California are filled with illegal marijuana farms. Hundreds of them. Some are on federal or state lands, and some are on private properties.

Bill, a friend at the University, was getting ready to retire. He'd planned on spending a good bit of his time at a cabin fifty miles southwest of Lake Tahoe on land he and his brother inherited from their parents. He has many fond memories of fishing and hiking there with his dad. Recently he drove up to the plot and found his cabin occupied by squatters. Bill is a calm guy, just said hello, and walked around a bit. He soon realized the squatter had developed his land into a marijuana farm, including cutting down large shade trees and installing a major irrigation system.

He left and immediately reported the crimes and trespass to the local Sheriff. The commander was unimpressed and said he had over sixty similar cases in the county and couldn't get an officer out there anytime soon to investigate. He suggested a private detective. Bill hired one, but the detective made just one visit and quit. The squatter was a felon with weapons, too dangerous.

Consulting yet another PI, the suggestion was to hire off-duty officers to remove the perpetrator. This is apparently a common solution to the problem.

> "Most of the time, marijuana growing is happening out in the open," said Fresno County Sheriff Margaret Mims, who has to put every one of her 15 deputies in the narcotics unit — and even some off-duty officers — on the case during the fall harvest. "During the season, everyone's working marijuana," Mims said. "We can't even call them plants anymore. They are really trees."[1]

---

1   Haya El Nasser, "Armed Guards Defend Illegal California Marijuana Farms," Aljazeera, January 30, 2014, see http://america.aljazeera.com/articles/2014/1/30/armed-farmers-combatille galcaliforniamarijuanafarms.html.

Bill's only cost would be gas money. Usually officers making these kinds of "raids" end up with substantial amounts of loose cash the farmers stash somewhere handy. But that's not the end of it, even if this works. Bill would still have to eliminate about twenty acres of harvest-ready marijuana. A wood chipper is the prescription. Ultimately the squatter was prosecuted and convicted – but the district attorney recommended that Bill stay away from the property for a very long time if he was interested in his personal safety. Awful, just awful. This lawlessness is reminiscent of the aforementioned Whiskey Rebellion of 1794 for which George Washington raised an army of thirteen thousand to quell.

Other Consequences. On September 21, 2011, the Rand Corporation issued a startling report based on "the most rigorous independent examination of its kind" that crime near medical marijuana dispensaries in Los Angeles *increased* after they were forced to close by local authorities. A benefit of legalization reversed?

Los Angeles city attorneys were outraged and demanded a retraction. They had argued in court that the key reason for closing the shops was increased crime in the area. The Rand study showed the opposite. Less than a month later, on October 12 Rand pulled the report from its website. On October 25 they retracted the report based on admitted errors in their analyses. They have promised to fix the errors and republish the results – I cannot find these corrections at this writing. Rand, if nothing else, is politically savvy. On June 8, 2012, a UCLA report conducted a similar study and found no link between medical marijuana outlets and crime in Sacramento.[1]

Even more recently researchers at Western universities[2] report: "The current study examines the relationship between the legalization of medical marijuana and traffic fatalities, the leading cause of death among Americans ages 5-34. The first full year after coming into effect, legalization is associated with an 8-11 percent *decrease* in traffic fatalities." The researchers don't suggest

---

1   Press release, describing a study (sponsored by the National Institute of Drug Abuse) by Bridget Freisthler and Nancy Kepple at the Luskin School of Public Affairs at UCLA.

2   D. Mark Anderson, Benjamin Hansen, and Daniel I Rees, "Medical Marijuana Laws, Traffic Fatalities, and Alcohol Consumption," *Journal of Law and Economics*, 56, May 2006, pages 333-345.

that driving under the influence of marijuana is safe. Rather it appears that where marijuana is legalized, consumption of alcohol declines. These will be interesting lines of research to follow.

Ways to Reduce the Consumption of Marijuana

When written in Chinese, the word for
"crisis" is composed of two characters.
One represents danger and the other represents opportunity.

– JOHN F. KENNEDY

Perhaps the first attempt at controlling a cannabis-consumption crisis came from the Vatican. Michael Pollan tells us:

> In 1484, Pope Innocent VIII issued a papal condemnation of witch-craft in which he condemned the use of cannabis as an "antisacrament" in satanic worship. The black mass celebrated by medieval witches and sorcerers presented a mocking mirror image of the Catholic Eucharist, as in it cannabis traditionally took the place of wine – serving as a pagan sacrament in the counterculture that sought to undermine the establishment church.[1]

Pollan further explains that the papal decree then and now made marijuana something that outsiders, foreigners, and strangers partook. Indeed, in the current laws and their enforcement, there is an uncomfortable racist element associated with the bans on heroin, marijuana, and cocaine. For heroin it's the Chinese opium den. Sit back in your chair for a moment, and conjure and contemplate that image. About the same time opium arrived from China, marijuana was arriving in Texas via the border with Mexico. Law enforcement officials there associated its use with Mexicans and Blacks into the 1930s. So

---

1 Ibid. *The Botany of Desire*, page 173.

for marijuana, it's the lower-classes, the Latino and African-American drug of choice. Think Rastafarian Bob Marley, "Don't worry, be happy." The Crips and Bloods gangs in Los Angeles. It's the same for cocaine, the 1980s crack-house image comes to mind.

The legal regime for marijuana that Nixon and Anslinger (we'll get to the latter villain soon enough) cooked up is one based on lies. It is now collapsing. And the chaos caused here has consequences for the planet.

Let me be crystal clear on this topic. The hedonic consumption of marijuana is a bad thing for society. Bad laws surrounding its marketing have exacerbated the damage it causes. The current crisis contains elements of both danger and opportunity.

My fundamental recommendation is simple. Prohibition does not work. Interdiction and eradication efforts have failed with marijuana. Regulations regarding distribution can have limited effects. They should be focused on controlling access for minors. There is encouraging news here – Microsoft is developing cloud systems to monitor the distribution channels of cannabis, from seed to sale. Better information will allow for closer regulation.

With legalized and organized production, big companies will take over which can more easily be regulated and taxed.[1] Some rightly worry about big companies' marketing (particularly with respect to children)[2] and lobbying power. Certainly, multinationals in tobacco, alcohol, and pharmaceutical industries would be in that game. Stanton Glantz and his colleagues at UCSF make the strongest arguments on this topic and recommend either limiting the size of firms in the industry or government ownership.[3] Regarding government ownership, the completely unethical state-run lottery advertising demonstrates an unhealthy revenue seeking motivation among our legislators. But my key point here is all three options are better than the current black market that operates on our street corners and around the world.

---

1   Rachel Ann Barry, Heikki Hiilamo, and Stanton A. Glantz, "Waiting for the Opportune Moment: The Tobacco Industry and Marijuana Legalization," *Milbank Quarterly*, 92(2), 2014, pages 207-242.

2   Eliza Gray, "Dope Dreams," *Time*, April 20, 2015, pages 46-48.

3   Even the editors at the libertarian Economist magazine advocate government ownership. See "How to Smack It Down," *Economist*, November 7, 2015, pages 12-13.

The key tools to reduce consumption are price and promotion. Colorado and Washington are on the right path. Yes, retail prices are low in those states at the moment. Taxes should be raised at the retail level to the highest levels that don't encourage black markets.

Mass-market advertising promoting the products must be completely banned including print, television, radio, billboards, sporting event sponsorship, and so on. This approach has worked to great effect against tobacco in recent decades and spirits previous to the last few years. Branding is fine, but the ban should preclude attractive packaging and in-store displays. Informational advertising on brand or store websites is fine, but not pop-up ads and the like. Emotion-based appeals should be disallowed. Here, think of the travesty and lies of "get rich" appeals for the state lotteries.

We know that anti-tobacco ads have had an important impact on consumption. We applaud Colorado's explorations of educating teens via television PSAs. See

http://www.denverpost.com/marijuana/ci_26308424/colorado-ad-campaign-tests-new-message-prevent-teen. Part of the tax revenues garnered from sales of marijuana should be dedicated to supporting such educational campaigns. Treatment programs for addiction should also be part of the advertising efforts.

I am heartened by the very recent publication of the *Pathways Report* by the Blue Ribbon Commission (BRC) on Marijuana Policy (see www.safeandsmartpolicy.org, July 22, 2015). In approach and its reliance on science, it is reminiscent of the Shafer Commission Report published thirty-three years earlier. The BRC correctly anticipated legalization in California in 2016 or shortly thereafter. The Steering Committee is chaired by California Lieutenant Governor Gavin Newsom portending political support. Particularly laudable are its emphases on research-based policy making with consideration of ideas from other states and industries (alcohol and tobacco), prevention of consumption by children, and regulatory justice across races and economic levels. See Stanton Glantz's detailed comments: http://tobacco.ucsf.edu/moving-discussion-possible-marijuana-legalization-business-frame-public-health-frame.

Finally, there is a huge opportunity associated with the coming argument over marijuana advertising. All the First Amendment, "freedom of speech" and "companies are people" issues will be debated. But, the key bargain to be made is to eliminate mass-media advertising of alcoholic beverages, rather than legalizing mass-media advertising of marijuana. Logic dictates either eliminating or allowing mass-media advertising for both. More on this in Chapter 14.

Marketing Miscreant – Marijuana

Candidates for our award in this chapter must start with Pope Innocent VIII, Richard Nixon (he was clearly not innocent), and the winner, one Harry J. Anslinger. The common thread among the three is their contribution to the public's misunderstanding of the threat of marijuana. While I do respect the evinced efficacy of non-secular appeals for sobriety such as that prescribed by the Mormons, the Pope's witch thing is both silly and dangerous. Of course, "I am not a crook" Nixon is one of the biggest liars in history. Indeed, it's a toss-up whether his lies about Southeast Asia or marijuana caused more deaths for Americans. But most directly culpable for the marijuana mess today is Anslinger.

We need to go back and take a look at the 1972 Shafer Commission's work advising Congress and the President on the marijuana matter. The title of the report is salient – "Marihuana, A Signal of Misunderstanding." The Commission blamed the widespread, decades-long public misperception of the drug on: "the absence of adequate understanding of the effects of the drug" combined with "lurid accounts of [largely unsubstantiated] marijuana atrocities" and users being labeled as "physically aggressive, lacking in self-control, irresponsible, mentally ill and, perhaps most alarming, criminally inclined and dangerous." They were describing Anslinger's tactics specifically.

The Commission research showed a different effect of the drug: "pacifying the user… and generally producing states of drowsiness, lethargy, timidity and passivity." The Commission concluded, "Looking only at the effects on the individual, there, is little proven danger of physical or psychological harm from the experimental or intermittent use of the natural preparations of cannabis."

Harry J. Anslinger was a clean cop during the Prohibition years. In 1930 he was appointed by President Herbert Hoover as the first Commissioner of the Federal Bureau of Narcotics. He held that office until 1962. About the time marijuana was making its way around the country from the Texas-Mexico border he got very interested in the drug. In the mid-thirties he began a national public relations campaign against the drug that included Congressional testimony and print media. In his popular press articles he often quoted police reports to vilify marijuana. Here is perhaps the most infamous example of his "journalism:"

> An entire family was murdered by a youthful addict in Florida. When officers arrived at the home, they found the youth staggering about in a human slaughterhouse. With an axe he had killed his father, mother, two brothers, and a sister. He seemed to be in a daze… He had no recollection of having committed the multiple crime. The officers knew him ordinarily as a sane, rather quiet young man; now he was pitifully crazed. They sought the reason. The boy said that he had been in the habit of smoking something which youthful friends called "muggles," a childish name for marijuana.

Then in 1936 his campaign got a big boost from the release of *Reefer Madness*, a sixty-eight-minute B-movie depicting murder and mayhem under the influence of marijuana. Unforgettable is the scene where the former Mr. Nice Guy in the film pounds on a piano manically, a reefer in his mouth. I recommend you download the film from Amazon and take a look through it. It's a bad movie, but it well reflects the thinking at the time. While Anslinger's words surely inspired the script, the imagery of the motion picture was even more powerful.

Anslinger's crime? He preferred his anecdotes over the much better evidence that was accumulating. That might be called hubris or conviction, but it's really just madness. The tragedy – his madness held sway for more than thirty years.

Ten

COCAINE
Primary chemical ingredient: benzoylmethylecgonine, $C_{17}H_{21}NO_4$

*Cocaine isn't habit forming. I should
know, I've been using it for years.*

TALLULAH BANKHEAD

*I lost a beautiful lady to a bitch.... That bitch took
my lady...to sell her body for smoke....Stole her heart
and body and soul. A once beautiful body looks like
a bag of bones....I pray she will break that chain. To
get away and stay away from that bitch cocaine.*

SOUTHERN COMFORT, STREET POET
ON A WALL ON SKID ROW, LOS ANGELES[1]

The story of cocaine is filled with inconsistencies. Panacea, poison, leaf of
the gods, fruit of the devil, the champagne drug, racism, the all-American
drug, the rush, all these terms are associated with cocaine. And the effects vary

---

1   From David Ferrell, "A Ruthless Rule of the Streets," *Los Angeles Times*, December 19, 1994,
online.

233

from person to person. Thus, even its often useful anesthetic side is ruined for the healthcare community.

Tallulah Bankhead was a deep-voiced daughter of a prominent Alabama political family. Her father had been Speaker of the US House of Representatives and an uncle and her grandfather served as US Senators. She debuted on Broadway and in film in 1918, at age sixteen. By the 1940s she led the pack of hedonistic Hollywood heartthrobs with proclamations such as, "If I had to live my life again, I'd make the same mistakes, only sooner." Sooner than sixteen? Apparently so. Perhaps her reputed description of her experience with rape is one of the most scandalous party pronouncements ever: "I was raped in our driveway when I was eleven. You know darling, it was a terrible experience because we had all that gravel."

Actually, Bankhead knew she was addicted: "My father warned me about men and booze, but he never mentioned a word about women and cocaine." She died at age sixty-six of pleural pneumonia, complicated by emphysema and malnutrition. Appetite suppression and dangerous weight loss are consequences of cocaine addiction. Perhaps she was finally tired of stimulants? Her last words were, "Codeine ... bourbon." Two depressants. Or perhaps those at her bedside misheard her request for cocaine?

About five miles and fifty years away, Southern Comfort described his very different experience with cocaine. Of course, Southern Comfort and Bankhead were reporting their experiences with two different forms of the hedonic compound – he crack cocaine, and she the white powdery Hollywood sort. The settings were also different, a South Central crack house versus the glamour of movie land. Yet in the end, beauty became a "bag of bones" for both.

History

The coca tea they served my family and me at a posh Cuzco, Peru restaurant I thought was rather bland, both in taste and effect. They say it's supposed to relieve altitude sickness for tourists traveling from sea level. I really didn't notice the downer from the high altitude or upper from the tea. I guess it could be, as my wife often says, "John has no taste...except in women!"

Chewing on coca leaves has always been deeply imbedded in Inca culture. Given by the gods, it provides stimulation for surviving in the thin air above ten thousand feet. It's both a practical matter and a religious practice. Medicine and magic. Tim Madge, in his excellent book *White Mischief*, describes the depth of the relationship:

> As with the [Japanese] tea ceremony, there are religious undertones. Once the coca bag is opened, an individual will blow on the bundle while waving it in front of his or her mouth, invoking the earth (*Pacha Mama*) or sacred places or the community. For Andeans every landmark is experienced as alive and powerful, possessing a name and personality The earth as a whole is thought to be alive and to be primarily female. This is by no means based on some cloying sentimentality about 'mother earth', but on profound and meaningful connections with the natural world. Coca is the medium by which men and women talk to the earth and its powerful, unpredictable deities.[1]

The Inca culture of the Andes was only about three hundred years old when the Spaniards arrived in Peru in 1524. Most recently archeologists have found evidence of coca's sacred use in the region as early as 8,000 years ago. The Spaniards tried the leafy chew, but were generally unimpressed. They became interested in other forms of treasure: gold, silver, chocolate, vanilla, maize and potatoes were more to their tastes. Three and a half centuries would pass before the real (in both English and Spanish senses of the word) value of coca became apparent. By the way, the Spaniards did notice coca's importance to the locals, and began to tax the crop at 10 percent.

Cocaine is derived from coca leaves, but the two are very different things. In the 1850s scientists on both sides of the Atlantic were investigating the properties of the leaf. An Austrian doctoral student, Albert Niemann working

---

1 Tim Madge, *White Mischief, A Cultural History of Cocaine* (New York: Thunder's Mouth Press, 2001). His book has been invaluable in my development of this chapter.

in Friedrich Wohler's chemistry laboratory, is credited for isolating cocaine, and he reported his results in 1860. Merck, then with headquarters in Darmstadt, Germany began to produce small quantities of the pharmaceutical soon thereafter. Prices remained high and distribution was limited. Its use as an anesthetic was being noticed.

Then, in 1863 everything changed forever. A Corsican chemist named Angelo Mariani, unfamiliar with the "invention" of cocaine, patented and marketed a product mixing coca extract (not cocaine) and Bordeaux wine. More a marketer than a scientist, he paid attention to product quality and advertising and rolled out Vin Mariana across Europe and the United States. His brew was attractive, and he garnered and advertised endorsements by the likes of Alexander Dumas, Thomas Edison, President McKinley, Oscar II (king of Sweden and Norway), Jules Verne, the Czar, the Prince of Wales, and even Ulysses S. Grant!

In 1884 an obscure young Sigmund Freud bought a gram of cocaine from Merck to explore its effects. He dissolved a small portion in glass of water, drank it, and proclaimed it exhilarating. In a scientific paper – I love the title, "Über Coca" – the young doctor wrote that summer, he listed its potential uses for depression, digestive disorders, morphine and alcohol addictions, asthma, and the big two, as both an anesthetic and an aphrodisiac. Freud gave amounts of the drug to colleagues.

One of them, Carl Koller, is credited with demonstrating cocaine's importance as a local anesthetic. At one scientific meeting he put a little cocaine in his eye, then stuck it with a needle. While the audience produced perhaps the greatest group wince ever, Koller showed no pain, just numbness. Brave man? Not really – he had tried it with frogs before. Ultimately cocaine proved to be unreliable and therefore dangerous in the operating room and was obsolesced by the development of Novocain a decade or so later.

About this same time Parke-Davis in the States was advertising the stuff. Our morphine addicted druggist John Pemberton from Chapter 3 mixed a little cocaine, caffeine (from kola nuts), alcohol, soda water, and sugar. Like its predecessor, Vin Mariana, Coca-Cola became the biggest-selling snake oil in history. Ultimately, Freud has been vilified as the "author of the third scourge of humankind after alcohol and morphine." Pemberton is at least a co-author of the fourth scourge, and the most damaging, added sugar.

During the next couple of decades – including the proverbial "gay nineties," Parke-Davis executives must have partied hearty. Big sales, and they could celebrate with their own drug. Nice. Parke-Davis, good marketer that they were (are), paid fast-becoming-famous Freud to endorse their product over Merck's. The drug apparently also made impressions on both Arthur Conan Doyle (he had his *Sherlock Holmes* injecting it) and Robert Louis Stevenson (*Dr. Jekyll and Mr. Hyde*). Cocaine's promotion peaked with the 1901 publication of Dr. W. Golden Mortimer's *Peru: History of Coca*, in which he prescribed the drug for everything and everyone, even tired athletes. Soon enough, the Mr. Hyde side of the drug would start to emerge with increasing reports of use, abuse, addiction, and death.

Widespread demand led to firms ramping up production and reduced prices. Consumption in the United States exploded by 500 percent in the last years of the 1890s. Prices plummeted to $2 per ounce. With purity levels high, this was a cheap high even taking into account a century of inflation. Seeing an opportunity to boost production, employers around the country began to provide it free to their factory and farm workers. And race entered the fray. The drug was blamed for violence by black men and prostitution by black women. Prohibition exacerbated the problem. The "lower class" couldn't get alcohol, but they could get cocaine. Recall that racism had been used in garnering support of reigning in opium dens. And so the tide turned.

State and local laws prohibiting sales of cocaine began to pop up around the country, particularly in the South. For example, Georgia banned the sale of any form of cocaine in 1902. The federal government finally began to take control with the Pure Food and Drug Act of 1906. It said nothing about food safety or drugs, but mandated accurate labeling of products. The impact on the patent medicine industry (snake oil) was devastating.

Named for the New York Congressman that introduced it, the Harrison Narcotics Tax Act was passed into law at the end of 1914. Prohibition of alcohol was in the winds at the time, finally coming in 1920. The specific wording is important:

An Act to provide for the registration of, with collectors of internal revenue, and to impose a special tax on all persons who produce, import, manufacture, compound, deal in, dispense, sell, distribute, or give away opium or coca leaves, their salts, derivatives, or preparations, and for other purposes.

The courts interpreted "for other purposes" to mean that doctors could use the drugs for medical purposes, but could not prescribe opium or cocaine to treat addiction to these drugs. The record-keeping requirements and the specter of taxation amounted to a tacit prohibition forcing the medical community and pharmaceutical companies out of the trade. And as trade always finds a way, it continued underground, thus initiating a growing illicit cocaine commerce.

Cocaine consumption in the United States and internationally subsided during World War II. It was something that happened on Sunset Strip, but not so much on Main Street. But then, in the 1960s, the tide turns again as American baby boomers begin to change the country.

The next two waves of cocaine consumption came in quick succession. First was the glitzy game of Hollywood, Wall Street, New York, and the jet set of the 1980s. Then crack cocaine became king of the mean streets of the country during the 1990s. As baby-boom college students reintroduced the mass consumption of marijuana, many of them graduated to the harder drugs once their incomes took off. Two factors boosted cocaine sales – Vietnam acquainted two million GIs with the drug (demand) and the Columbian marijuana producers shifted their product line to cocaine (supply). It was easier to smuggle (smaller and lighter) than weed and the profits were greater. They also found a surplus of unemployed American military pilots to fly it into the country from Columbia. Innovations in the supply chain included submarine deliveries and high-tech radio systems.

In business school we teach that an important tool for growing markets and profits is new product introductions. That lesson wasn't lost on the drug cartels and their American distributors. Thus we saw the introduction of crack cocaine that became a flood tide in the '80s and '90s. Crack delivers a cheaper, quicker, shorter high. It hits the "bliss point" of consumption (that the

American food processors treasured in Chapters 2 and 3) that creates a *craving* for more, more, more. The consequences of that bliss point Southern Comfort so compellingly put into poetry.

There is some good news in this story. The tide again has turned. Now in the second decade of this century, cocaine consumption is falling in the United States and around the world. Some attribute the change to successful law enforcement and others to generational shifts in fashion.

Consumer Behavior

In some countries cocaine is still used as a local anesthetic – for mouth ulcers in Australia, for example. However the medical uses are a minor matter. What is important is its use as a hedonic molecule. A spice.

Cocaine is a central nervous system stimulant. It delivers its high for fifteen to sixty minutes. Depending on how it's imbibed and its form, it can take up to thirty minutes to deliver its effects, which include increased alertness, euphoria, increased physical and mental energy, feelings of confidence and competence, and sexuality. David Ferrell at the *Los Angeles Times* reports:

> Gordon Marble lost his job, his family, his home and everything he owned. He said he first fully understood the seductive power of the drug the second time he used it – in bed with a woman in a hotel room. "Once I took a drag off the cocaine pipe, I didn't want the sex," Marble said. "I just wanted the cocaine."

Hmm. For some I guess it doesn't deliver the increased sexuality. It's just better than sex.

> "You immediately feel like you can handle the world, no problem," said Marble…"Let's say I'm depressed and concerned about the job and my wife nagging me about the money that's gone. One blast off the cocaine and I start to feel the sensation where my head gets light. I start to get kind of excitable. Where I was depressed and low, now

I'm up and standing tall. Then my thoughts are saying, 'I can manipulate my wife, I can manipulate my job, I can manipulate the Internal Revenue Service…'[1]

In *Newsweek* actor Dennis Quaid describes the culture that influenced his addiction:

My greatest mistake was being addicted to cocaine. It started after I left college and came to Los Angeles in 1974. It was very casual at first. That's what people were doing when they were at parties. Cocaine was even in the budgets of movies, thinly disguised. It was petty cash, you know? It was supplied, basically, on movie sets because everyone was doing it. People would make deals. Instead of having a cocktail, you'd have a line. So it was insidious, the way it snuck up on everybody. Coming from where I came from—lower-middle-class life, from Houston into Hollywood—and all of a sudden this success starts happening to you, I just didn't know how to handle that. Doing blow just contributed to me not being able to handle the fame, which, at the time, I guess I felt I didn't deserve.[2]

Note the 1974 date. Quaid also brings up a key consideration, the psychological-dependence dimension of the drug. More on this soon.

In Exhibit 10.1 below is a comparison of the prevalence of consumption across selected countries. Many of the low-income countries that have reported consumption levels of other hedonic compounds don't even bother with cocaine. Higher incomes seem to favor the champagne drug. Proximity to the Andes also seems to make a difference, as does a Spanish language connection. While Colombia and Mexico are deeply involved in cocaine commerce, the low incomes of the residents seem to limit their prevalence of consumption. I should also mention that the Scots explain their numbers as "errors in the

---

1   David Farrell, "A Ruthless Ruler of the Streets," *Los Angeles Times*, December 19, 1994, pages A1, A22-3.
2   Dennis Quaid, "On How He Blew It Straight up His Nose," *Newsweek*, April 18, 2011, page 56.

data." With a Scottish surname I guess I should be more interested in the arguments over this datum. But I'm not.

Exhibit 10.1
Consumption and Prices of Cocaine by Country

Countries	Cocaine Consumption* (percent prevalence of last-year use, ages 15-64, 2014)	Retail Prices** ($/gram of salts)
Scotland	3.9%	--
Argentina	2.6	$ 6
Spain	2.6	79
UK (w/o Scotland)	2.5	62
United States	2.4	169
Chile	2.4	21
Canada	1.4	100
Germany	0.9	84
Colombia	0.8	4
S. Africa	0.8	33
Brazil	0.7	12
Nigeria	0.7	33
France	0.6	84
Netherlands	0.6	73
Finland	0.5	103
Sweden	0.5	148
Mexico	0.5	
Hong Kong	0.3	140
Russia	0.2	206
Afghanistan	<0.1	
Iran	<0.1	
Globally	0.4	

* World Drug Report 2014.
** UNDOC and U.S. Office of Drug Control Policy
Most Africa, Asian, and Middle Eastern countries do not report

The huge variance in prevalence of use across American states is interesting. I cannot see a regional pattern in the data – see Exhibit 10.2. A variety of studies find African-American prevalence rates to be higher than Hispanics and whites. However, when you focus on just the powder form, whites are more likely to consume it. African-American preference rates dominate for crack usage. Generally, prevalence rates for males are higher, but there is a stronger female prevalence for crack, well representing the subject of Southern Comfort's poem. Employment category and age made big differences in prevalence rates – highest consumption rates were centered in the unemployed and eighteen to twenty-five age groups. Finally, Whites were more likely to get treatment, then come Hispanics, and then Blacks.[1]

Exhibit 10.2
Cocaine Consumption and Selected States

State or Province	Cocaine Consumption (% prevalence of last-year use, ages 12+)
District of Columbia	3.01%
Rhode Island	2.62
Colorado	2.41
New York	2.11
Vermont	2.08
New Mexico	2.07
Arizona	2.02
California	1.90
Illinois	1.79
Utah	1.69
Texas	1.39
Iowa	1.16

Source: National Survey on Drug Abuse and Health, see
http://www.samhsa.gov/data/NSDUH/2k12State/NSDUHsae2012/Index.aspx.

---

1 Edward Bernstein, Judith Bernstein, Katherine Tassiopoulos, Anne Valentine, Timothy Heeren, Suzette Levenson, and Ralph Hingson, "Racial and Ethnic Diversity among a Heroin and Cocaine Using Population: Treat System Utilization, *Journal of Addictive Diseases*, 24(4), 2005, pages 43-63.

Perhaps the most interesting recent study in this area looked at prevalence rates for American high school students. Students who earned or had access to more than $50 per week spending money tended to have higher prevalence rates of cocaine use. The researchers also report Hispanics with higher usage rates of crack, and females' usage rates as lower for powder. Finally, they emphasize the importance of separating data on prevalence across the forms, crack and powder.[1]

Finally, back to the good news – consumption in the US has been declining. We quote from the 2014 World Drug Report:

> The general behavior of the cocaine market in the United States from 2006 onward appears to be that of a tight market where use patterns were constrained by, and thus to a certain extent followed, the available supply. In particular, the apparent rebound in cocaine use in 2012 may be associated with a slight comeback in cocaine availability towards late 2011. However, in 2013 seizures returned to a declining trend, suggesting that was only a transitory aberration. Moreover, the increase in past-year use in 2012 appears to have been driven by the consumption patterns of older users, including past users returning to the habit, rather than a predisposition of younger people at risk of initiating cocaine use; indeed, the number of first-time users actually declined in 2012, while the trend in past-year use was increasing only in the older age categories.[2]

What I like about this quote is the illogic of their argument. If it were a "tight" supply constrained market during the last decades, prices would be on the increase. However, prices have remained flat or declined depending on the measure. The US Office of National Drug Control reports the 1990 street price at $167 per gram compared to $169 per gram in 2010. If you adjust for inflation, then it declines from $278 to $169 over the same period. Had supplies

---

1 Joseph J. Palamar and Danielle C. Ompad, "Demographic and Socioeconomic Correlates of Powder Cocaine and Crack Use among High School Seniors in the United States," *American Journal of Drug and Alcohol Abuse*, 40(1), January 2014, pages 37-43.
2 UNODC, *2014 World Drug Report*, page 36.

shrunk because of attacks on production and successful interdiction, prices would have gone up, assuming constant demand. But, instead, the stronger case is a fall in demand associated with (and perhaps causing) the lower prices and cutbacks in production.

I do like the optimism warranted by their analyses of first-time users in the United States. The number of users of cocaine has fallen to its lowest level in a decade at about 5.2 million Americans, from a peak some 25 percent higher in 2006.

The Global Consumption and Supply. The UNODC estimates coca bush cultivation in hectares. The three countries in the game are Peru, Colombia, and Bolivia with a combined total of 137,000 hectares (that's about 500 square miles) in 2012. Land under cultivation peaked about 180,000 hectares in 2007. Now, for the first time, Peru has become the largest producer, at over 400 tons, overtaking Colombia at 309 tons (its lowest level of production since 1997), and Bolivia at 130 tons.

On the demand side, there were some seventeen million users around the world (0.4 prevalence), with the United States consuming about a third of that production.

Marketing

Product. Cocaine is used in three basic ways – snorting the white powder, free basing, and smoking crack. We will focus on those in our discussion. But for the sake of completeness, as humans are creative creatures, there are other routes of infusion as well – oral (tea, chewing, rubbing on gums, or swallowing whole wrapped in a smoking paper), injection, and suppositories. The slang terms make for a gross little guessing game as to which applies to which imbibing technique: numbies, gummers, cocoa puffs, parachute, snow bomb, snorting, sniffing, blowing, bumps, lines, rails, stems, horns, blasters, straight shooters, brillo, chore, rock, and plugging.

The process of converting dried leaves into pure cocaine is a relatively complex chemical process involving acids, caustic soda (bases), and solvents. One traditional approach calls for a little cement, gasoline, and battery acid.

Yummy! Obviously the manufacturing process is more sophisticated now. A ton of leaves will yield a couple of pounds of pure cocaine. Once purified, it then is often "cut" or adulterated by the addition of other white chemical substances (sugars, baking soda, or other anesthetics) that lowers the cost of production. There's no truth in packaging laws operating here, so what you get depends on a chain of trust among the distributors.

The powder form that most people snort is usually cocaine hydrochloride, a salt (pure, slightly alkaline cocaine mixed with hydrochloric acid). This sells at the retail level as "dime bags," a ten-dollar bag containing about a tenth of a gram. Basic or "free base" cocaine is usually smoked, which produces an almost immediate effect compared to the twenty-minute time fuse when snorting the salt. "Crack" cocaine is really just a crude mix of the salt with sodium bicarbonate and when smoked produces a crackling noise when the impurities burn. Like free basing, crack delivers the rush faster, but because of the impurities the effect is shorter. Tim Madge compares it to "having a chocolate bar snatched away after having only a taste."[1]

And we must go back to Bankhead for a moment: "Here's a rule I recommend: Never practice two vices at once." Good advice, Tallulah. A "speedball" is an injected mix of cocaine and heroin. Among those who apparently ignored Tallulah's admonition about this often lethal combination have been John Belushi, River Phoenix, Chris Farley, and Philip Seymour Hoffman, to name a famous few.

Place. The typical supply chain starts with a farm in Peru, production in Colombia, a small plane flight to the coast of Florida for a radio drop, a boat ride to shore, delivery to Miami, then distribution and cutting by other derivative distributors around the country, and eventually to teenage boys on street corners or in crack houses. Nothing fancy. We've all seen it on TV. Download *Cocaine Cowboys* for a creepy, gory report on the riches and violence involved in the illicit trade. The recent book by Roberto Saviano, *Zero, Zero, Zero* (Penguin 2015) is a most graphic and very scary resource.

Price. See Exhibit 10.1 for a sampling of international prices and Exhibit 10.3 for a longitudinal comparison of US and Dutch prices. International

---

1 Ibid. *White Mischief,* page 17.

prices are all over the place with Colombia at $4 per gram and Russia at $206 per gram for cocaine salts. We pay about twice the price in the United States compared to the Europeans. Please notice in Exhibit 10.3 the very low prices and consumption rates in the Netherlands.

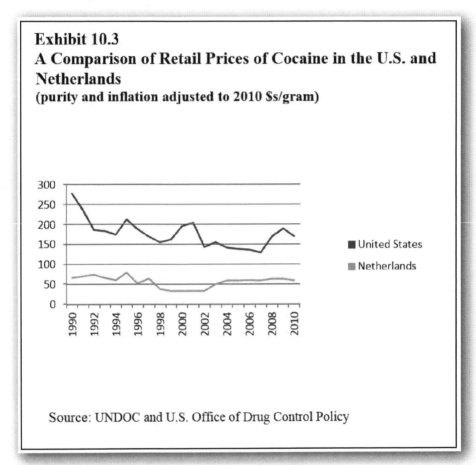

Exhibit 10.3
A Comparison of Retail Prices of Cocaine in the U.S. and Netherlands
(purity and inflation adjusted to 2010 $s/gram)

Source: UNDOC and U.S. Office of Drug Control Policy

At a street price of $169 per gram, that translates of the total US market for cocaine to be in the neighborhood of $43 billion.

Promotion. There are two main ways that cocaine consumption is promoted. First, of course, is your local drug dealer using personal selling approaches.

Second, and more subtle, is the promotion of what some have called "glamorous consumption" in movies and television. The recent *Wolf of Wall Street* is a good example. Snorting coke is something rich, successful people enjoy. Historically, such portrayals in film were prohibited by the film makers themselves via the 1934 Hayes Code. More on this in Chapter 14.

Consequences of Cocaine Consumption

Effects on Users. The rush was described earlier. Cocaine allows dopamine to accumulate at the synaptic level in the brain, thus strengthening the pleasure felt. Better than sex, and so on. Sometimes other unpleasant psychological effects include irritability, paranoia, restlessness, anxiety, and post-high depression.

The WebMD's list[1] of potential side effects is scary:

- **Heart.** Cocaine is bad for the heart. Cocaine increases heart rate and blood pressure while constricting the arteries supplying blood to the heart. The result can be a heart attack, even in young people without heart disease. Cocaine can also trigger a deadly abnormal heart rhythm called arrhythmia.

- **Brain.** Cocaine can constrict blood vessels in the brain, causing strokes. This can happen even in young people without other risk factors for strokes. Cocaine causes seizures and can lead to bizarre or violent behavior.

- **Lungs and respiratory system.** Snorting cocaine damages the nose and sinuses. Regular use can cause nasal perforation. Smoking crack cocaine irritates the lungs and, in some people, causes permanent lung damage.

- **Gastrointestinal tract.** Cocaine constricts blood vessels supplying the gut. The resulting oxygen starvation can cause ulcers, or even perforation of the stomach or intestines.

---

1 "Cocaine Use and Its Effects," *WebMD*, see http://www.webmd.com/mental-health/addiction/cocaine-use-and-its-effects, accessed September 2014.

- **Kidneys.** Cocaine can cause sudden, overwhelming kidney failure through a process called rhabdomyolysis. In people with high blood pressure, regular cocaine use can accelerate the long-term kidney damage caused by high blood pressure.
- **Sexual function.** Although cocaine has a reputation as an aphrodisiac, it actually may make you less able to finish what you start. Chronic cocaine use can impair sexual function in men and women. In men, cocaine can cause delayed or impaired ejaculation.

Other physical problems include teeth grinding, flu-like symptoms, breathing difficulties, throat soreness, and hoarseness. One has to wonder if cocaine use contributed to Ms. Bankhead's deep, sexy voice?

Societal Effects. Of course, the worst consequence of cocaine use is premature death, for both the user and his or her family and friends, and the larger society as well. There were 6726 cocaine related deaths in the United States in 2012, the last year reported in the 2014 World Drug Report.

Other measures of damage are the number of past month users – 2.4 million; the prevalence of past month use age twelve and above – one percent; ER visits – 184 per 100,000; treatment admissions – 267,256.

You will recall that in the last chapter, Exhibit 9.3 I reported that of Americans that have tried cocaine, 17 percent become dependent on the drug. As described in *Lancet*, British researchers[1] have developed a multi-dimensional "rational scale" to measure the relative damage done by use of twenty different substances. In particular, they use a Delphi technique for combining the separate ratings of a wide variety of healthcare and drug-abuse experts.

On that scale, heroin is judged the worst across all dimensions with a damage rating of 9.3[2] on a scale of 0 to 10, 10 being greater damage. Cocaine is second, with a damage rating of 7.7. See the entire array of scores in Chapter 12. The major difference between heroin and cocaine

---

1 David Nutt, Leslie A. King, William Saulsbury, and Colin Blackmore, "Development of a Rational Scale to Assess the Harm of Drugs," *Health Policy*, 369, March 24, 2007, pages 1047-1053, see TheLancet.com.

2 Here I have adjusted the scores reported in the 2007 Nutt et al. scale from a 0-3 to a 0-10 scale.

is in the nature of the addiction/dependence. Heroin delivers the maximum scores of 10 across all three dimensions of Dependence. Cocaine scores 10 on Pleasure, 9.3 on Psychological Dependence, but only 4.3 on Physiological Dependence. Many maintain that cocaine causes little in the way of physiological dependence, and fewer problems with withdrawal. But overall, cocaine is still a powerfully addicting drug. That is, one of six who try it, become dependent. Tim Madge is equivocal on the addictiveness of cocaine. However, when he wrote his otherwise excellent book *White Mischief* in 2001, he did not have access to this systematic research and its recommendations.

One critic of the *Lancet* paper pointed out that the researchers had omitted what I will call the Bankhead principle. Mixing is really bad – one can only imagine how high a score John Belushi's speedball would yield!

Of particular concern are cocaine consumers that use hypodermic needles to inject drugs. Across all drugs (heroin, cocaine, and so on), about 1.6 million users in the United States employ needles. Injection and shared needle use spread of HIV/AIDS and hepatitis C and B infections.

Another cost associated with cocaine use is the two million Americans incarcerated. More are serving time for marijuana related crimes, but cocaine is number two in this area. For example, among all US inmates (state and federal) 78 percent reported having used marijuana, 47 percent cocaine/crack, 23 percent heroin/opiates, and 29 percent stimulants (such as methamphetamines).

Finally, you will recall the estimated total costs of all illicit drugs to the country is $193 billion, as reported by the National Institute on Drug Abuse (NIH) in 2014.

How to Reduce/Control the Consumption of Cocaine

Based on the prices of cocaine in Exhibit 10.3, I conclude that prohibition and interdiction has not worked. To reiterate, if consumption and prices are down, logic suggests the decreases are demand driven, not supply driven.

Interdiction efforts during the Reagan administration resulted in huge federal expenditures targeted at the cocaine pipeline between Colombia and the United States. Now involved are the FBI, Immigration Service, US Marshall Service, Customs Service, Internal Revenue Service, the Pentagon (including satellites and nuclear submarines), the Department of Agriculture Forest Service, and, of course, the DEA. President Obama has requested a 6 percent increase in the budget for his US National Drug Control Budget totaling $24.5 billion. This does not include state and local expenditures which yield estimates in the $50 billion range. Most of this money is misspent.

Other aspects of the panic lawmaking in Washington, DC have yielded at least three unintended consequences. First is the current drug-testing regime. Because marijuana remains in the bloodstream longer than either cocaine or opiates, the prospect of testing pushes users in the direction of these stronger, yet harder-to-detect drugs including cocaine.

Tim Madge points out that the US/Mexican efforts to eliminate the Mexican marijuana crop in the 1980s via paraquat spraying perhaps made things worse. Paraquat is a weed killer that is strongly toxic to humans. First, it served to move marijuana cultivation further south to Colombia, and further from US control assets. Second, American marijuana consumers may have switched to "safer" opiates and cocaine products for fear of paraquat poisoning.[1]

Perhaps the worst effect of the coercive lawmaking of the time was the Anti-Drug Abuse Act of 1986. Its tacit racism well reflects the prejudiced fears of the crack cocaine epidemic. It introduced mandated sentencing for cocaine violations – a minimum of five years for possession of 500 grams of cocaine powder or five grams of crack, likewise a ten-year sentence for one kilogram of powder and ten grams of crack. Race-based fears yielded an overestimation of the damage done by the two different forms of the drug. This heinous law was mitigated a quarter century later by the Fair Sentencing Act of 2012. It reduced the ratio of the sentencing law from 1:100 to 1:18 and eliminated the mandatory sentence for crack possession. President Obama commuted

---

1 Ibid. *White Mischief*, page 158.

the sentences of eight prisoners under the auspices of the new law. There are thousands that deserve such consideration.

Governments in other countries are doing a much more effective and efficient jobs of reducing the consumption of cocaine. Consider the numbers on the Netherlands included in this chapter. Our approach is not only wasteful, it is shameful.

Ultimately legalization will allow us to control the distribution of cocaine, to tax it, to control its personal selling, and to invest appropriate amounts of our tax dollars into credible consumer education and treatment programs.

Marketing Miscreant – Cocaine

So many candidates: Mariani, Niemann, Merck, Parke-Davis, Escobar, Paraphernalia HQ of California (the producer of the first freebasing kit in 1978), Freud, Jung? The last two sound like part of the reading list for my graduate psychology classes at Berkeley, coincidentally in 1978. My choice is Jung, but George, not the Carl of my psych course or Chapter 2.

George Jung was released from prison on June 2, 2014. He spent the last twenty years in federal prisons. In 1994 he was arrested with almost two tons of cocaine. Download *Blow* – Jonny Depp plays George – for two-hour version of the story. It's a pretty good movie.

Jung got into marketing honestly, starting a program in advertising at the University of Southern Mississippi. There he began smoking pot, got into dealing the stuff in 1967, and dropped out. He was a natural. He began transcontinental trafficking via air using a stewardess friend. He moved into the airplane business, bringing marijuana from Mexico north in small civilian aircraft he had stolen. He was arrested in Chicago in 1974 with 660 pounds of marijuana. His first stay in federal prison ensued.

In jail he met Carlos Lehder Rivas, who introduced him to Pablo Escobar and the Medellin Cartel. They began flying small plane loads of cocaine from Colombia to California for his local distributor, Richard Barile. He banked hundreds of millions of dollars in Panama.

His villainy? George Jung, perhaps more than anyone else, turned on the cocaine tap to the United States in the 1980s. The big difference between Jung and most of the others on the list above is that Jung completely understood the damage he was doing to his fellow man. A very bad person indeed.

Eleven

The Continuing Alchemy

And by strange alchemy of brain
His pleasures always turn'd to pain –

Edgar Allan Poe

It's never been just about making gold. *Webster's* defines alchemy a bit differently: "A medieval chemical science and speculative philosophy aiming to achieve the transmutation of the base metals into gold, the discovery of a universal cure for disease, and the discovery of a means of indefinitely prolonging life." That is, money *and* a longer life to enjoy it.

No modern has taken a greater interest in alchemy than Carl (not George) Jung. The concept was essential for his theories about dreams and the unconscious:

> Before having discovered *alchemy* I had dreamed repeatedly dreams which that treated each time the same theme: next to my house was another one, more precisely a wing or an added construction that was strange to me. Each time I would amaze myself in my dream because I did not know this part of the house which apparently was there from the beginning.[1]

---

1 Carl G. Jung, *Memories, Dreams and Reflections* (New York: Vintage, 1989), page 202.

I'm not trying to get mystical on you now. And the only drugs I consumed before writing this were two chocolate donuts, one cake and one old fashioned. Oh, and the coffee.

My point is a simple one. In order to understand the continuing search for new, better hedonic molecules – the subject of this chapter – we must consider the motivations for the explorations. Take Freud and cocaine for example. He was interested in discovering a panacea and making money on it. This dialectic persists. The modern pharmaceutical industry is interested in these same two goals. Where the explorers get into trouble is when the money matters more. Then bad things start to happen.

Poe's own death is somewhat related. In 1849, at age forty he was found on the streets of Baltimore in another man's clothes and delirious. He was taken to a hospital, where he expired before his coherence returned. The medical records were subsequently lost. The conjecture about cause of death runs from suicide to murder, cholera, rabies, syphilis, influenza, alcohol, and opium. Perhaps a fitting demise for the father of mystery. In his poem above, the potion that delivered the pleasure and pain was love, not drink nor drug.

The UN Office on Drugs and Crime (UNODC) tracks the work of the new alchemists in 103 countries. As of December 2013 it had received reports of 348 "new psychoactive substances." This avalanche is more frightening than any Poe pendulum.

This chapter is similar to Chapter 4 on Chocolate and the other good spices. Here we consider a compendium of bad chemistry, of *Breaking Bad* if you like. We briefly report on six categories of mostly synthetic compounds that well represent the continuing alchemy of hedonic compounds: barbiturates, amphetamine-type substances (ATS), club drugs, dissociative drugs, hallucinogens, and inhalants.[1] Their prevalence of use is listed in Exhibit 11.1

---

1 Several excellent references have been consulted for this chapter: Leslie Iversen, *Speed>Ecstasy>Ritalin: The Science of Amphetamines* (Oxford: Oxford University Press, 2008); Leslie Iversen, Susan D. Iversen, Floyd E. Bloom, and Robert H. Roth, *Introduction to Neuropsychopharmacology*, (Oxford: Oxford University Press, 2009); Martin A. Lee and Bruce Slain, *Acid Dreams* (New York: Grove Press, 1992); Cynthia Kuhn, Scott Swartzwedler, and Wilkie Wilson, *Buzzed: The Straight Facts about the Most Used and Abused Drugs from Alcohol to Ecstasy* (New York: Norton, 1998); Nicolas Rasmussen, *On Speed: The Many Lives of Amphetamine* (New York: NYU Press, 2008); and Stephen M. Stahl, *Stahl's Essential Psychopharmacology* (Cambridge: Cambridge University Press, third edition, 2008).

Exhibit 11.1
Prevalence of Use of Selected Psychoactive Substances
in the U.S. and Globally (percentages)

Molecule	United States			Globally
	12ᵗʰ graders past year*	age 18-25 past year**	age 12+ past year***	age 12+ past year****
Alcohol	62.0%	76.8%	66.3%	
Cigarettes	--	57.9↓	25.3	
Illicit drugs	40.3	35.8	15.9	
Cocaine	2.6	4.4	1.6	0.4
Crack	1.1	0.3	0.2↓	
GHB	1.0	--	--	
Hallucinogens	4.5	6.7	1.7	
LSD	2.2	2.0	0.4	
MDMA	4.0	4.0	1.0	0.4
Heroin	0.6	0.7	0.3	0.4 (opiates)
Inhalants	2.5	1.4	0.7	
Ketamine	1.4	--	--	
Cannabis	36.4	31.6	12.6	3.8
Methamphetamine	0.9	0.9	0.5	
PCP	0.7	0.1↓	0.0↓	
Rohypnol	0.9	--	--	
Vicodin	5.3↑	--	--	
Amphetamine	8.7	--	--	0.7 (ATS w/o MDMA)

↑ = a statistically significant increase from the previous year
↓ = a statistically significant decrease from the previous year

* Monitoring the Future Study, National Institute on Drug Abuse (NIDA),
http://www.drugabuse.gov/trends-statistics/monitoring-future/monitoring-future-study-trends-in-prevalence-various-drugs, accessed September 2014.
**AdAge.com, 2014.
*** National Survey of Drug Abuse and Health, NIDA, http://www.drugabuse.gov/national-survey-drug-use-health, accessed September 2014.
****2014 World Drug Report, UNDOC

Barbiturates
Primary chemical ingredient: Barbituric acid, $C_4H_4N_2O_3$

This large family of central nervous system depressants is derived from barbituric acid. One example is Amytal (a.k.a. $C_{11}H_{17}N_2NaO_3$ or Amobarbital). Adolf von Baeyer (not the Bayer of aspirin fame), a German chemist whose dissertation was supervised by Robert Bunsen (of Bunsen burner fame), won the 1905 Nobel Prize for his body of work. One of his discoveries was the synthesis of barbituric acid in 1864. Do I sound like a chemistry major? He condensed urea with diethyl malonate, basically mixing horse urine and apple juice to produce a white powdery substance. Rumor has it that the barb- prefix comes either from a waitress named Barbara or from the holiday celebrating the feast of Saint Barbara. The first medical use was discovered in 1903 – scientists at Bayer found barbiturates useful to put down dogs. That makes the boys from Bayer the alchemists in this story. For people, medical uses included treatment for anxiety, insomnia, seizure disorders, and migraine headaches. More recently barbiturates have been used in physician assisted suicides and executions.

Barbiturates did not become popular until the 1950s, and about the same time started killing people. Both Marilyn Monroe and Judy Garland died from barbiturate overdoses. They are a dangerous set of drugs – the reactions vary according to the specific drug and across different people. A small dose may make someone sleepy but kill another person. Long-term use often results in addiction including tolerance and sometimes serious withdrawal symptoms. The Global Information Network about Drugs (GINAD) provides a summary of barbiturate prevalence:

In the USA around 300 tons of barbiturates are legally produced every year and it is estimated that the drug can be found in around 1 in 3 medicine cabinets across the country. There are around 2,500 different types of barbiturates produced in the USA, yet only about a dozen of these are in common usage. The most popular barbiturates are prescribed as sleeping pills, and 19 million prescriptions are written out for them every year.

Federal investigations into the illicit supply of barbiturates in the USA have found that the majority are produced legitimately by pharmaceutical companies, shipped to Mexico and then smuggled back into the country for sale on the black market.[1]

Barbiturates are prescription drugs, listed in Schedule III and IV under the US Controlled Substance Act of 1970. Recreational users report feelings of relaxed contentment and euphoria. Phenobarbital has a ninety-two-hour half-life causing a long hangover effect. Popular with recreational users are short- and medium-acting versions such as Amytal with onset of effects after about forty minutes and lasting about five to six hours.

The medical use of barbiturates has declined. They have mainly being replaced by a safer class of depressants, benzodiazepines. I used the word "safer" rather than "safe" – a combination of drugs including benzodiazepine killed Michael Jackson. Both are harmful drugs scoring 60 on the 0-to-100 scale[2] for physical dependence developed by Nutt and his colleagues (henceforth I will refer to this as the Harm Scale).[3] Only heroin and methadone score higher (worse) on that scale. Across all dimensions of the Harm Scale barbiturates are the third worst, less harmful than only heroin and cocaine, worse than even alcohol, tobacco, amphetamines, LSD, and cannabis.

While these drugs have generally fallen out of favor for recreational users, American teens are beginning to take a new interest in such pills in our medicine cabinets. Perhaps they are attracted by the colors of the pills – slang terms include blue velvet, yellow jackets, purple hearts, red devils, pink ladies, and rainbows, as well as downers, goofballs, and double trouble. Of course, they are also called sedatives and sleeping pills.

---

1 Global Information Network about Drugs (GINAD), http://www.ginad.org/en/drugs/drugs/222/barbiturates-. See also *WebMD* for their material on barbiturate abuse.

2 Note that I converted Nutt et al. 2007 scale to 0-100, rather than their original 0-3. See the next references.

3 David Nutt, Leslie A. King, Willam Saulsbury, Colin Blackmore, "Development of a Rational Scale to Asses the Harm of Drugs of Potential Misuse," *www.thelancet.com*, 369, March 24, 2007, 1047-1053.

ATS (Amphetamine-type stimulants)
Primary chemical ingredients: Amphetamine, $C_9H_{13}N$ and
Methamphetamine, $C_{10}H_{15}N$

Perhaps an entire chapter should be devoted to meth – it's a nasty stimulant (as is cocaine) that's just become a problem in the last decade. Indeed, the Harm Scale which was published in 2007 doesn't even list it. It does list the damage caused by amphetamines, the eighth most harmful drug on their list of twenty. Simple amphetamine is more harmful than tobacco, cannabis, solvents and a host of other compounds.

Amphetamine was first synthesized in German in 1887. Smith, Kline, and French commercialized it as a decongestant and anti-depressant under the trade name Benzedrine in the late 1930s. During World War II soldiers on all sides used the drugs – Americans to combat battle fatigue (we call it PSTD now) and to promote wakefulness.[1] You may recall from the Introduction that back in 1965, I took a "benny" to pull an all-nighter for a philosophy final. I also think my mother was addicted to the drug about the same time as a pre-scribed weight-loss medicine.

The UNODC *2014 World Drug Report* numbers included in the fourth column of Exhibit 11.1 are not broken down by amphetamine vs. methamphetamine, while MDMA is broken out. While world consumption has held about steady for ATS (excluding MDMA), prevalence rates in the United States grew about 20 percent with about 4.1 million Americans reporting use during the last year. Much of that increase is licit, prescription sales of amphetamines to treat ADHD. These are almost always lower doses than in the illicit market.

In the United States about 20 percent of ATS consumed is methamphetamine (I'll call it "meth" from now on). Meth consumption has remained flat during the last few years at about 1.2 million Americans reporting past-year use. For illicit meth wholesale prices have fallen steadily since 2007 by 35 percent and purity levels have risen from 45 percent to 95 percent in the same time frame.

---

1 Ibid. *On Speed*, pages 50-55.

A Japanese chemist first synthesized methamphetamine in 1893. Perhaps its first use was in World War II, when it was distributed to German pilots by Berlin-based Temmler, our alchemist for meth. German pilots and soldiers consumed thirty-five million meth tablets during the first three months of the war, yielding a reputation for ferocity during the Blitzkrieg. German scientists soon became doubtful of its efficacy and concerned about its potential for abuse, and began banning meth and amphetamines later in the war. In the 1950s it was marketed in the States by Obetrol Pharmaceuticals as a diet aid. Perhaps my mother was actually on that one. Meth is now legally prescribed as a Schedule II drug and manufactured in Denmark using the trade name Desoxyn.

Meth is, of course, a much more powerful stimulant that is more like cocaine in effect than amphetamine. All methods of imbibing are used. Its main recreational value comes as an aphrodisiac and it delivers an accompanying euphoria.

The list of potential physiological and psychological side effects is shocking: anorexia, hyperactivity, dilated pupils, flushed skin, excessive sweating, restlessness, dry mouth, teeth grinding, headache, irregular heartbeat, rapid breathing, high blood pressure, low blood pressure, cardiac system damage, high body temperature, diarrhea, constipation, blurred vision, dizziness, twitching, numbness, tremors, dry skin, acne, pallor, a general unhappiness, memory loss, apprehension, insomnia, aggression, irritability, grandiosity, obsessive behaviors, and psychosis. Perhaps its worst effect is the agonizingly long withdrawal symptoms that can persist for months. Meth is a known neurotoxin, that is, a poison. Overdoses can lead to brain damage (both in structure and function) and death, often preceded by convulsions and coma. Given the impurities in the street drug during the last decade, some of these awful consequences might be attributed to them. But, overall the sex and good feelings must be really great to make up for that profusion of pains.

The US National Institute on Drug Abuse (NIDA) reports that societal harm by meth abuse continues to threaten entire communities with lawlessness and crime waves, unemployment, child neglect and family abuse. A Rand report estimated meth abuse to cost the nation $23.4 billion in 2005.

Amphetamines are marketed illicitly on the street as speed, truck drivers, and uppers. The past-year prevalence of use for American twelfth graders was 8.7 percent last year. The street names for meth are much more entertaining: ice, crank, crystal, glass, shard, fire, Okie coke, tweak, chicken feed, and also speed. The prevalence of meth use rate in the last year for Americans was 0.9 percent.

Club Drugs

This is a classification of convenience used by the National Institute of Drug Abuse. It includes MDMA ("ecstasy," a stimulant and a hallucinogen), fluni-trazepam (a depressant), and GHB (another depressant). All three have been popular during the last three decades at nightclubs around the world. Ecstasy is the major current problem, and I will cover it last.

Flunitrazepam ($C_{16}H_{12}FN_3O_3$, a.k.a. Rohypnol, roofies, forget-me pill, roach, roofinol, rope, Mexican valium) was developed by Hoffman La-Roche in 1963. Leo Sternbach was the alchemist there. Its first use was as a hypnotic/sedative and it is in the benzodiazepine family. Benzodiazepines are listed as #7 on the Harm Scale, just ahead of amphetamines. As a powerful Schedule IV drug it is abused recreationally and as a method of suicide. It is also known as a "date-rape" drug that not only induces unconsciousness but also memory loss. When consumed with alcohol, it is often associated with being robbed and/or sexually assaulted. Neither are nice side effects. Other consequences of consumption are muscle relaxation, confusion, dizziness, impaired coordination, and addiction. The prevalence rate is estimated to be 0.9 percent for American twelfth graders. See Exhibit 11.1.

GHB ($C_4H_8O_3$, gamma-Hydroxybutyric acid, a.k.a. Xyrem, G, Georgia home boy, grievous bodily harm, liquid ecstasy, soap, scoop, goop, fantasy, and liquid X) was first synthesized in 1874. The alchemist for GHB is a French physician named Henri Laborit. On my alchemy scale Dr. Laborit, was more interested in helping humans – his work in the area was with wounded French soldiers in Vietnam. GHB has been medically used as an anesthetic, and oddly enough, it is FDA approved as a treatment for a type of narcolepsy. For this narrow application it is considered a Schedule III drug. As a recreational drug is it classified as a Schedule I drug because of its high rate of abuse. Euphoria, disinhibition, and sexuality are its attractive attributes. At higher doses or mixed with alcohol it can induce a very undesirable pair of consequences, vomiting and drowsiness, which in turn can lead to fatal choking. GHB is also a known "date-rape" drug. It is simple to manufacture and thus attractive in the illicit market. GHB is listed as #17 on the Harm Scale. The drug is addictive and has sometimes serious withdrawal symptoms including delirium. As can be seen in Exhibit 11.1, the prevalence rate of American twelfth graders is about 1.0 percent.

MDMA ($C_{11}H_{15}NO_2$, 3,4-methylenedioxy-N-methamphetamine, a.k.a. ecstasy, Molly, E, X, XTC, clarity, lover's speed, peace, uppers), an amphetamine derivative, was stumbled upon by scientists at Merck in 1912. MDMA was patented two years later as an intermediate compound in the production of a substance to stop abnormal bleeding. The US Army experimented with it in the 1950s for interrogations, among other purposes.

In the 1970s MDMA became quite popular for use by psychotherapists, particularly in California. Alexander Shulgin, a Berkeley-trained biochemist is credited with its initial description and promotion in a paper in 1978. Shulgin, the so-called "god-father of psychedelics," led quite an interesting life, but recently died in June 2014. On my alchemy scale, he was interested mostly in the topic, not the money. He held a most valuable patent on an insecticide he developed for Dow Chemical that allowed him the financial independence and free time to synthesize, discover, and personally try over two hundred psychoactive compounds. Of note, he worked with the DEA, giving seminars and writing reference materials, and was given a license to work with Schedule I drugs. In 1994 the DEA raided his private lab, his license was revoked, and he paid a $25,000 fine for possession of a wide variety of illicit compounds.

Shulgin describes his own response to 120 milligrams of MDMA, what he later called "my low-calorie martini":

I felt absolutely clean inside, and there is nothing but pure euphoria. I have never felt so great or believed this to be possible. The cleanliness, clarity and marvelous feeling of solid inner strength continued throughout the rest of the day, and evening, and through the next day. I am overcome by the profundity of the experience, and how much more powerful it was than previous experiences, for no apparent reason, other than a continually improving state of being. All the next day I felt like a 'citizen of the universe' rather than a citizen of the planet, completely disconnecting time and flowing easily from one activity to the next. [1]

The subjective experiences of MDMA differ from person to person and by dose. Descriptors include: relaxing, clarity, disinhibited, euphoric, extroversion, hallucinations, dazed, emotional excitation, sensuality, and, of course, ecstasy. The effects are felt twenty to sixty minutes after taking a pill, and last for three to five hours.

A variety of adverse side effects have been reported: concentration difficulties, teeth grinding, lack of appetite, dehydration, and attentional and memory impairment. Overdoses can yield confusion, delusions, anxiety, convulsions, a range of cardiovascular problems, organ failure, unconsciousness, coma, and death. Of course, the impurities associated with illicit production and distribution add greatly to the list of potential harms. One website[2] has tracked purity levels using convenience sampling techniques since 1996, and they report scary variations: In 2014 only 20 percent of the samples they received contained only MDMA, for 2009 only 8.7 percent, while in 2000 45.6 percent contained only MDMA. The purity has declined precipitously since 2003. Finally, MDMA is #18 on the Harm Scale and #16 on the "dependence" dimension.

The US National Institute of Drug Abuse reports the "prevalence of consumption during the last year" for MDMA as holding steady over the last few years: As can be seen in Exhibit 11.1, for Americans age twelve and older the prevalence rate is 1.0 percent in the past year, for twelfth graders at 4.0

---

1 Alexander Shulgin and Ann Shulgin, *PiHKAL: A Chemical Love Story* (Berkeley: Transform Press, 2014), page 736.

2 www.ecstasydata.org/stats.pjp,accessed September 2014.

percent, and eighteen to twenty-five year olds at 4.0 percent. The global prevalence of use rate (for the *last year*) has also held steady at 0.4 percent for the last two reporting periods. We're not quite done with ecstasy yet – we'll return to the topic at the end of this chapter.

Dissociative Drugs

According to the National Institute of Drug Abuse:

> Dissociative drugs can produce visual and auditory distortions and a sense of floating and dissociation (feeling detached from reality) in users. Use of dissociative drugs can also cause a user to experience anxiety, memory loss, and impaired motor function, including body tremors and numbness. These effects, which depend on the amount of the drug taken, are also unpredictable—typically beginning within minutes of ingestion and lasting for several hours (although some users report feeling the drug's effects for days).

Three are considered here: Ketamine, PCP, and DXM. Common effects of the three are hallucinations, memory loss, physical distress (heart, breathing, tremors, numbness, and nausea), marked psychological distress (panic, fear, anxiety, paranoia, invulnerability, and aggression), and when mixed with alcohol and other depressants respiratory distress or arrest, and death.

Ketamine ($C_{13}H_{16}ClNO$, a.k.a. Special K, K, vitamin K, cat Valium) was first synthesized by a consultant at Parke-Davis in 1962. After animal and human testing, it was approved by the FDA in 1970 for use as a short-duration anesthetic. Initially it was given to wounded soldiers in the Vietnam War.

It immediately became a popular recreational drug in the United States. It is now classified as Schedule III drug, available for prescription use for pediatric and ER settings, and at low doses to treat depression and pain. It is listed as #8 on the Harm Scale with a relatively high "psychological dependence" score of 57 on a 0 to 100 scale.

As listed in Exhibit 11.1, Ketamine was used by about 1.4 percent of American twelfth graders in the past year. They might find it in your medicine cabinet or know a drug dealer in school who can supply it.

PCP ($C_{17}H_{25}N$, phencyclidine, a.k.a. angel dust, boat, love boat), first synthesized in 1926, was brought to market by Parke-Davis in the 1950s as an anesthetic. It was pulled from the market in 1964 because of competition with similar drugs like Ketamine, and PCP's awful side effects such as mania, aggression, and violence. Some studies suggest these latter effects are exaggerated. While it is not included on the Harm Scale, it surely would rank worse (higher) that Ketamine which is PCP's nice Parke-Davis sister. It is listed as a Schedule II drug in the United States. While never really popular in the 1970s, PCP is even less so now with some of the lowest prevalence use scores listed in Exhibit 11.l.

DXM ($C_{18}H_{25}NO$, dextromethorphan, a.k.a. robotripping, robo, triple C, dex, and skittles) is commonly found in cough syrups in the United States. The "robo" refers to Robitussin, an over-the-counter cough medication produced by Pfizer. The DEA provides a concise description of its availability:

> DXM is a cough suppressor found in more than 120 over-the-counter (OTC) cold medications, either alone or in combination with other drugs such as analgesics (e.g., acetaminophen), antihistamines (e.g., chlorpheniramine), decongestants (e.g., pseudoephedrine), and/or expectorants (e.g., guaifenesin). The typical adult dose for cough is 15 or 30 mg taken three to four times daily. The cough-suppressing effects of DXM persist for 5 to 6 hours after ingestion. When taken as directed, side-effects are rarely observed.
>
> DXM abusers can obtain the drug at almost any pharmacy or supermarket, seeking out the products with the highest concentration of the drug from among all the OTC cough and cold remedies that contain it. DXM products and powder can also be purchased on the Internet.[1]

---

1 *Drugs of Abuse*, 2011 Edition, US Department of Justice, Drug Enforcement Administration, page 76, see www.dea.gov.

High doses bring the effects desired by recreational users: Euphoria and visual and auditory hallucinations. Over doses and mixing with alcohol are believed to produce all the nasty side effects described above for the other dissociative drugs. At the moment this drug is unregulated by the US government and its consumption rates are unknown.

Hallucinogens

The three most famous hallucinogens are, of course, LSD, mescaline, and psilocybin. All provide the recreational user hallucinations, altered states of perception and feeling, and often nausea. Other common effects are increased body temperature, heart rate, and blood pressure, loss of appetite, sweating, sleeplessness, numbness, dizziness, weakness, tremors, impulsive behavior, and rapid shifts in emotion. The side effects list for psilocybin is shorter – nervousness, paranoia, and panic. The only health risk listed by a National Institute of Drug Abuse (NIDA) summary is flashbacks (or hallucinogen persisting perception disorder) for LSD.

Two other risks are worth note: Because of the black market nature of the drugs, nobody can be sure of the purity or even the contents of a dose of hallucinogens. With respect to psilocybin, while some mushrooms may yield the desired recreational effects, other, very similar looking mushrooms are quite poisonous.

All have a colorful history filled with controversy. For example, the DEA lists death as a potential overdose effect of LSD – this is not mentioned by NIDA. Which is correct?

LSD ($C_{20}H_{25}N_3O$, lysergic acid diethylamide, a.k.a. acid, blotter acid, dots, mellow yellow, window pane, sunshine, and blue heaven) was first synthesized by Albert Hofmann, working at Sandoz Laboratories in Basel, Switzerland in 1938. He was looking to create new molecules ultimately from ergot, a grain fungus.

Hoffmann did not recognize the hallucinogenic effect of the compound until he accidently absorbed a dose through his fingertips in 1943. He was the first person to feel its effects, and here's how he described his surprise walk on the moon:

... affected by a remarkable restlessness, combined with a slight dizziness. At home I lay down and sank into a not unpleasant intoxicated-like condition, characterized by an extremely stimulated imagination. In a dreamlike state, with eyes closed (I found the daylight to be unpleasantly glaring), I perceived an uninterrupted stream of fantastic pictures, extraordinary shapes with intense, kaleidoscopic play of colors. After some two hours this condition faded away.[1]

In 1947 it was commercialized by Sandoz for psychiatric uses. It was well accepted at the time.

The drug takes effect after about twenty to thirty minutes and its half-life of duration is reported to be between three to five hours. Beyond the effects listed above, Hofmann and others have reported a strong metallic taste during the high from LSD. Generally both the physiological and psychological effects vary from person to person and with setting and mindset. Most in the medical community believe it is not physically addictive, but has a powerfully attractive psychological impact. Thus, LSD is listed as #14 on the Harm Scale with a physical dependence score of 10 (compared to heroin at 100), among the lowest of the twenty hedonic molecules studied.

The psychiatric community identifies several potential uses for LSD: treating alcoholism, end-of-life anxiety, cluster headaches, and pain management. Claims are made even about its spiritual enhancement qualities. It is classified as a Schedule I substance and so is unavailable for any of these purposes in the United States. While accidents have occurred because of its effects on judgment and physical movement, there have been no documented reports of death from overdose on LSD.[2] The DEA is either misinformed, or just plain lying about this issue.

Perhaps the most interesting controversy regards its effects on human creativity. The DEA says no. I am agnostic on the causal effect of hedonic

---

1 Albert Hofmann, *LSD – My Problem Child* (Santa Cruz, CA: MAPS, 2009, page 47.

2 Torten Passie, John H. Halpern, Dirk O. Stichtenoth, Hinderk M. Emrich, and Annelie Hintzen, The Pharmacology of Lysergic Acid Diethylamide: A Review," *CNS Neuroscience and Therapeutics* 14, 2008, pages 295-314. This is an important peer-reviewed article. I would be interested in the DEA's comments on it.

compounds in general on human performance, physical or mental. There have been a series of experiments on LSD and creativity. My favorite was done by a UCI colleague, Oscar Janiger MD in the 1950s. He and his coauthor had 250 artists render still-life paintings of Kachina dolls, before and one hour after taking LSD. Then a professor of art history judged the creative differences across the treatments. Janiger and another colleague summarize the findings: "Several of the artists altered their styles from representational to expressionistic; changes in figure/ground and boundaries; greater intensity of color and light; oversimplification; symbolic and abstract depiction of objects, and fragmentation, disorganization, and distortion."[1]

Certainly different before and after, but more creative? The last three descriptors don't sound like more creative to me. And what would have happened if the artist were simply asked to take a more impressionistic approach? Of course the study was conducted in the 1950s, so we must excuse the sloppy methods. The good news here is now research on the effects of LSD is being resumed around the world.

My absolute favorite attribution of enhanced performance to LSD is the story told by a Pittsburgh Pirates all-star and world-champion pitcher, Dock Ellis, about his only major league no hitter:

"I was in Los Angeles, and the team was playing in San Diego, but I didn't know it. I had taken LSD..... I thought it was an off-day, that's how come I had it in me. I took the LSD at noon." At 1pm, his girlfriend and trip partner looked at the paper and said, "Dock, you're pitching today!"

"That's when it was $9.50 to fly to San Diego. She got me to the airport at 3:30. I got there at 4:30, and the game started at 6:05pm. It was a twi-night doubleheader.

I can only remember bits and pieces of the game. I was psyched. I had a feeling of euphoria.

1 Oscar Janiger and Marlene Dobkin de Rios, *LSD, Spirituality, and Creative Process* (Rochester, VT: Park Street Press, 2003), pages 86-87.

I was zeroed in on the [catcher's] glove, but I didn't hit the glove too much. I remember hitting a couple of batters and the bases were loaded two or three times.

The ball was small sometimes, the ball was large sometimes, sometimes I saw the catcher, sometimes I didn't. Sometimes I tried to stare the hitter down and throw while I was looking at him. I chewed my gum until it turned to powder. They say I had about three to four fielding chances. I remember diving out of the way of a ball I thought was a line drive. I jumped, but the ball wasn't hit hard and never reached me.[1]

The Pirates won the game, 2-0, although Ellis walked eight batters. Reporters at the game question his credibility, but his teammates weren't surprised. He was known as "outspoken" and he admitted after retirement to never pitching without drugs, usually amphetamines. But I have to say the detail of his story works pretty well with what we now know about LSD. So for a second or ten, let's assume he did pitch a no-hitter that day. My question is, might he have pitched a perfect game (without the eight walks) if he were sober?

Mescaline ($C_{11}H_{17}NO_3$, 3,4,5-trimethoxyphenethylamine, a.k.a. buttons, cactus, mesc, peyote), unlike the semisynthetic LSD, is a natural plant. Synthesized by nature, so to speak like, marijuana – you just need to know how to find it. Native Americans in the Southwest found it some 5,700 years ago and have used it since in religious ceremonies. It was synthesized in 1919 by Ernst Späth, an Austrian chemist. Its effects are similar to LSD but not the same. Potential medical uses are for treating alcoholism and depression. But, it is a Schedule I substance in the United States preventing further scientific research until the last decade.

Psilocybin ($C_{12}H_{17}N_2O_4P$, a.k.a. magic mushrooms, shrooms, purple passion, little smoke) comes naturally from some two hundred varieties of mushrooms. Prehistoric man used the drug in the Mediterranean region and

---

1   http://www.sirbacon.org/4membersonly/docellis.htm. This is not even close to being a scientific source, but the story is fun, and still makes my point. Ellis and his biographer, Donald Hall, confirm the LSD no-hitter story in *Dock Ellis: In the Country of Baseball* (New York: Fireside, 1989) pages 316-7.

Mesoamerica. Spanish explorers were the first to document its use in the Americas in the 1500s. Centuries later Albert Hofmann was sent a sample, and he applied scientific techniques in both his laboratory and stomach to discern it chemistry. He and others at Sandoz also worked out how to purify the compound.

Divinity was the vehicle that my Nebraska grandmother used to deliver sugar to her grandchildren. It was a candy that came in pink and white. Good stuff. In the early 1960s Timothy Leary conducted research on both LSD and psilocybin at Harvard. One of the topics he and his colleagues were interested in was divinity (not the candy) and its relationship to hallucinogens.

A graduate student at Harvard's Divinity School, Walter Pahnke, under the auspices of Leary's Psilocybin Project, designed and carried out an experiment to determine whether psilocybin delivered enhanced religious experiences. In what is now known as the Marsh Chapel Experiment, twenty graduate divinity students from the area were invited to participate on the campus of nearby Boston University on Good Friday, 1962. Half the group was given psilocybin and the control group was given nicotinic acid (Niacin). Pahnke concluded:

> The results of our experiment would indicate that psilocybin (and LSD and mescaline, by analogy) are important tools for the study of the mystical state of consciousness. Experiences previously possible for only a small minority of people, and difficult to study because of their unpredictability and rarity, are now reproducible under suitable conditions. The mystical experience has been called by many names suggestive of areas that are paranormal and not usually considered easily available for investigation (e.g., an experience of transcendence, ecstasy, conversion, or cosmic consciousness); but this is a realm of human experience that should not be rejected as outside the realm of serious scientific study, especially if it can be shown that a practical benefit can result.[1]

---

1 Wlater N. Pahnke, "Drugs and Mysticism," *International Journal of Parapsychology* 8(2), Spring 1966, pages 295-313.

Not long after scientific scandal over Leary's work in chapels and prisons (he reported a drop in recidivism from 60 percent to 20 percent among the prisoners given psilocybin) the drug was banned in the United States and is now listed on Schedule I. Sandoz stopped producing the drug that same year.

Leary was fired from Harvard because of his research. He spent a great deal of time in jail in the following years for his hallucinogen-marketing efforts. His slogan, "Turn on, tune in, drop out," moved the drugs along quite well. The illicit drug became popular with recreational and spiritual users, and grow-your-own books proliferated in the 1980s. In the 1990s and early this century the mushrooms were marketed in the Netherlands and UK and online.

The effects of the drug are in the ballpark with LSD. Physical dependence seems not a consequence of use. However, there have been two documented cases of death from psilocybin overdose. The prevalence of recreational use across all hallucinogens is 6.7 percent in the past year for Americans aged eighteen to twenty-five. This is too high, so to speak.

Inhalants

These mundane industrial chemicals are used recreationally primarily by very young people who cannot afford the other drugs listed in this chapter. The prevalence of use during the past year for American eighth graders is 5.2 percent, 3.5 percent for tenth graders, and 2.5 percent for twelfth graders. See Exhibit 11.1.Most of these molecules are not controlled by the federal government and are available in retail stores around the country.

Three categories are defined by NIDA: *solvents* (paint thinners, gasoline, glues); *gases* (butane, propane aerosol propellants, nitrous oxide); *nitrites* (isoamyl, isobutyl, cyclohexyl). Street names include laughing gas, poppers, snappers, gluey, huff, rush, and whippets.

Inhaling these gases produce an intoxicating effect that can include dizziness and euphoria, but only for ten minutes or so at a time. Thus, users repeat frequently. With long-term use they can cause weight loss, muscle weakness, inactivity, lack of coordination, irritability, depression, brain and/

or cardiovascular damage, and in overdose, sudden death. In most localities restrictions on sale to youths are the only form of control. Fortunately, the kids seem to grow out of these nasty practices.

The Newest Alchemy

That brings us back to the creepiest datum in this book: 348. That's the number of newly identified psychoactive substances at the global level since 2009. For the first time the UNODC has included this monitoring of the coming threats in its *2014 World Drug Report*. See Exhibit 11.2 which illustrates the accelerating efforts of the alchemists around the world.

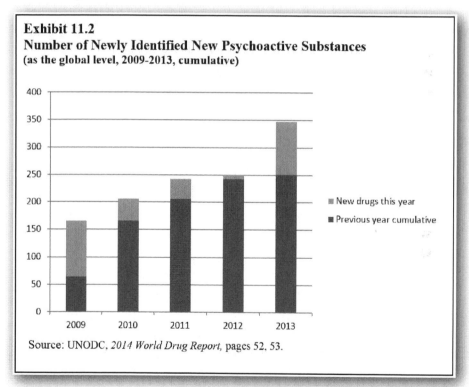

Exhibit 11.2
Number of Newly Identified New Psychoactive Substances
(as the global level, 2009-2013, cumulative)

Source: UNODC, *2014 World Drug Report*, pages 52, 53.

Enforcement and research regarding effects cannot keep up with this onslaught of alchemy, that is, creativity and greed. Ninety countries reported new substances in 2013. In contrast to the 348 new ones, there are only 234 substances currently controlled by international treaty. Of the 97 new substances "released" (or discovered by regulators) in the last year, 50 percent are cannabinoids, 17 percent are phenethyamines, and 8 percent are synthetic cathinones (for example, bath salts). The only good news in the report is the failures of a couple of these new molecules to launch effectively in the United States. Among American high school students synthetic cannabinoid past-year prevalence of use fell from 11.4 percent to 7.9 percent between 2011 and 2013. Likewise use of bath salts (cathinones) fell from 1.3 percent to 0.9 percent in the same time period. Of course, the risk is that with so many new product launches, some will take hold.

Back to the bad news for a moment – an article in *Bloomberg Businessweek* illustrates the problem:

It's a Friday afternoon in April, and Wesley Upchurch, the 24-year-old owner of Pandora Potpourri, has arrived at his factory to fill some last-minute orders for the weekend. The factory is a cramped, unmarked garage bay adjoining an auto body shop in Columbia, MO. What Upchurch and his one full-time employee, 21-year-old Jay Harness, are making is debatable, at least in their eyes. The finished product looks like crushed grass, comes in three-gram (.11 ounce) packets, and sells for about $13 wholesale. Its key ingredient is a synthetic cannabinoid that mimics tetrahydrocannabinol (THC), the active ingredient in marijuana. Upchurch, however, insists his product is incense. "There are rogue players in this industry that make the business look bad for everyone," Upchurch says. "We don't want people smoking this."[1]

But he does want them inhaling it. The reporter says Upchurch is just plain lying. He's really making $500,000 a year on $2.5 million in revenues selling synthetic cannabinoids, which may or may not be subject to federal or state

---

1 Ben Paynter, "The Drug is Fake, the High is Real, the Money is Huge:The Unlicensed, Ingenious, and Increasingly Scary World of Synthetic Drugs," *Bloomberg Businessweek*, June 20-26, 2011, pages 56-64

laws. And worse still, the high delivered is often real. The ironic part of this story is that the first product among the new synthetics to warrant the attention of the DEA was produced in Europe, shipped to the United States and branded as "Spice." And this synthetic spice is now causing overdoses all over the country.[1]

Governments are behind the curve on this issue. In New Zealand, a test market for synthetics these days, the government has made a conscious decision to test, not ban. But the queue for testing is so long that none are being approved. In the short run this helps the illicit market. In the longer run, depending on the testing results, appropriate regulations can be applied. The UK is also trying to develop a system for faster testing as well.

Alchemy and Intelligence

A classic scene from the dominant network TV show, *The Big Bang Theory*, shows Drs. Sheldon Cooper and Amy Farah Fowler arguing over which is the more fundamental science, Sheldon's theoretical physics or Amy's neurobiology. They are actually arguing over who is the smarter between them. Another entrant in that contest would be the science of intelligence. Richard Haier, my good friend and neighbor, would never make the claim himself, but he may be the smartest person in the world on the subject of intelligence. I think his claim would be stronger than either Sheldon's or Amy's. Being smart about being smart – I would think there's some sort of exponential effect.

From among Rich's many important works, I'm going to borrow from his lecture series "The Intelligent Brain," from *The Great Courses*, www. thegreatcourses.com. As a Johns Hopkins-trained psychologist he treads where others fear to go. For example, in the series, one lecture is entitled "Genes and Intelligence," another "Sex and Intelligence," and another "Race and Intelligence." For the topic of this book, his Lecture 18 "The IQ Pill" is most pertinent. Indeed, the lecture title is sexier than even the *The Big Bang Theory*. He explains:

---

1 Soumya Karlamangla, "Skid Row's 'Cheapest Buzz,'" *Los Angeles Times*, August 26, 2016, pages B1, B5.

The concept of an IQ pill is metaphorical. It may be a drug that affects synaptic growth, neuron efficiency, gray matter thickness, or white matter integrity, or it may be a way to stimulate brain function with electricity or magnetic fields.

Many drug companies are already working on new drugs to improve memory and learning for patients with Alzheimer's disease, but if these new drugs work in patients, could they also work in people without brain disease to enhance memory and learning – two of the key components of general intelligence?

Few people would be against using such drugs if they improved cognition for people with Alzheimer's disease, stroke patients, in patients with brain damage, or people with mental retardation – but what about people with no brain problems using such drugs?

There are already drugs that improve attention in children with attention deficit disorder (ADD) like Adderall and Ritalin. Many parents want these drugs for non-ADD teenagers before they take the SATs and other exams. These drugs are also in demand by many college students; estimates range from seven to 25 percent of college students use these drugs before exams. Despite their popularity, there doesn't seem to be any research that supports these uses. Nonetheless, the idea of cognitive enhancement seems to be not only acceptable, but there also seems to be a strong demand from parents as well as from students.

Then he asks some tough questions for all of us to ponder:

- Assuming no side effects, would you give an IQ pill to your children if it put them in the top one percent of students?
- If an IQ pill existed, and it was not cheaply available to everyone, what would you be willing to pay for it?
- If an IQ pill were possible, should the government ban it for any use?[1]

---

1 Richard J. Haier, *The Intelligent Brain Course Guidebook*, (Chantilly, VA: The Great Courses, 2013), pages 124-127.

I can tell you that in an online survey of *Nature* (a top scientific journal) readers, 69.4 percent of the professors asked if they would take a cognitive enhancing drug said "yes." When specifically asked, "Have you ever taken any of the following drugs: modafinil (Provigil), methylphenidate (Ritalin), or beta blockers like propranolol (Inderal)?" 20.2 percent answered "Yes, either these or other drugs for nonmedical reasons to improve concentration or cognition." Yikes![1]

Marketing Miscreant among Alchemists

So many possibilities among the alchemists in this chapter. But, I'm going to go with a classic marketing alchemist who's in it only for the money. Human progress comes in far below a new Lamborghini.

Part of the reason for the aforementioned decline in the purity of MDMA (ecstasy) during this century in the United States has been the relatively successful control of precursor chemicals for manufacture. Most of those chemicals (for example, piperonyl methyl ketone or PMK) are now manufactured in China (a country with a known purity problem even when the drugs are legal), and an important pipeline moves them to the Netherlands for synthesis and tablet production. Much of this illicit international trade is managed by Chinese Triad gangsters. The DEA estimates that 80 percent of the MDMA consumed in the US is smuggled in from the Netherlands. The problem then is how to get the pills from there to the US rave scene?

An enterprising twenty-three-year-old Dutchman solved that problem, at least for a time. His alchemy was combining the Internet and ecstasy. The *Chicago Tribune* headline on June 10, 2014 read: "World's Most Prolific Online Drug Dealer Pleads Guilty in Chicago."[2] The article makes the point that the Dutchman trafficked millions of dollars' worth of illicit drugs simply using his laptop and a backpack. The feds met him at the Miami airport – he was in the States to party, and had rented a Lamborghini. He was given

---

1 Richard Monastersky, "Some Professors Pop Pills for an Intellectual Edge," *The Chronicle of Higher Education*, April 25, 2008, pages 1, 10.

2 See Kim Janssen's "World's Most Prolific Online Drug Dealer Pleads Guilty in Chicago," *Chicago Sun Times*, June 10, 2014, online.

fifteen years in federal prison as part of a negotiated guilty plea. Actually the best source of details on Cornelis "SuperTrips" Slomp, comes from his plea bargain:

…from in or about January 2011 to in or about October 2013, an underground website known as "Silk Road" allowed vendors and buyers to exchange goods and services online. Silk Road was dedicated to the sale of illegal drugs and other illicit, black market goods and services using the digital currency "bitcoins" and was designed to facilitate illegal commerce by ensuring anonymity among its users.

SLOMP, a citizen and resident of the Netherlands, used the username "SuperTrips" to advertise, market, and sell illegal drugs on Silk Road. SLOMP was the world's largest drug-trafficking vendor on Silk Road by volume of business and customer base, conducting sales of illegal drugs in the millions of dollars and deriving his livelihood from drug-trafficking criminal activities. In total, for the eighteen months from March 2012 through in or about August 2013, SLOMP distributed worldwide approximately: 104 kilograms of powder 3,4-methylenedioxy-N-methylamphetamine (MDMA); 566,000 ecstasy pills containing MDMA; four kilograms of cocaine; three kilograms of enzodiazepine; and substantial quantities of amphetamine, lysergic acid diethylamide (LSD), and marijuana, in addition to allowing for substantial quantities of methamphetamine, ketamine, and Xanax to be distributed on his SuperTrips vendor account. SLOMP received approximately 385,000 in bitcoins as payment for his illegal drug sales, which spanned across more than 10,000 transactions.

SLOMP was the "boss" of the SuperTrips identity and controlled virtually all aspects of the identity, including the exercise of decision-making authority, recruiting accomplices, claiming a right to a larger share of the drug proceeds, planning and organizing his drug-trafficking business, and exercising control and authority over others…

At the time of his arrest, SLOMP possessed not less than $3,030,000 in illegal drug proceeds and assets, some of the latter of which have been converted into cash, from the sale of illegal drugs on Silk Road through his SuperTrips account.

The *Chicago Tribune* article also has a link to the entire plea agreement. Anyone that is involved in illegal trafficking should read this article. There is an explicit statement about Slomp's required cooperation in additional cases to be brought against his accomplices. Recall that George Jung (our miscreant from the last chapter) was given a sixty-year sentence, but only served twenty years because he ratted on his partners. Perhaps Slomp will get off after only five years after testifying against his ten partners in crime? The implication is that even if it's your partner who gets caught, you may be prosecuted and ultimately spend more time incarcerated. If you're the last to be prosecuted, you may serve the longest term.

Twelve

The Consequences of Consumption: A Summary

*Research is always a work in progress; no single study can answer
complex questions, and there are always
more questions than answers.*

Richard Haier

One of the consequences of the consumption psychoactive substances is the pleasure for the consumer. This is obvious. Indeed, this is so by definition.

Almost all of the psychoactive substances have historically been used as paths to spirituality, aphrodisiacs, and medicines. Most have not delivered on those promises. But, some still do, and for others great controversy still surrounds their usefulness. Many of the hedonic substances are painkillers, for example.

The topic of pain killers came up about twenty years ago at a wonderful meeting I had with E.T. Hall, my intellectual hero. Ned was a world renowned anthropologist who had much to say about how Americans conducted business in other countries. He was the seminal author in the area of cultural differences in perceptions of space and the science of proxemics. We had simultaneously and independently produced books on how to negotiate with Japanese. He sent me a copy of his that included a nice note about mine.

We agreed to meet for lunch at a patio café in Santa Fe. We were seated at a nice shady table. Then the surrealism showed up. He decided our table was too close to the adjacent one. So the two of us stood up and adjusted our space by moving the table. For me, it was a little like watching Paul McCartney changing the channel on my car radio.

We talked about Japan and other topics of mutual interest. I asked him why he thought illicit drugs were beginning to dominate the cultural discourse of America. Anthropologists are good at answering "why" questions. He responded immediately, "Vietnam." It was an awful experience for the country and the soldiers who traveled there. Many died, and many came home with both physical and psychological wounds. Soldiers have always managed the pain of killing and seeing killing with drugs. In the World War II Ned Hall had experienced, it was mostly alcohol. He pointed out that in Vietnam 2.7 million Americans were exposed to a new variety of psychoactive drugs, along with the pain that made them attractive. They brought the pain, the pain relievers, and their addictions home with them. Sadly we lost Professor Hall in 2009 – he was ninety-five.

Author of *Illegal Drugs*, an excellent book, Dr. Paul Galinger makes a similar point:

> I have seen morphine kill people and, during my years in the Emergency Department, I have seen it save countless lives. I have seen people destroy themselves with cocaine, and I have applied it to stop bleeding in patients who might have hemorrhaged to death without it. In the hospice, I am thankful that such a drug exists. Clearly, these drugs have the potential for both great benefit and great harm.[1]

So, while the main topic of this chapter is the harm, I thought it essential to provide the larger context of their use first.

---

1 Paul Gahlinger, *Illegal Drugs: A Complete Guide to their History, Chemistry, Use, and Abuse* (New York: Plume, 2004), page x.

Measuring Harm

Dr. David Nutt's qualifications couldn't be stronger – he's a fellow of the Royal College of Physicians, Royal College of Psychiatrists, and the Academy of Medical Sciences in the UK. He has been president or vice-president of the British Association of Psychopharmacology, the European College of Neuropsychopharmacology, the British Neuroscience Association, and the European Brain Council. He certainly can compete with Sheldon Cooper, Amy Farrah Fowler, and Richard Haier in the world's smartest person category. He also seems an affable man, kind of an older Ricky Gervais with a mustache. By his physical stature, I'd guess he's also a sugar addict. You can see him make his case on *YouTube* – go to http://www.youtube.com/watch?v=2TookjqAqF4.

His name probably doesn't help his cause. But it is certainly is memorable.

The British medical journal *Lancet* is one of the most respected in the world. Recently it ran a nasty little war of words regarding Nutt's work under the title "Nutt Damage." First the note by his critic, medical journalist William Cullerne Bown:

> In October, 2009, David Nutt was sacked as chair of the UK's Advisory Council on the Misuse of Drugs (ACMD). The central issue was Prime Minister Gordon Brown's decision to upgrade cannabis to a class B drug in the face of contrary advice from the ACMD, and Nutt's public resistance to that move. Nutt is entitled to dispute Brown's decision, but he should be precise about the grounds on which he does so. Framing the issue as "government *vs* science" is misleading.
>
> The question of the classification of drugs is not one on which science has provided a verdict. Nutt, in his paper in 2007, rated drugs on nine categories of harm and reported agreement among experts on the scores in each category. But that still leaves open the questions of what the categories should be and what weightings should be given to them. Why give "intensity of pleasure" the same weight as "other social harm"?
>
> The upshot is that there is no "scientific" answer to this ranking question. Consequently, the broader question of classification, with all its social and political dimensions, also cannot have an answer provided by science. In reality, the dispute over cannabis crystallises a

broader dispute over whether to rely on policing or, as Nutt wants, public-health strategy in drugs policy.

Nutt has overstated what the science tells us and other scientists have not stepped up to clarify the position. Consequently, science itself has become a passive accomplice in Nutt's campaign, undermining the integrity of science and the goal of evidence-based policy.

I declare that I have no conflicts of interest. [1]

Adjacent in the February 27, 2010 issue is Nutt's reply:

Presumably William Cullerne Bown agrees that harm-based drug ranking for the determination of punishments is, in a just society, both desirable and necessary. The Misuse of Drugs Act 1971 requires such a system, but has never explicitly defined how ranking should be done—hence the unsatisfactory and, in places, arbitrary state of the current classification system.

Our attempts at improved ranking used a systematic and transparent analysis based on nine parameters of harm derived from knowledge of addiction and rated by many of the UK's top experts in the field by use of a Delphic process. We pointed out in our paper that the lack of weightings was a weakness that could be rectified. Fortunately, over the past year, with support from the Home Office and Medical Research Council, the Advisory Council on the Misuse of Drugs (ACMD) undertook a more sophisticated approach using multicriteria decision-making. From first principles we derived 16 independent parameters of harm and weighted each. The report was in the process of being finalised just before the ACMD went into meltdown, but I can safely say that the conclusions of this analysis strongly support the arguments for which I was sacked. Certainly they make the harms of alcohol even more stark and hopefully they will soon be made public.

The repeated claims by Gordon Brown's government that it had scientific evidence that trumped that of the ACMD and the

---

1 William Cullenre Bown, "Nutt Damage," *The Lancet* 375(9716), February 27, 2010, pages 723-4.

acknowledgment that it was only interested in scientific evidence that supported its political aims was a cynical misuse of scientific evidence that breached the principles of the 1971 Act and was insulting to Council.

Since my sacking and the resignation of five members (all scientists), the council is now fatally depleted in scientific expertise. Given that the subsequent Drayson report and the Home Secretary's answer to a parliamentary question both affirm the current government position that chief scientific advisers can be sacked at the will of ministers, I doubt whether the ACMD will be able to recruit adequate scientific expertise to replace that it has lost.

For these reasons we are setting up an Independent Scientific Committee on Drugs that will comprise most of the ACMD scientists and another dozen or so leading scientific experts. This group will provide a truly independent and authoritative voice of science in relation to drug harms for the benefit of the public, the media, and other scientists. Perhaps the government will also take our outputs as *the best available scientific evidence* [my italics], so the ACMD can then focus on sentencing and treatment guidelines, education, and drug policy.[1]

Nutt reminds me of my own colleague, Connie Pechmann. Like her, he received a medal for his valor under fire – the 2013 John Maddox Prize "for promoting sound science and evidence on a matter of public interest, whilst facing difficulty or hostility in doing so."

This little argument is pertinent, as you will recall that I used his 2007 ranking (I called it the Harm Scale, avoiding using his name) in the last chapter. In Chapter 7 I presented a summary of his 2010 improved version which I will now call Nutt's Scale for short. Please see Exhibit 7.1 on page 148.

I respect the science behind it and its usefulness. It is quite a bit more systematic than a bunch of politicians sitting around guessing about harms. And, of course, this controversy is all reminiscent of tricky Dick Nixon's manipulation of the Shafer Commission's Report in 1972. Nixon, certainly one of the

---

1 David Nutt, "Nutt Damage – Author's Reply," *The Lancet* 375(9716), February 27, 2010, page 724.

biggest liars in history about all things, including marijuana, is well emulated by Prime Minister Brown some four decades later. I must also point out that in the United States circa 2016, the DEA has made the same bad choice as Gordon Brown. The agency is refused to reclassify marijuana as a Schedule II drug. Eight US legislators had requested the change from Schedule I to II.

On Nutt's Scale (2010) alcohol is the worst, mainly for the awful consequences its consumption burdens the British. For the UK heroin, crack cocaine, and methamphetamine are almost equally the worst for users. Nutt's argument in *The Lancet* exchange is basically that this best harm metric (that is, measure of consequences) should be used to make policy decisions about controlling the marketing and consumption of psychoactive substances. And as Richard Haier would predict, Nutt's work raises more questions.

For example, can we apply his analysis here in the United States? Also in the *Lancet*, another of Nutt's critics says no: "Comparison with studies published in the USA and the Netherlands is difficult because, by Nutt and colleagues' own admission, different availability and legal status of drugs in these countries influences their harmful effects."[1] As listed in Exhibit 7.3, the alcohol consumption rate in the UK is 13.4 liters per capita per year and only 9.4 in the United States. You would expect the harm to others by alcohol consumption in the US would be less prominently bad. Of course, it's still a disaster here, so imagine what things are like in the UK.

The big advantage of having Nutt's work available is the listing of his sixteen different consequences. And we will order the discussion in the rest of this chapter accordingly. I should also repeat that his listing of drugs ignores the biggest killer in this country, sugar, to which both he and I are apparently addicted.

I also note that Dr. Nutt is currently working with other scientists at Imperial College London to produce an alcohol substitute. They are crafting a benzodiazepine derivative that yields the same relaxation effect as alcohol but avoids physical addiction, loss of responsibility, and other toxic effects like liver damage. Interesting alchemy.[2]

---

1 Maria Viskaduraki and Diamanto Mamuneas, "Drugs and Harm to Society," *The Lancet* 377(9765), February 12, 2011, pages 553-554.
2 "Can David Nutt Wean Us off The Demon Drink with His Alcohol Substitute?" *The Guardian*, February 27, 2014, online.

Premature Death and the Associated Illnesses

The US Centers for Disease Control (CDC) collects data from death certificates of Americans. These are summarized in Exhibit 12.1 below. Of the 2.5 million people who died in 2011 (the last year for which data are available) the consumption of hedonic molecules are potentially involved in about 75 percent of them.

Exhibit 12.1
Causes of Death in the United States and
Related Consumption of Psychoactive Substances

CDC Cause	Number (%)*	Psychoactive Substances Implicated
Cardiovascular disease	778,503 (31.1%)	sugar, alcohol, tobacco, salt, stimulants, inhalants
Cancers	575,313 (23.0%) ↑	tobacco
Chronic lower respiratory diseases	143,382 (5.7%) ↑	tobacco, crack cocaine
Accidents	122,777 (4.9%) ↑	alcohol, all intoxicants
Diabetes	73,282 (2.9%) ↑	sugar, alcohol
Renal failure (kidney disease)	43,682 (1.7%)	sugar, alcohol, tobacco, salt, cocaine
Suicide	38,285 (1.5%)	alcohol, depressants
Homicide	19,766 (0.8%)	alcohol, illicit drugs
Alcoholic liver disease (cirrhosis)	16,634 (0.7%) ↑	alcohol
Hepatitis and HIV	15,422 (0.6%)	injection of illicit drugs

already included in categories above

Drug induced deaths	40,239 (1.6%) ↑	depressants (except alcohol)
Injury by firearms	32,163 (1.3%) ↑	alcohol, illicit drugs
Alcohol induced deaths	26,256 (1.1%)	alcohol

↑ = increased over the previous year on a per capita basis

Source: U.S. Center for Disease Control, 2011 is the most recent year available

While both stimulants and inhalants can both cause cardiac arrest in overdose, most of the damage done is from chronic over consumption of licit hedonic molecules – sugar (which causes obesity), alcohol, tobacco, and salt.

Tobacco is the dominant risk factor in cancers and respiratory diseases.

The huge numbers of accidents represent three main categories: auto accidents at 35,000 per year (~33 percent involve drunk driving); falls at about

26,000 per year; and poisoning (~90 percent are drug overdoses). Of the 40,239 drug induced deaths, more than half are related to licit pharmaceuticals – primarily opioids and benzodiazepines (the latter are the "safer" synthetic barbiturates).

The over consumption of sugar causes obesity, metabolic syndrome, and in turn both diabetes, cardio vascular disease, and renal failure.

The US Justice Department estimates the 40 percent of homicides involve drinking and about 5 percent are drug related.

The CDC estimates that in about 20 percent of US suicides, drug and/ or alcohol are used. For 2011 that would amount to almost 2000 Americans. Firearms are used in 50 percent of suicides, and hanging and other methods account for the rest. In 79 percent of the drug related suicides, prescription drugs are used – opioids or benzodiazepines.

The CDC estimates that some one million Americans use injection methods for imbibing hedonic substances. About one half of new HIV infections in the United States are among injection drug users (IDUs). With hepatitis, 90 percent of injection drug users are infected.

When It Rains It Pours – Addiction

The vast majority of the deaths listed in Exhibit 12.1 are due to chronic abuse of the psychoactive substances. Yes, there were 66,495 deaths directly related to overdoses and another 9,865 deaths from drunk driving. And many other lethal accidents involved intoxication of one sort or another. But, these are tiny numbers compared to the millions who will die early deaths because of their hedonic molecule addictions. Indeed, I will be one of those data unless I curtail my own sugar intake dramatically.

The signs of addiction are quite clear. Leslie Iverson[1] and his colleagues describe six hallmarks of the downward spiral toward distress based on the World Health Organization (WHO)[2] guidelines:

---

1   Leslie Iversen, Susan D. Iversen, Floyd E. Bloom, and Robert H. Roth, *Introduction to Neuropsychopharmacology*, (Oxford: Oxford University Press, 2009).

2   The Tenth Revision of the International Classification of Diseases and Health Problems (ICD-10), see http://www.who.int/substance_abuse/terminology/definition1/en/.

1. Tolerance – successively larger doses are needed to duplicate effects
2. Withdrawal – physiological distress when doses are eliminated or reduced, use of alternative substances to reduce this distress
3. Uncontrolled use in terms of onset termination or levels of use
4. Neglect of alternative sources of pleasure or interest, or an increase in time spent to obtain, use, or recover from the effects of use
5. Continued use despite clear signs of physical or psychological damage
6. Compulsion to use the substance

The WHO suggests a clinical diagnosis of dependency if three or more of these symptoms are experienced in one year.

The best measure we can find of dependency is the 2007 ranking developed by David Nutt and his colleagues. See the scores for dependency below in Exhibit 12.2. We would expect the values to be relatively universal as they represent the relationships between people and substances, without respect to societal differences.

Exhibit 12.2
The Relative Dependency Power of Twenty Drugs

Hedonic Molecule	Mean	Pleasure	Psychological Dependence	Physiological Dependence
Heroin	100	100	100	100
Cocaine	77	100	93	43
Tobacco	74	77	86	60
Street methadone	69	60	74	74
Barbiturates	67	67	73	60
Alcohol	64	74	63	53
Benzodiazepine	61	53	70	60
Amphetamine	58	67	63	37
Buprenorphine	55	67	50	50
Cannabis	53	63	57	27
Ketamine	51	63	57	33
4-MTA	43	33	57	27
Methylphenidate	42	47	43	33
LSD	41	73	37	10
GHB	39	47	37	37
Ecstasy	38	50	40	23
Khat	35	53	40	10
Solvents	34	57	40	3
Anabolic steroids	29	33	27	27
Alkyl nitrite	29	53	23	10

Source: David Nutt, Leslie A. King, William Saulsbury, and Colin Blackmore, "Development of a Rational Scale to Assess the Harm of Drugs," Health Policy, 369, March 24, 2007, pages 1047-1053, see Lancet.com. All the scores from Nutt's original 0-3 ranking were converted to a 0-100 point scale, 100 = most harmful on the dependency dimensions

In Exhibit 9.3 I reported the finding of a US Institute of Medicine study using self-report and archival data (very different methods from Nutt and colleagues' studies). The percentage of those who had tried the following substances and became dependent on them are: Tobacco 32 percent, heroin 23 percent, cocaine 17 percent, alcohol 15 percent, anti-anxiety drugs (stimulants) 9 percent, and marijuana 9 percent. The order between the two studies is relatively consistent indicating the validity of both studies.

So the most addictive drugs are heroin, cocaine (particularly crack cocaine), and tobacco. Two molecules that are advertised in the mass media around the world are tobacco at #3 and alcohol #6. And the most harmful and addictive molecule of all – sugar – isn't considered in any of these studies.

The Nutt et al. 2010 analysis considers three other sorts of harms to individuals: impairment of mental functioning, loss of tangibles (property, income, and so on), and loss of relationships. Crack cocaine, LSD, and mushrooms are the standouts when it comes to impairment of mental functioning. When it comes to losses of both tangibles and relationships, heroine, crack cocaine, and methamphetamine are the most damaging.

Finally, the Nutt et al. 2010 analysis includes the lack of purity as a dangerous quality of illicit drugs. This is of course almost impossible to study. We did get a glimpse of this problem with respect to ecstasy purity in the previous chapter. I had to laugh when I saw a potential TV advertisement for licit marijuana that asked hypothetically, "Would you buy sushi from a street vendor?" But this is really no laughing matter. Given the incredible array of substances that have been used in cutting illicit drugs, the harms in the forms of overdose and poisoning can only be imagined.

Harms to Society

The 2010 Nutt et al. accounting includes seven dimensions of societal harm: injury, crime, environmental damage, family adversities, international damage, economic cost, and community harms. The top three substances that dominate the societal harm scores are alcohol, heroin, and crack cocaine. The researchers clearly list the lack of data and necessary judgment calls in assessing these latter harm scores. But I cannot find any systematic studies that disagree with the prominence of harm by alcohol, heroin, and crack cocaine.

One important measure of harm to US society is the cost to the medical system in terms of emergency department visits associated with the various drugs. See Exhibit 12.3 below:

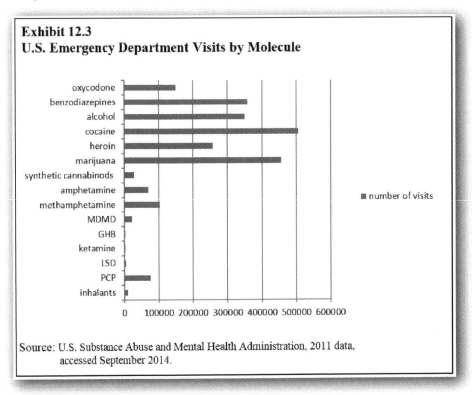

Exhibit 12.3
U.S. Emergency Department Visits by Molecule

Source: U.S. Substance Abuse and Mental Health Administration, 2011 data, accessed September 2014.

Of the 2.5 million total ED visits, 56 percent involved more than one substance. Mixing in not a good idea. You will also notice the prominence of the prescription drugs and alcohol at the top.

Harm and the Interactions among Consumption across Substances

Here the data are very fuzzy indeed. Mostly I will list the anecdotal evidence about such problems that I have found in the literature.

The Consequences of Consumption: A Summary

Perhaps the best known of these is the idea that marijuana is a gateway drug for cocaine, heroin, and so on While the folks at the *New York Times* don't see this as a problem (see Chapter 9, page 9-11), others do. Another author suggests that ambiguity of the term "gateway drug" helps the myth persist despite the preponderance of evidence against the effect. We do know that product lines often include marijuana and harder drugs. For example, the product line of our Marketing Miscreant from the previous chapter, Cornelis "SuperTrips" Slomp, included MDMA, cocaine, benzodiazepine, amphetamine, LSD, and cannabis. Thus, a correlation is evident from dealers selling across their product lines to single buyers. But, correlation is not causation. A more parsimonious theory suggests that people vary in the liability to consume addictive products.[1] Thus, we see some folks shopping across the product lines, and this produces the commonly observed correlation. Indeed, an interesting test for this mild controversy is happening in Colorado and Washington at the moment. If sales of other harder drugs decline in the face of licit marijuana sales, then the "gateway" theory loses what is left of its very limited credence.

Experts are suggesting that as the DEA and other authorities have cracked down on prescription opioid availability and abuse, users have begun to increasingly favor heroin as a substitute.[2] In many cases the prices are lower. For example, the street price for one oxycodone pill is about $29 and a comparable hit of heroin (about 100 mg) is about $10. Another recent study has identified opioid abusers switching to medical marijuana in a similar manner.

Many others have commented on the substitution effects among various drugs. Indeed, it is quite clear that enforcement efforts are spurring the alchemy efforts globally. Synthetic cannabinoids are substituting for cannabis in the United States, for example. Meth labs are even popping up in Afghanistan.

Perhaps the most interesting study in this area appeared last year in the *Journal of Law and Economics*. Researchers[3] found that in the states where

---

1   Michael M. Vanyukov, et al., "Common Liability to Addiction and "Gateway Hypothesis:" Theoretical, Empirical, and Evolution Perspective," *Drug Alcohol Dependency*, 2012, 123 (Suppl 1), pages s13-17.

2   Peter Weber, "Why is Heroin So Cheap?" *The Week*, February 4, 2014, online.

3   D. Mark Anderson, Benjamin Hansen, Daniel I Rees, "Medical Marijuana Laws, Traffic Fatalities, and Alcohol Consumption," *Journal of Law and Economics*, 56(2), May 2013, pages 333-369.

medical marijuana is allowed, traffic fatalities have fallen. In particular, they report that in the first full year after medical marijuana was allowed, traffic fatalities fell by 8-11 percent. Legalization is also associated with declines of both marijuana prices and alcohol consumption. They do, however, caution that their study says nothing about the relative safety of driving under the influence of marijuana. Of course, the study does raise more questions and begs more definitive studies. For example, how do government controls on one substance cause unintended harm related to potential substitutes?

Finally, there is an important debate going on about the legalization of marijuana in the United States and its impact on the efficacy of Mexican cartels and violence. I keep reading articles about falling murder rates around the United States, and almost always the causes suggested are more effective policing. But, then we have the Rand and UCLA reports mentioned in Chapter 9 suggesting the decline in violence is more a result of legalizing marijuana. Which is correct? The law enforcement folks refuse to even talk about the benefits of legalization, much less support systematic studies. Fortunately, we should learn shortly as the Washington and Colorado experiments proceed.

The Incarceration Complex

As Dwight Eisenhower left the Oval Office in 1961, he warned, "In the councils of government, we must guard against the acquisition of unwarranted influence, whether sought or unsought, by the military–industrial complex." As a nation, we have pretty much ignored his wise words, and we continue to spend more on our military than most of the rest of the world put together.

Not only are we trying to manage international relations through coercion, we are doing the same thing at home. Law enforcement is really not interested in Americans' freedom, just its control. Thus, we have the highest incarceration rate in the world. Half of federal prisoners and 17 percent of the prisoners of the states are serving time for drug offenses. We have more than 2,500 prisoners serving life sentences for non-violent drug crimes.

Many argue this incarceration complex began in early in the last century, when drugs became a criminal problem rather than a medical one. Others blame the 1964 riots in Harlem that ushered in crime-fighter, Richard "I am not a crook" Nixon. But, really the cause is less important than potential solutions.

There is also a much greater cost than dollars to this pathogen of policy. When it comes to drug-law enforcement, the system is fundamentally unjust. How can it be that racism is deeply imbedded in American society's views about relative harm and federal and state sentencing guidelines? How can it be that George Jung and Cornelis Slomp were sent to jail, but not the greedy miscreants at Purdue Pharma who duped the American public about the dangers of OxyContin, Michael Friedman, Howard Udell, and Paul Goldenheim? And government policy is also perverted by fear mongering politicians who are very willing to ignore evidence and even lie, for the sake of scared law-and-order votes and campaign contributions from law enforcement and prison guard unions. And, as the *Economist* bluntly puts it, "American prisons are full of old men, many of whom are well past their criminal years, and non-violent drug users, who would be better off in treatment."[1]

August Vollmer was chief of police in both Berkeley, CA and Los Angeles. He was the founder of the University of California School of Criminology. In his 1936 book on the topic he wrote:

> Stringent laws, spectacular police drives, vigorous prosecution, and imprisonment of addicts and peddlers have proved not only useless and enormously expensive as means of correcting this evil, but they are also unjustifiably and unbelievably cruel in their application to the unfortunate drug victims. Repression has driven this vice underground and produced the narcotic smugglers and supply agents, who have grown wealthy out of this evil practice and who, by devious methods, have stimulated traffic in drugs. Finally, and not the least of the evils associated with repression, the helpless addict has been forced to resort to crime in order to get money for the drug which is absolutely indispensable for his comfortable existence.

---

1 *Economist*, July 20, 2013, page 9.

The first step in any plan to alleviate this dreadful affliction should be the establishment of Federal control and dispensation – at cost – of habit-forming drugs. With the profit motive gone, no effort would be made to encourage its use by private dispensers of narcotics, and the drug peddler would disappear. New addicts would be speedily discovered and through early treatment, some of these unfortunate victims might be saved from becoming hopelessly incurable.

Drug addiction, like prostitution, and like liquor, is not a police problem; it never has been, and never can be solved by policemen. It is first and last a medical problem, and if there is a solution it will be discovered not by policemen, but by scientific and competently trained medical experts whose sole objective will be the reduction and possible eradication of this devastating appetite. There should be intelligent treatment of the incurables in outpatient clinics, hospitalization of those not too far gone to respond to therapeutic measures, and application of the prophylactic principles which medicine applies to all scourges of mankind.[1]

Vollmer's prescience is astonishing.

A Welcome Tipping Point. The good news is that sometime during the hot summer of 2015 we seem to have hit a tipping point in this madness in our legal system. Simultaneously at the federal level[2] and in some states such as California[3] we see a bipartisan push to relax sentencing laws and a growing movement toward granting clemency. The excellent recent news from California is that felony arrest rates dropped precipitously by 28.5 percent in 2015, primarily due to Proposition 47 mandated lower penalties for minor drug offenses. The Richard Nixon coercion approach to the drug problem has finally begun to wane. But *not fast enough* for those still serving time for bad laws.

---

1   August Vollmer, *The Police and Modern Society: Plain Talk Based on Practical Experience* (Berkeley, CA: University of California Press, 1936), page 118.

2   Jennifer Steinhauer, "Bipartisan Push Builds to Relax Sentencing Laws," *New York Times*, July 29, 2015, page A1,12.

3   Editorial, "California Leads on Justice Reform," *New York Times*, October 30, 2014.

Lawlessness and Distrust of Authority

In chapter 9 on cannabis, we already discussed this issue. When a teenager hears the DEA say that LSD can kill you, and when there is no documented case of a LSD overdose, distrust of government authority is inevitable. David Nutt comments on this consequence of drug-policy making by misinformation:

> The general public, especially the younger generation, are disillusioned with the lack of balanced political debate about drugs. This lack of rational debate can undermine the trust in government in relation to drug misuse and thereby undermining the government's message in public information campaigns. The media in general seem to have an interest in scare stories about illicit drugs, though there are some exceptions. A telling review of 10-year media reporting of drug deaths in Scotland illustrates the distorted media perspective very well. During this decade, the likelihood of a newspaper reporting a death from paracetamol was 1 per 250 deaths, for diazepam it was 1 in 50, whereas for amphetamine it was 1 in 3 and for ecstasy every associated death was reported.[1]

Actually the best part of his article is not the actual quote, but instead its context. Nutt compares the risks of "equasy," an addiction to horseback riding, with ecstasy. He reports that horseback riding in the UK delivers "acute harm to person" once for every 350 riding episodes, while ecstasy once every 10,000 episodes. Yet there are no restrictions on horseback riding in the UK. Nutt's entire article is included online – see www.Spiced.World/appendix. It will indeed be quite interesting to see how the government, the NFL PR armies, and the press handle an *estimated brain-damage rate of 33 percent* among National Football League retirees compared to the regulation of many of the psychoactive substances addressed in this book.

---

1 David J. Nutt, "Equasy – An Overlooked Addiction with Implications for the Current Debate on Drug Harms," *Journal of Psychopharmacology*, 23(1), 2009, pages 3-5.

The Bottom Line

We close this chapter with a cold economic analysis of hedonic consumption. Please see Exhibit 12.4 for details:

Exhibit 12.4
Annual U.S. Consumption of Psychoactive Substances ($) and Harm ($)

Molecule	Retail Revenues	Economic Costs of Harm
Salt	$3.5 billion	$26 billion
Sugar	$41 billion	$1 trillion
Chocolate	$30 billion	--
Caffeine	$46 billion	unknown
Tobacco	$112 billion	$300 billion
Alcohol	$170 billion	$279 billion
Prescription Opioids	$8.3 billion	$250 billion
Opiates	$12 billion	part of $193 billion
Marijuana	$285 billion	part of $193 billion
Cocaine	$43 billion	part of $193 billion

The total annual cost of our consumption of psychoactive substances is about $2.8 trillion. That's trillion with a *T*. Obviously all these estimates are flawed, but they represent the best evidence we have. Moreover, I cannot find estimates of the costs of the harm associated with caffeine consumption.

To provide some context on these numbers you might consider:

- The gross domestic product of the United States in 2015 was $17.9 trillion
- The GDP for China was $10.9 trillion
- US military expenditures in 2015 were $595 billion
- World military expenditures were $1.7 trillion, Chinese $215 billion, and Russian $66 billion in 2015
- US expenditures on education (public and private) in 2015 were $1.0 trillion

We Americans must be having a good time. Using this calculus we are spending 16 percent of our income on partying. Of course, the expenditures listed in the right-hand column above suggest we're spending more on the hangover than the actual party. At the end of Chapter 1 I asked which of the chemicals was worst for the public health. Unequivocally the answer is $C_{12}H_{22}O_{11.}$ Sugar, particularly the refined stuff big companies and restaurants add to our food, kills the most Americans and is the only psychoactive substance that causes more than a trillion dollar problem. Sugar costs us more every year than our kids' educations. We spend more cleaning up the sugar mess than we do on our military. We spend almost as much money buying alcohol as the Chinese do on missiles and troops. We spend more buying cigarettes than the Russians spend on tanks and satellites.

How can this be? And there is no metric or calculus for the dollar costs of lost years and wasted lives.

Thirteen

IDEAS FROM FOREIGN COUNTRIES

*We have smart people here at Philips, but
we don't have all the smart people.*

I've had the good fortune to travel the world as part of my international
business research, student programs, and consulting. In 2007 I visited one
of the centers of world innovation, the square mile General Motors Research
and Development Center in Warren, Michigan. In the latter half of the last
century, the place was filled to the brim with some of the brightest engineers
in the United States. On a cold spring day I was given a tour. Many of the
buildings were empty, and all the buildings looked shabby inside and out. The
company seemed out of new ideas, and within the year it was almost out of
money.

Even during its heyday, GM was missing out. Indeed, while GM was
hawking the "unsafe at any speed" Chevy Corvair that Ralph Nader railed, the
single most important safety feature ever was developed at Volvo in Sweden
in 1959. A thirty-nine-year-old Swedish mechanical engineer named Nils Ivar
Bohlin invented the three-point seat belt. It's the one we all buckle up every
time we get into a car, even now more than fifty years later. He applied some of
the ideas from designing ejection seats for military jets at SAAB. After making

it standard equipment in Volvos, the company then opened the patent for all to use in the interests of safety.

Over the years I took students on international business residential courses to China, Russia, Brazil, Vietnam, and the European Union. One of my favorite visits was to Aachen, Germany where the Dutch company Philips has a major R&D Center. It was not shabby. At the time they were developing systems (smart clothes, telemetry, and so on) to manage cardiovascular disease. Germany was a good place to do that because the German diet is a heart attack waiting to happen. That's where I heard the words in the epigraph above, from the Dutch Director of the Center. His point? "At Philips we have always collaborated with others around the world not only in our product development, but also our marketing efforts." Both he and Nils Bohlin had the small-country advantage. It never occurred to them that they knew everything.

I can tell you that at GM in the roaring sixties, they thought they knew everything. Now, not so much. My point? Americans are incredibly ethnocentric. We suffer from the big-country *disadvantage*. But, people in other countries have good ideas. We should pay attention. Not only are experiments targeting reductions in consumption of psychoactive substance going on in our states around the country, but also new ideas are being tested in countries around the world. We should pay attention (yes, I said it twice on purpose). Let's start with salt. Then we'll take a look at sugar and so on. In the last section of this chapter we will visit the ongoing calamity that is Mexico, and that is in large part caused by our devilish demand for hedonic molecules.

Finland – Reductions in Salt Consumption

Too much salt was killing people in Finland in the 1970s, and they knew it. If you think we have a salt problem in this country, try Finland. At the moment the average consumption for an American adult is about 3.4 grams per day, much too high according to all medical authorities. In 1977 in Finland the average adult consumed about twelve grams. Yikes! And they could see the consequences in their hospitals and funeral parlors. The Finns were dying like flies from stroke and coronary heart disease (CHD). Since they undertook a focused long-term effort to reduce salt intake, the average adult consumption rate has fallen steadily to about 7 grams. Over 30 years that's about a 40 percent improvement. This is a remarkable achievement that has yielded major improvements in health outcomes: 10 mmHg declines in blood pressure, 75-80 percent reductions in stroke and CHD mortality, and a five to six year increase in life expectancy. How'd they do it?

First, they started with a small experiment. About 5.5 million people live in Finland. The salt reduction project was initiated in the 1970s in the province of North Karelia, with a population of about 175,000. The approach was two pronged – education via the mass media and garnering the cooperation of food producers. As they saw things working in North Karelia, they rolled out the program nationally with even greater effect.

Key has been the reporting about salt's dangers and more healthful alternatives in the *Helsingin Sanomat,* the most popular newspaper in the Nordic countries, and the most influential medium in Finland. The television networks, radio stations, and local papers picked up many of their stories about salt.

In part spurred by this reporting, the Finnish government and health authorities targeted a 5 gram consumption rate over the then 10 gram rate. The legislature also passed a comprehensive salt labeling law in 1993. Foods that were traditionally large contributors of salt to the Finnish diet (bread, sausages, cheese, butter, and breakfast cereal) were required to post warning labels on packaging. The food companies responded to the labeling requirement by lowering salt content – by 20 percent in breads and 10 percent in sausages, for example.

Since the 1980s food companies in Finland (both foreign and domestic) have also replaced common salt with sodium-reduced options, potassium- and magnesium-enriched mineral salt. Even McDonald's hamburgers (no Carl's Jr. there!) display a "Pansalt" logo signifying having met national standards for salt content. Since 2000 specific salt reduction criteria for each food type was also been set by the Finnish Heart Association for the use of their "Better Choice" label.[1]

---

1 Information for this section was gleaned from www.worldactiononsalt.com, www.medscape.com/features/slideshow/salt, and Pirjo Pietinen, "Finland's Experiences in Salt Reduction," a presentation in Brussels, October 21, 2009.

The key lessons from the Finnish example are several. First, start with a small experiment. Success is yielded in the long term and via a long-term, sustained effort. Government, media, and companies must cooperate. Consumer education is key.

Hungary – An Experiment in Sugar Consumption Reduction

The *dobostorta* cake, a five-layer vanilla and chocolate buttercream dessert with a caramel-glazed top layer [yum], is probably Hungary's best-known treat – at least after goulash. The cake can be seen in the vitrines of coffee houses and bakery shops lining the streets of Budapest.

"Hungarians are really into desserts," said Carolyn Banfalvi, co-founder of Taste Hungary. On the topic of fatty foods, she added, "What they call bacon here is often pieces of pure lard."[1]

I gained a pound just reading this. How ironic that in Hungary they've instituted a government so-called "fat tax." And there is fat in Hungary. The *dobostorta* cakes and so on have delivered an obesity rate of 18.8 percent, three points higher than the European Union average, and that compared to 13.6 percent for Germany and 7.9 percent for Romania (the EU low). Hungary also has the highest salt consumption rate in the EU. And, life expectancies are four to five years shorter in Hungary compared to the EU average.

Beginning in September 2011 Hungarians started paying a 10-*forint* (about 5¢) tax on foods with high fat, sugar, salt, and caffeine content, and increased taxes on soda and alcohol. The anticipated $90 million in revenues was to go toward state health care costs. The Prime Minister has said, "Those who live unhealthily have to contribute more." This is, of course, a controversial

---

1 Catherine Cheney, "Hungary Introduces 'Fat Tax,'" *Spiegel Online*, September 1, 2011, online.

fundamental philosophical issue. Indeed, Romania axed such a tax based on fears of further damaging the diets of its low income residents.

Three years out we can begin to get a glimpse of the consequences of the tax. The energy-drink companies have changed formulas in response, this consistent with the goals of the tax. These reformulations also resulted in decreased revenues of about $13 million but also decreases in caffeine consumption. Consumption of salty and sugary foods has declined, although the causality in the short run is hard to determine. Another possible explanation is the overall economic decline in Hungary.

Other European countries are experimenting as well. For example, Finland and France have instituted a soda tax. Perhaps the most useful example is that of Denmark's 2011 tax on saturated fats. Within the year the Danes rescinded the law. Most blame related political battles, food-industry complaints and lobbying, and a population that just shopped across the border in Germany. However, the health advocates in Denmark have been undeterred and have succeeded in beginning a smaller experiment, taxing butter. It's a little bit tougher to out-shop for a perishable. Maybe this one will stick.

I have been quite happy to see a 2014 report entitled "Sugar Reduction, Responding to the Challenge" published by Public Health England, the UK Department of Health. In the report they list potential strategies to reduce sugar consumption. I particularly appreciate the attention they allocate to education, regulation of advertising, and fiscal levers.

The Europeans are leading the way on these important issues, and I notice that often they compare their problems to the "fat" United States. Where obesity rates in the UK are about 23 percent, in the America we are at 35 percent. We need to pay attention to the progress of their experiments. We obviously don't know what we're doing.[1]

In both Mexico and Japan we can see strong evidence that higher prices for sugar yield lower consumption rates. A preliminary study conducted by the Mexican National Institute of Public Health in collaboration with researchers

---

[1] Other useful references for the sugar section: William Harless, "Taxes of Unhealthy Foods Gain Traction in Europe, *PBS News Hour*, June 7, 2012, online, www.pbs.org; and Suzanne Daley, "Hungary Tries a Dash of Taxes to Promote Healthier Eating Habits," *New York Times*, March 2, 2013, online.

at the University of North Carolina report that the 10 percent tax on sugared sodas resulted in a 6 percent drop in consumption in 2015. Japanese authorities report that a sugar-price spike in the early 1970s caused a steady decline in per capita consumption of 15 percent between 1973 and 2012.[1]

Finally, we have a strange bit of evidence that reducing sugar consumption will lead to better health. The Cuban economy collapsed in the first half of the 1990s, after the disintegration of the Soviet Union and their withdrawal of economic and energy subsidies. The country teetered on the brink of famine with average caloric intake dropping 40 percent to starvation levels. During those five miserable years of austerity the average Cuban lost twelve pounds with food being rationed and no fuel for autos and trucks. Also during those years, deaths from cardiovascular disease fell by a third and type-2 diabetes by half. More modest drops occurred in stroke and overall mortality rates. Later in the decade, when caloric intakes recovered, so did the previous weights and death rates.

Lithuania – Reductions in Caffeine Content

Kids and caffeine? In May 2014 Lithuania banned the sale of high-caffeine drinks such as Red Bull and Monster to minors. The American Medical Association recommends we do the same thing. A few years earlier the governments of Colombia and Latvia preceded Lithuania on banning the beverages for minors. Some expect the Lithuanian ban to have a substantial effect on overall sales. The European Food Safety Authority reported in 2013 the following prevalence of consumption rates by age group for Europeans: 3-10 years – 18 percent; 10-18 years – *68 percent;* and 18-65 years – 30 percent.

Other countries are trying to control caffeine consumption as well. Australia limits the amounts of caffeine in energy and soft drinks, as well as, labeling the drinks with the caffeine content and a warning to limit consumption to two cans per day. It is also interesting that the Australian authorities are looking at the risks involved in mixing high doses of caffeine with high doses

---

1 Takamasa Akiyama and Michael Corbin, "The Japanese Sugar Market," *Proceedings of the Fiji/ FAO 1997 Asia Pacific Sugar Conference*, online.

of sugar. Canadian regulations are fast headed in the direction of Australia's with respect to caffeine content labeling. South Africa also requires caffeine content on the label. France and Norway initially banned the drinks all together, but both have now relaxed those regulations.

Assuming the Colombians, Latvians, and Lithuanians keep their bans for minors in place, we should be able to discern their effectiveness in the long run. But the key lesson from Lithuania is that setting policies for youths different from adults is important. I will take up this theme in more detail in the next chapter.[1]

Australia – Prohibition of e-Cigarettes

We all know that prohibition doesn't work – right? The state of Western Australia is giving the concept another test by completely banning the tobacco product or delivery mode or whatever you want to call e-cigarettes. So far the retailers (neither bricks-and-mortar nor online) are getting the message. Also, possession is still legal, only selling in the state is prohibited. So residents can still make the long treks to neighboring states to make purchases.

Of course, e-cigarettes are following the path of burgeoning sales similar to energy drinks. Regulators around the world are trying to catch up. Most recently the European Parliament approved new rules that make e-cigarettes subject to the same regulations for other tobacco products: advertising is banned, child-proofing is required, safety warnings on labels, and a limit of 20 mgs of nicotine.

So far in the United States the Food and Drug Administration is still debating how to regulate the products here. Perhaps by 2016 we will see some clarification of policies and rules, but as of this writing, there are no rules to the game. More on this one in the next chapter as well.[2]

---

1 Useful references on caffeine and energy drinks was gleaned from: Sam Fritzell, "Lithuania Is Banning Red Bull for Some Reason," *Time*, May 16, 2014; Sabrina Bachai, "Lithuania Bans the Sale of Energy Drinks to Minors," *Medical Daily*, May 16, 2014, online; and *Food Regulation Policy Options Paper: The Regulation of Caffeine in Foods*, Australia and New Zealand Food Regulation Ministerial Council, The Food Ministry, August 2013.

2 Quite helpful in this section were articles by Alesiha Orr, "E-Cigarettes Message Goes up in Smoke," *WAToday.com.au*, June 26, 2014, online and Eliza Gray, "Europe Sets New Rules for E-Cigs While the US Drags Its Feet," *Time*, February 27, 2014, online.

I must also mention China, the biggest smoking problem in world history. Estimates are a hundred million will die from smoking this century. Little is done to curtail smoking – only half-hearted, lightly enforced bans on smoking in public places. The World Health Organization recommends several strategies, among them research on use, bans on all marketing and advertising, and the heavy weaponry of taxation. Heavy taxation has worked everywhere, in countries rich and poor, such as France and South Africa. Taxes have also been effective in the United States. China needs to pay attention. The semi-monopoly government tobacco company makes nice profits now. But at some point, those profits have to be balanced against the huge medical costs of the looming cancer epidemic.

The United Kingdom and Alcohol Consumption

"He (or, quite often, she) stands accused of turning the centers of British cities and towns into 'no-go areas' on Friday and Saturday nights as he vomits, fights and falls over, often at the same time."[1] I witnessed this nasty little ritual myself, on a train ride back from Stratford-upon-Avon after a very nice performance by Jeremy Irons in *A Winter's Dream*. The sad part is, even though the play was much better, the Oxford drunks were the more memorable.

Nobody knows more about the British binge drinker than the Brits themselves. They poke fun at themselves – "Britons drink as often as Mediterraneans and as much as Scandinavians." Yet, after more than 500 years of complaining, they're still experimenting with how to reduce consumption of the hellish hedonic molecule. They claim these complications:

Britain's battles with the bottle have always involved a heady mixture of anxieties about health, morality and social class. Britain's first licensing act, passed in 1552, made an early distinction between rich and poor boozers by enforcing strictures on "common alehouses" which did not apply to wine taverns. Elizabethan antis,

---

1 Charles Nevin, "Britain's Drinking Problem," *New York Times*, August 10, 2014, page 4 opinion.

in an early example of censorious scapegoating, were also minded to blame growing levels of public drunkenness on decadent foreign, or Catholic, influences. (Meanwhile, they also carefully maintained that Brits could outdrink any foreigner. "The great drinkings of foreign countries compared to ours are but sippings," wrote one 17th-century pamphleteer.)[1]

But the Brits never give up. So now two new ventures are on the table.

First is a price floor on alcohol, not a tax. The floor would serve to raise prices overall, but of course will affect the lower rungs of society more. Sounds like the five-hundred-year-old problem rearing its head again. Perhaps another reason the Scots are considering secession?

Second, the Brits are borrowing an idea from Lindsay Lohan – ankle bracelets. The Mayor of London has proposed tagging those committing minor crimes while under the influence toward barring (an interesting use of the term) them from drinking for 120 days. In America we refer to Lindsay's jewelry as Secure Continuous Remote Alcohol Monitoring (SCRAM) or sobriety tags. They're made by a company in Colorado. More interesting experiments to follow.

Some of the Canadian states have taxed alcohol, with positive effects on consumption, associated crime, and hospital admissions. The Russians, even bigger drinkers than the Brits, have recently tightened their alcoholic beverage advertising regulations: no more health claims, cartoons, Internet campaigns, or hard liquor (read vodka) ads in the mass media. In Mumbai they're starting to enforce outdated prohibition laws. The Chinese are often accused of being enigmatic – lowering alcohol taxes while strengthening drunk-driving penalties does seem a bit strange. Finally, alcohol consumption is prohibited in most Muslim countries – Iran, Libya, Pakistan, Saudi Arabia are examples. It is tolerated in others – Egypt, Lebanon, and Turkey. As governments change, the laws will become more volatile. But, there is no binge drinking in those lands.

---

1 Bagehot, "Their Cup Runneth Over," *Economist,* January 5, 2013, page 44.

Opium and Control in Afghanistan

If ever there was a marriage made in heaven, it's the meeting of the opium crop in Afghanistan and pain ridden and dying American baby boomers.[1] There are seventy-five million of us. The accelerating demand is easy to see coming. Now we just need legalization of the crop. Anybody working in hospice knows the truth of this. Yes, the abuse of illicit opiates and licit opioids is a huge problem worldwide. But prohibition has not and will not work. Legalization and then taking control of the flow of the drug can work if we're careful about it.

A little flashback is useful in the argument. Consider what the *Economist* had to say about opium in Afghanistan in 1997:

> The UNDCP has been trying to put a stop to Afghan heroin production for years, and saw the Taliban's rise to power as an opportunity. The deposed government of President Burhanuddin Rabbani had endorsed UN conventions forbidding production, but did not have enough control to enforce them. Taliban rule is strict. The UNDCP assumed that Islamic *sharia* law outlaws the production of drugs such as heroin. But *sharia* law relies on interpretation, and the UNDCP has had to enlist the help of Islamic scholars to make its case. The Taliban, however, insists that it alone has the authority to interpret the law—and so far it has made no clear ruling on heroin.[2]

If ever there was an understatement, it's "Taliban rule is strict." In the waning days of our war in Afghanistan, our own military used opium control as a strange justification for continuing our intrusion there, our longest war in history.

Afghanistan's production of opium virtually died in 2001 after substantial decreases under Taliban rule. With the presence of the American military, it remained volatile in the last decade. It peaked at over 7,000 tons in

---

1 I cannot take credit for this practical idea. I was attending a conference of peace scholars at the University of Notre Dame a few years back. One of the participants who had spent time on the ground in Afghanistan and worked in the healthcare aid area suggested the potential opportunity.

2 "Drug and Islamic Law," *Economist*, September 6, 1997, page 44.

2007, and has bounced around with production in 2013 at over 5,000 tons.[1] Production has boomed mostly in the south in places such as Helmand Province where the American military "helped out" by drilling water wells. Indeed, much of the water in those wells paid for by American tax dollars isn't sweet enough to drink, but is just right for irrigating opium fields.

The US Department of State described the situation on the ground circa 2012:

> The Government of the Islamic Republic of Afghanistan (GIRoA) generally relies on assistance from the international community to implement its counternarcotics strategy. Greater political will, increased institutional capacity, enhanced security, and more robust effort at all levels of government are required to decrease cultivation, combat trafficking, and respond to a burgeoning domestic addiction problem. Afghanistan is party to the 1988 UN Drug Convention.[2]

Judging by the increases in production coinciding with the American troop withdrawal, the State Department analysts were quite correct – "relies on assistance."

Finally, a dangerous side effect of heroin abuse is the spread of infectious diseases by the reuse of hypodermic needles. Governments in several countries around the world support needle-exchange programs. Switzerland and New Zealand are two pioneers in this area, but not the United States. We specifically ban federal support for such programs. This is a lethal policy mistake. The empirical certainty that needle exchanges cause lower morbidity is being traded off against a fanciful potential decline in addiction. Fortunately, in other countries, reason and experimentation prevail. In Melbourne, Australia, they have even considered syringe vending machines. The authorities there reason, "...syringe vending machines and 24-hour access to sterile injection

---

1 UNODC, *2014 World Drug Report.*

2 US Department of State, *International Narcotics Control Strategy Report (volume I)*, March 2012, page 91.

equipment could help clean up heroin hot spots."[1] Innovative marketing? A crazy idea? We will learn which, if we pay attention.

The Netherlands and Marijuana Consumption

I mentioned earlier my trips to Aachen, Germany with MBA students in tow. We always stayed in nearby Maastricht – that central city in the southern tip of the Netherlands let us travel easily among Brussels, Aachen, and Amsterdam. The Dutch have always been among the most innovative peoples in the world. Because their country is small, it must be cosmopolitan. They are constantly importing new ideas and keeping the good ones.

In 1990s' Amsterdam you could not only buy marijuana in local "coffee shops" – their name for an actual coffee shop is the French, "*café*" – you could even buy seeds in sidewalk flower markets. The laws prohibited such purchases, but the police ignored the bricks-and-mortar of places such as the Bull Dog. Tourists did not ignore them. On the menu at the Bull Dog, they include twenty different brands of cannabis from around the world, from Dutch Star to Purple Haze. Yes, I still have the picture I took two decades ago. I also have a pamphlet distributed on the street – a map of city center Amsterdam with the twenty-nine best coffee shops according to the Cannabis Retailers Association. Among them were Rookies, Sensi, Stones Café, and Big Fun.

In 2012 some Dutch provincial and local governments approved "weed pass" laws, which limited coffee shop entrance to Dutch citizens that had registered. Amsterdam did not adopt these restrictions and still draws huge numbers of tourists to its two hundred coffee shops. Their federal government has stayed out of the controversy for now.

This combination of public availability and liberal, blind-eye policing must have resulted in a very high cannabis consumption rate for the Dutch. Right? As you know from Chapter 9, page 212 that our American past-year

---

1 Birdie Byrne, "Drug Experts Propose Needle Vending Machines for Footscray," *Herald Sun*, May 28, 2013, online.

prevalence of use rate is 13.7 percent of adults, and for the Dutch it's 5.4 percent. Perhaps what they've been doing in the schools is more important than what they've been doing in their streets:

> The class, which teachers call "the confrontation," is part of the curriculum, and pupils can miss the trip to a police station cellblock only if they have a note from their parents.
>
> In six years with the project, police Sgt. Linda Van den Broek hasn't seen a child excused yet. As frightening as it may be to send a child to sit at a junkie's knee, Dutch parents are frightened enough of drugs to try anything, she said.
>
> About 5,000 of Amsterdam's schoolchildren visit the jailed addicts each year. They are encouraged to write letters to the junkies after the encounter or send them drawings to express their feelings.
>
> "The addict is not telling a story, and he is also not saying, 'Don't do it,' " Van den Broek said. "We give the children information, and they have to decide if they will do drugs or not. That's the key."[1]

Uruguay is another interesting case. In 2001 their seventy-three-year-old President advocated drug legalization. He served just one term, but he apparently planted a seed. In 2013 Jose Mujica, the current president proposed not only legalizing marijuan but also producing it as a government monopoly. In a tiny article in the *New York Times* the big story was broken regarding the details of the new laws in Uruguay:

> Uruguayan citizens and legal residents 18 or older may now register for licenses to cultivate up to six marijuana plants per household and harvest 480 grams a year, or join a marijuana growing club with 15 to 45 members and no more than 99 plants. Pharmacies are expected

---

1 Paul Watson, "Jail Doubles as Classroom in Fight against Drugs," *Los Angeles Times*, November 11, 1998, page B2.

to stock government-approved marijuana cigarettes for sale by year's end. Licensed buyers will be able to purchase up to 10 grams a week or 40 grams a month, at a cost starting at about 90 cents a gram, to be adjusted to compete with illegal marijuana.[1]

The odd thing about this is my *New York Times* just today ran a very nice "Travel Guide" article for visiting the tiny country.[2] Tourism must be up in Uruguay? For those of you considering traveling there to learn about how drug policy changes work, I'd say you ought to wait a couple of years.

Cocaine – Brazil, Russia, and China, Pay Attention!

The good global marketer will always look for new markets in the face of falling demand in traditional ones. Brazil, Russia, and China all appear to be such an opportunities for coke producers and traffickers. Use is rising in in all three countries. But the law makers there aren't paying attention to what's worked and what hasn't worked in other big countries, such as the United States. In late 2012 the Brazilians passed an anti-cocaine law that features double penalties for crack versus. powder. Perhaps now that the 2014 World Cup and 2016 Olympics have worked well, the Brazilians can make some reasoned (as opposed to panicked) decisions about drug regulation. Coercion-based crack downs are also being mounted in Russia, the Philippines, and China.

The current President of Bolivia is also suing for a change in strategy. Evo Morales who also leads a coca-growers' union, would like to see the leaf itself removed from the UN's banned substances list. Indeed, the constitution

---

1 "Uruguay: Government Sets Rules for Legal Sales of Marijuana," *New York Times*, May 7, 2014, page A9 (in a little tiny box).
2 Paola Singer, "In Uruguay, Bohemian-Chic at the Beach," *New York Times*, September 18, 2014, online.

passed in 2009 refers to coca as part of Bolivia's cultural heritage. He'd like to use as an ingredient in drinks and creams.

Singapore, Malaysia, India, and so on – The Death Penalty

About thirty nations around the world have a potential death penalty on their books for drug traffickers. Some even put it on their immigration forms, along with a hearty welcome. Here are three examples:

- India – TRAFFICKING IN NARCOTICS IS A SERIOUS OFFENCE AND IS PUNISHABLE WITH IMPRISONMENT OR EVEN A DEATH SENTENCE
- Malaysia – **BE FORWARNED DEATH FOR DRUG TRAFFICKERS UNDER MALAYSIAN LAW**
- Singapore – **WARNING DEATH FOR DRUG TRAFFICKERS UNDER SINGAPORE LAW**

All three used all caps on their form, and the last two used emboldened red. A friend from Singapore always refers to it as a "fine, fine country" because they fine you for everything. At one point they banned chewing gum because they didn't like seeing wads left on their very clean streets. And not only do they have it on their immigration cards in Singapore, they also deliver the death penalty message on billboards as you enter the immigration area of their wonderful international airport.

Judging by their low consumption rates, maybe the harsh penalties work. But as usual, the causality is hard to sort out, perhaps with strong cultural norms causing both the lower consumption rates and the signage? I can only wonder what they might have done with caffeine-laced chewing gum?

All jokes aside, sadly, I note that since 2011 five convicted Filipino drug traffickers have been executed in China. More recently seven foreigners were executed in Indonesia for the same crimes.

Mexico – The Calamity and a Remedy?

Unfortunately "death" makes a good segue here.

Poor Mexico, so far from God, so close to the United States.

So goes the old saw about Mexico's relationship with the United States. Books have been, are, and should be written about the continuing tragedy of awful drug war violence in Mexico. The odd thing is that we live in a world of peace. The percentage of people that die by violence in the world is at the lowest level in centuries, if not millennia.[1] And humans are nonviolent by nature – 99.9 percent of us have never killed a fellow human.

Yet during the last decade between 50,000 and 100,000 Mexican citizens have died in horribly violent ways. Estimates vary greatly. And this violence is spread to other parts of Central America. Thus, we see tens of thousands of Latin American youths fleeing north to the safe United States. Other reports list 27,000 as missing. Fifty-eight reporters, more than a thousand children, and over five-hundred US citizens have died.

But we Americans, safe here in *Estados Unidos,* are the greater part of Mexico's problem. We are the consumers over which the drug cartels fight their wars.

The cartels are the marketers. In many ways they operate like Apple or Nike. Someone else manufactures, and they manage the distribution of the products. The fighting is over distribution channels. But instead of low prices and good service, they fight with automatic weapons and terror.

Vicente Fox, Mexico's first opposition-party President, was elected in 2000 to a six-year term of office to change things ("*Cambio*"). He grew steadily dissatisfied with the old coercion of sending in the federal troops to quell the cartel violence.

He proposed legalizing everything *for users* – cocaine, heroin, LSD, marijuana, PCP, opium, synthetic opioids, mescaline, peyote, psilocybin mushrooms, amphetamines, and meth. The law allowed for substantial quantities

---

1   Steven Pinker, *The Better Angels of Our Nature: Why Violence Has Declined* (New York: Viking, 2011).

for personal use. At the time Colombia allowed personal use of marijuana, cocaine, and heroin, but not PCP and LSD. You already know what the Netherlands was doing. So Fox's list was revolutionary. The Mexican Congress passed the measure, and Fox of course, promised a signature. Then he had a conversation with George W. Bush and perhaps Dick Cheney and changed his mind. A few months later he left office, and the violence really began to accelerate as the Colombian cartels lost control to the Mexican ones.

Then, in 2009, after the Bush boys had left office, the new Mexican president, Felipe Calderon, signed off on an almost identical bill. Use was decriminalized, and government forces could focus on the cartels and the flow of illicit drugs through the country into the United States. The Obama administration has taken a wait-and-see attitude. The violence has escalated further.

A very rough measure of the effects of the Mexican relaxation of possession laws comes from the UNDOC annual prevalence of use for adults. The rising consumption rates appear to coincide with the change in the laws. Between 2008 to 2011 past-year consumption of opiates increased from 0.04 percent to 0.18 percent; cannabis 1.0 percent to 1.2 percent; and cocaine 0.4 percent to 0.5 percent. As we all should, the critics of the Mexican liberalization decry the increases.[1] But, causality is tough to assign. And, the consumption rates remain small compared to the United States where the comparable past-year consumption rates are opiates 0.6 percent, cannabis 13.7 percent, and cocaine 2.4 percent. And, of course, the benefits of this change in Mexican drug policies are hard to measure as the violence among traffickers there remains staggeringly high.

In 2010 Calderon publically opposed California's Prop. 19 to legalize marijuana. He complained it would damage his efforts at defeating the cartels. What an interesting dance. Of course, the California proposition failed, but similar laws have been approved in Washington, Colorado, Oregon, Alaska, and the District of Columbia. And medical marijuana is for sale in twenty-three states as well. And, certainly Mexico's 2006 legislation inspired legalization moves around the world. Indeed, legalization is on the proximate horizon

---

1 Laura Villagran, "As Mexico's Traffickers Ship Drugs North, The Leave Addicts in Their Wake," *Christian Science Monitor*, January 25, 2013, online.

in Canada, and most recently approved in California, Massachusetts, and Nevada.

At an Organization of American States (OAS) the presidents of Colombia, Guatemala, and Mexico argued for legalization. They agreed that eradication was impossible and only ending prohibition, not just decriminalization, would eliminate the profits from trafficking, and reduce the competition and violence. At the moment this a just one more quiet issue on President Obama's lame duck plate.

The new Mexican President, Enrique Pena Nieto, came into office in 2012 opposing legalizing the marijuana trade. But most recently he's expressed a willingness to engage the debate despite his personal misgivings. Pena has also said Mexico's policies must stay in step with the United States and prohibition has been a colossal failure. And, finally Vicente Fox is drumming up support for legalization around the continent, suggesting he himself would farm marijuana. The new legalization wave is building, oddly enough from the south.

Fourteen

My Prescriptions for Change

Coercion is so last century.

First a little philosophy, then I'll get to the action items. About fifty years ago I found myself sitting in a room with two of my favorite fraternity brothers. They were pissed. At each other. The topic was marijuana. One was quitting the house. I was able to muddle through that encounter and settle things down. That's also the purpose of this book. To settle things down.

In the last century millions have died around the world because of the same disagreement. Even before 1900 alcohol had been killing, through poisoning and violence, for millennia. There were salt riots and opium wars as well.

Now we live in an age of ubiquitous information. Truth, to the extent that we know it, is in your pocket, just a Google away. And in this age of reason we really don't need to fight anymore. We really don't need to coerce others. Evidence and negotiation are the keys to peaceful human interaction. Not the swords, bludgeons, and bombs of our fathers.

I say all this recognizing that rule of law is also essential for a peaceful society. We will always have police and prisons. But with reasoned laws, their numbers will be small. It also seems that we will always have wars in the

Middle East. But that's a subject for another book. And, even that business of barbarians will wind down sometime this century, under the weight of reason, markets, and negotiation.

Finally, laws and legal systems cannot solve all our problems. Our other institutions are more important. Schools, extended families, and neighbors must be depended upon. Religious organizations as well. The most prominent example is perhaps Mormon doctrine. It has been quite useful in reducing consumption of psychoactive substances. And it's not just the revelation given to Joseph Smith in 1833, in *Words of Wisdom*: "Strong drinks are not for the belly...." It's modern Mormon parents reading to their kids from a kind of religious comic-book beginning in early childhood. Of course, the parents' behavior is also imitated. The efficacy of their approach is readily evident in the Utah consumption statistics (the population is 58 percent Mormon). Yes, it takes a village.

In the paragraphs below I order my prescriptions using the perspective of a marketing manager, employing the *4 Ps* as guideposts. My prescriptions are broadly stated. I cannot provide details. They will have to be worked out through careful planning, innovative thinking, trial and error, political will, and inventive negotiations.

Marketing Research

Prescription 1 – Accelerate Investments in Marketing Research. Throughout the pages of this book we have run into questions without answers. Systematic research has yielded many useful, even surprising answers. For example, it is now quite clear that sugar is the most dangerous drug. But, we have no idea about the long-term consequences of marijuana consumption. We are beginning to learn about the societal costs of prescription pain medicines. But we know almost nothing about the long-term consequences of sugar substitutes. We need to continue the work of folks like Connie Pechmann so that we can fashion effective messages about hedonic molecules for mass-media advertising campaigns and classroom curricula, particularly for children.

Product

Prescription 2 – Freedom Will Yield Educated Consumers. Many of these molecules still have medicinal uses. But for most consumers, the attractive product attribute is the same – they entertain the brain. Their kind and level of titillation and their side effects do vary, but basically the purpose of their use is identical. From that extra $NaCl$ to LSD, they're all brain entertainment.

The two most dangerous molecules are sugar and alcohol. We are free to use and abuse them. They are advertised in the mass media. The companies that intrude into our daily lives with billions of dollars in advertising persuade and coerce us into craving them. Yes, advertising can be coercive when emotion-laden messages are repeated over and over again.

For the illicit drugs personal selling is out of control. So are the finances of the marketplace. Tremendous profits are extracted not only from the users, but also the greater society. Criminals compete with healthcare workers for the attention of consumers.

The current legal regime makes us all pay for the excesses of the abusers. Think date rape, drunk-driving accidents, diabetes insurance claims, and the DEA.

Legalization will allow problem cases to be treated by medical workers, rather than police investigators. Prohibition has not worked. We've tried it before, and we've been trying it for a long time. It doesn't work.

Legalization will also curtail the problems of product impurities that often have devastating effects.

On the issue of incremental changes – marijuana first, then so on – I prefer former Mexican President Vicente Fox's "big bang" approach discussed at the end of the last chapter. We now can take a look at Mexico and consumption levels there to see whether Fox was right in 2006.

Finally, it is my prediction that legalization will lower consumption of the now illicit drugs. Once legalized we will be able to limit distribution, raise prices, and reduce promotion, thereby reducing demand. The experiments in Washington and Colorado and other states and countries will soon begin providing empirical data on this question.

Place (Distribution)

Prescription 3 – Control Distribution. Once consumption is out in the open, we can control it. Ultimately, bigger companies will dominate the market place for all hedonic molecules. The big companies already do in the licit product areas. Forcing companies to obey the rules is simpler than corralling illicit-drug cartels or street-corner drug dealers. Government regulation agencies often work, and they are in fact constitutional. Section 8 of the US Constitution includes the following crystal-clear statement about its powers: "To regulate Commerce with foreign Nations, and among the several States, and with the Indian Tribes…" And as we know, states and local governments can also regulate commerce.

Of course, circa 2016, in many ways industry regulates Congress via the influence of corporate campaign contributions. This has to stop. But this is a topic of many a book these days. And we should be looking to see how other democracies handle this problem, paying attention to research on comparative democracy. While we might have invented modern democracy, other countries often do a better job of tweaking their systems.

Some of these substances will require control under the doctor's prescription program currently in place. We do know about the abuses of this channel of distribution. Consider the current tragedy of opioid abuse in this country. But board certification and licensing can be powerful regulation tools at the industrial level.

Distribution to minors is also an essential aspect of regulation of these products. We have practice with alcohol and tobacco. Issuing purchasing licenses at age eighteens is plausible. The technologies for enforcement (personal identification, product tracking, and so on) in this area are burgeoning and should be applied particularly with respect to minors.

Price

Prescription 4 – Controlling Prices via Taxes. Without question, raising prices works to reduce consumption. The efficacy of this marketing tool has been clearly demonstrated empirically, particularly with respect to alcohol and tobacco consumption in the United States. All these hedonic compounds should be taxed at the highest rate possible that doesn't support black markets. These taxes should be collected from producers, processors, and in some cases, consumers. That is, when the psychoactive substance is a natural part of the product – think specifically, tobacco, alcohol, marijuana, and other licit and illicit drugs – individual consumers should be charged a tax directly. When the psychoactive substance is an added ingredient – think salt, sugar, and caffeine – then the food and beverage processors should be taxed on their bulk purchase of such ingredients.

Really John, a tax on sugar? Yes, but not on specific products. Tax the stuff delivered to the food processors and the retailers (restaurants, and so on) in bulk, and at a high rate as I recent recommended in a letter to the editor of the *New York Times*. Let's say 500 percent.[1] That will lower their profit margins and affect all competitors in the same way. They will all begin to curtail the sugar content of their products to reduce costs and restore profits. Consumers will pay higher prices in the short run, as producers and processors pass along their increased costs. At least one empirical study well supports this prescription – see the new international study from McKinsey regarding the powerful efficacy of changing food-product formulas.[2] Ultimately, consumption of added sugar will decline, and prices to consumers will decline. Sugar bowls will reappear on tables.

Careful crafting of flexible taxation systems will be essential. Please recall that the Harrison Narcotics Tax Act of 1914 was not effective in either raising tax revenues or reducing consumption of cocaine and opium. The distribution of these drugs retreated to black markets. For example, regulators should be empowered to adjust tax levels perhaps quarterly as black market competition rises and wanes.

Finally, such taxes will allow us to capture some of the societal costs of hedonic consumption. Costs and benefits of the trade will be better aligned.

---

1 "How to Tax Sugar," letter to the editor, *New York Times*, May 26, 2016, online.
2 "Heavy Weapons," *The Economist*, November 22, 2014, page 55.

Promotion

Prescription 5 – Ban Mass Media Advertising of Psychoactive Substances.
This is so easy to do. We have plenty of practice at it. The last time someone saw
a cigarette ad on television in the United States was 1971. Only in the last few
years have the spirits folks been bold enough to return to TV advertising. We
know that such bans on mass-media advertising can work. Systematic research
demonstrates that reducing advertising reduces demand for alcohol and tobacco.

This is where the grand bargain comes in. Either governments will accept
marijuana advertising, or they must ban alcohol advertising. The latter is the
only logical option for leveling the playing field across the two types of products. I recommend the marijuana retailers sue over the issue, getting the courts
involved. And please recall the multinational companies' oft-repeated chorus
about a level playing field. Taxing the molecules and banning their advertising
levels the playing field across molecules, and between the largest and smallest
companies.

Certainly, banning psychoactive substance ads directed at minors is warranted. Even Coca-Cola thinks they are a bad thing. Other countries have implemented with success bans of all advertising to children – Sweden, Norway,
and in Canada, Quebec. The UK now prohibits ads for foods high in sugar
and salt in broadcast media to children. And the evidence continues to stack
up about the efficacy of this tool.[1] In the States Disney promises not to advertise junk food on their television programs for children. Such company and
industry measures are welcome but really not enough. And we know from
their behaviors in the 1980s that industry pledges in this area are almost always fleeting, the briefest appeasement at best. When public and press criticism fades away, so do their promises.

Fortunately, commercial television is waning. That's a good thing for us
all, particularly during the political campaign seasons. TV ads lean toward
emotional appeals (fear and humor) and contain little information about
products or politicians. The print media is also retreating fast. The magazines
I subscribe to are getting thinner and thinner.

---

1 Tirtha Dhar amd Kathy Baylis, "Fast-food Consumption and the Ban on Advertising Targeting
Children: The Quebec Experience," *Journal of Marketing Research*, 48(5), 2011, pages 799-813.

Presently a perfect storm is brewing that will may cause commercial television to follow the path of print. First, is the surge of growth in spending on digital media. Second, ad-skipping devices such as Dish's AdHop function are making ads disappear from your TV screen – see www.Spiced.World/appendix for an early view on this wonderful technology. Third, Netflix streaming and binge watching are also killing the appeal of TV advertising. Of course, all this is happening in the United States, but all such innovations tend to spread around the world. The big question then is how will American politicians spend the billions of dollars they are used to raising for their campaigns? One forecast predicts spending on digital advertising will surpass TV ads in 2017.[1] This is not soon enough.

That leaves us with the Internet. The advertising interruptions are perhaps most annoying there. Indeed, an ad-blocking battle is being waged between companies and consumers as you read this. All this suggests that consumers are already initiating their own Internet information searches. This is a wonderful trend we need to encourage. Of course, there are big dangers lurking in the social media with respect to illicit drugs and other criminal intent. But as a society we, are learning how to manage those.

Another viable proposal is a tax on advertising (across media) for psychoactive substances. Such taxes have proven useful in other contexts.

Prescription 6 – Product Labeling.

Reliable and information is crucial for good decision making, whether about products or policy. While studies often show food and ingredients labeling does not work well, we can teach consumers to pay attention. We have excellent empirical support for the efficacy of information-laden labeling in some contexts. Think of the Finland salt case in the last chapter, for example. It is more than annoying that Starbucks does not list the caffeine content on the one-pound bag I buy once a month. Other countries require detailed labeling. We should do the same.

---

1 Alexandra Bruell, "Digital Ad Spending to Pass TV in US by 2017, New Forecast Says," *AdAge*, December 8, 2014, online.

Prescription 7 – Education and Licensing Programs Focusing on Adolescents

Every person purchasing hedonic molecules, from salt to LSD, should know their benefits and dangers, short- and long-run. One attractive idea for controlling distribution to individuals is the Dutch "weed pass" idea applied more broadly. That is, licensing consumers the way we do drivers, or the way we should gun owners, makes all kinds of sense. As Tim Madge has suggested, we "license their use – not so that they had to be prescribed by medics, but so that a reasonable level of both self and official monitoring of individual use could be maintained."[1]

This would make imperative the development of a licensing course. On the front end would be a science-based educational program about the immediate effects and long term consequences of consumption. But of course, consumption decisions about psychoactive substances often involve emotions and peer pressure. Thus, the back end of such a curriculum must include experiential learning regarding concepts such as addiction, managing temptation, ego depletion, and social processes in the genre of Alcoholics Anonymous or the Mormon church.

This material can easily be packed into licensing exams for high school students. The more we learn about brain science, the more adolescents should become the focus of educational programs. Here's why:

> Studies reveal adolescence to be a period of heightened "plasticity" during which the brain is highly influenced by experience. As a result, adolescence is both a time of opportunity and vulnerability, a time when much is learned, especially about the social world, but when exposure to stressful events can be particularly devastating. As we leave adolescence, a series of neurochemical changes make the brain increasingly less plastic and less sensitive to environmental influences. Once we reach adulthood, existing brain circuits can be tweaked, but they can't be overhauled.[2]

---

1 Tim Madge, *White Mischief: A Cultural History of Cocaine* (New York: Thunder's Mouth Press, 2001).

2 Laurence Steinbert, "The Case for Delayed Adulthood," *New York Times*, September 21, 2014, opinion page 12.

Particularly because the laws about hedonic molecules will remain fluid and confusing for *adults* during the next decade, teenagers will need special attention. Tara Parker-Pope well summarizes the beginnings of such programs:

> Drug prevention experts say the "Just Say No" approach of the 1980s does not work. The goal of parents should not be to prevent their kids from ever trying marijuana. Instead, the focus should be on practical reasons to delay use of any mind-altering substance, including alcohol, until they are older.
>
> The reason is that young brains continue to develop until the early 20s, and young people who start using alcohol or marijuana in their teens are far more vulnerable to long-term substance-abuse problems.
>
> The brain is still wiring itself during adolescence, and any drug use during this period essentially trains the reward system to embrace a mind-altering chemical.[1]

During the next decade or so, while TV ads still hold some sway, public service announcement (PSAs) campaigns such as the following should accompany other educational efforts.

> The Partnership for Drug-Free Kids plans to continue its "Above the Influence" marketing campaign, which studies show has been an effective way of reaching teenagers about the risks of drug use. The campaign does not target a specific drug, but it teaches parents and teens about the health effects of early drug use and tries to empower teens to make good choices.[2]

Doing this right will perhaps be the most important thing we can do for our kids.

---

1 Tara Parker-Pope, "In Drug Fight, Erratic Cues for Teenagers," *New York Times*, August 19, 2014, science pages 1 and 4.
2 Ibid. Parker-Pope, 2014.

Conclusion – The Urgency of Political Will and Leadership

The amount of money US firms will spend against most of these initiatives is hard to imagine. For example, the American Beverage Association and friends spent $4.1 million to defeat soda taxes in two mid-sized California towns, Richmond and El Monte.

The proper path is pretty clear. Following any of the prescriptions above will require political courage. Legalization is essential for controlling (and reducing) the consumption of psychoactive substances in America. Two politicians are in an excellent position to fix Richard Nixon's dishonest and destructive approach to controlling hedonic molecules. Now that the elections are in the rear view mirror, both Jerry Brown and the new President have the opportunity to engage the debate on legalization, sign the legislation on legalization, and pardon the 300,000 or so prison inmates serving time for non-violent drug crimes. The tax dollars legalization will yield and the costs savings from smaller prisons can then go to "pre-criminal" education.

Finally, the whole world will follow America's lead on this. Mexican President Pena is correct. His policies on this must stay in step with the United States, the biggest market in the world. The whole world will benefit from policy making based on truth rather than political fortune.

Fifteen

A Glimpse of the Future, circa 2040

The ability to imagine is the largest part of what you call intelligence. You think the ability to imagine is merely a useful step on the way to solving a problem or making something happen. But imagining it is what makes it happen.

Michael Crichton, *Sphere*

Their eyes met as she walked into the car. Her smile had him at twenty feet. There weren't many empty seats on the train up to Pendleton International that time of day. She was funneled in his direction. After looking around a bit, she plopped down next to him.

She was wearing an old pair of jeans, running shoes, and a jade-colored blouse under a light-weight faux leather jacket. She had a backpack over her shoulder. She'd checked her bag in at Delmar. Her perky black ponytail was sticking out the back of her baseball hat. It was white with the word "AND?" emblazoned above the brim in orange and purple.

She popped off her earbuds, "I could tell by your smile that you wanna fuck[1] me. Most college guys do. Most guys do."

---

1 This language will seem too rough for some. I apologize. I am going for realism here. I also refer the reader to Kory Stamper's explanations about FUBAR, and so on in her "Yo Dude, Slang for the Ages," *New York Times*, October 4, 2014, page A19.

"*Want* to fuck you, or *do* fuck you?"

"Very funny. The former, of course!"

"Then why'd you sit here? Why'd you smile back?"

"'Cause I'm thinking about fucking you. Also, seeing *Romeo & Juliet* there on the seat helped your case. That for a class?" He was wearing an anteater T-shirt.

"Getting back to the fucking stuff for a minute, when are we going to do that?"

She laughed, "Maybe, with the emphasis on MAYBE, after I find out what kinda guy you are. At first glance you're yummy, what my grandmother would call vigorous. And we both have purple wristbands. That's a start. When'd you put yours on?"

"So you've seen the old *Zorro* flick – the one with Antonio Banderas?"

"Nope. My grandmother just usta call cute guys 'vigorous'. She'd fan her face fast with her hand and say 'my, my, he looks so vigorous.' Even when she was in her eighties. She told me about the movie I guess, but I never paid much attention."

"We, or you should watch it on the plane."

"Actually, you can watch anything you want on the plane. By yourself." With that smile, she asked again, "You didn't say when you put it on?"

He tried to focus on the conversation, "About halfway up Nutt Mountain. I took my roomies' challenge my freshman year. The LSD was crazy, but the Ketamine just put me to sleep. I really didn't like the GHB. Most important, I like playing tennis and running cross country and, once in a while, winning much better. A clear head helps with both."

He continued, "That was also about the time my grandfather left. He told me, 'If you're smart, you'll save something for your nineties. When you're decrepit like me, there aren't many new ways to have fun anymore.' He died with both heroin and LSD going through his veins, and he seemed serene."

"I got pure when my mom told me about my uncle's suicide. He jumped off the Coronado Bridge." She explained, "He'd caused a car accident. He was driving drunk, hit a tree, and killed his girlfriend and his best friend on the way to her prom. He drove onto the bridge two weeks later, stopped, and jumped. I don't know what was worse for his girlfriend, dying or not getting to go to her prom."

They both laughed. "That's dark," he opined.

"I swore off sugar and all the rest that day. The New Puritan reading list helped me along. I've had the bracelet on five years now. I feel great. God, you're cute!" She smiled again.

Looking up at her hat, he queried, "What's the 'AND?' for?"

Her large blue eyes rolled up as if to look at the hat too. "It's a creativity thing. I learned it in a drama class. An improv kinda thing. It's optimistic. It wants more. It's fun." She smiled again.

"To be honest, the book's a lure. In this case, it worked. But, I *am* actually reading it. Just started Act II."

"The honesty stuff gets you points, but not the lure bit. There will be a Shakespeare test at the end of this ride." The ride was a short one. Just 10 minutes on the bullet train from Delmar to Pendleton International Airport. She'd know whether he was telling the truth quite soon.

"Where ya going now?" he continued.

"I'm a senior at UCSD, and I'm going to the Holy Land for a two-week class."

"That with the Olive Tree Initiative?"

"Yeah. How'd you know about that?"

"This is nuts. Maybe I *am* gonna get laid. I go to Irvine. I was visiting my folks in San Diego before heading out with what must be the same OTI group! Wehrenfennig's the professor, a really old guy."

"You're shittin' me! What's your name?"

"No. I'm not. And where'd you get such a nasty mouth? And it's Adam Smith."

"I have a couple of older brothers."

"That explains it." He turned to glance out the window.

"So you're Adam Smith? We saw your name on the roster. I suppose you're headed to business school?"

"Nope. I'm a PoliSci major. I really don't know what I'm doing after school. And you are?"

"Lara. Lara Amador."

"Really? Lara the lover. Did you see *Doctor Zhivago*?"

"Really. I'm a ninth-generation Californian. You know, Amador County. And no, haven't seen that one either."

"Sure. The Sierra foothills were cannabis central before legalization. You been on a long flight like this before?" he asked.

"Nope."

"What are you gonna do all night?"

"I'll read and watch movies. You?"

He'd just trapped himself. What a dope. He was planning on popping a benzo to make him sleep for the eight-hour nonstop from San Diego to Tel Aviv. Of course, that meant breaking the promise, really just cheating on it a little. A sleeping pill was more medicine than recreation.

The thin purple braided leather band on his wrist proclaimed he was a New Puritan. It wasn't a religious thing. He and millions of others around the world had just pledged to put no more hedonic molecules into their bodies. The sugar and alcohol were easy for him to avoid, they hurt his athletic performance. The cannabinoids and hallucinogens damaged his competitiveness. He was attracted to the fitness (maybe even the vigor) of the Nupur women.

The comfort of rectitude was also attractive. People spoke their minds, and clear thinking prevailed. They still imbibed spices – apples, berries, chocolate – and the virtual ones – hiking trails, visiting new lands, reading great books, and crazy books, viewing movies and serials, playing creative games and competitive games, the thrill of victory and the agony of defeat. A Nupur favorite was trivia contests. Old card games and dancing with old and new music were both popular. Helping other people was also keen. And both sex and love. The latter proved best. Nothing's more fun than being unable to predict a potential life-long partner.

He'd found a new benzodiazepine that was perfect for the flight, really specific in its effect. No fun. Just sleep, with almost no hangover.

The airlines didn't allow them. The flight attendants didn't have time to run down the aisles slapping passengers to wake them in emergencies. But emergencies were quite rare. The AI-guided preventative maintenance was a kind of mechanical magic.

"Probably the same." That wasn't a lie until he made it so by popping the benzo.

As they were arriving at Pendleton X he said: "Where' you on the plane?

"First the R&J exam. I have three questions, get two right and you pass. How old was Juliet?"

He winced for effect, deep in thought. "Fourteen."

"Close enough. She was *almost* fourteen. How many times did he kiss her in Act I?"

"How do you know so much about the play?"

She tapped her chest, "Drama minor. Remember. I was a stage hand for the play. Don't change the subject. The answer is?"

Another faked wince. "Two."

"A romantic. Excellent. You passed. I'm in the back, 88J."

"Let me look – I'm in 73A. Also, I think you were going easy on me, maybe on purpose? Your Shakespeare exam was just numbers. What was your third question?"

"What *deus ex machina* lead to their meeting?"

He responded immediately, "Capulet's servant couldn't read the guest list he'd been given." And he displayed a cocky, self-satisfied grin.

With a bit of a British accent, "The lad does well. If we meet hence, I shall have questions a more." She returned his grin.

"Was your last word English or Italian?"

"Very funny," she laughed. "You guess."

The lines at airports had been pretty much eliminated about ten years earlier. Now you just walked up to the counter, looked into the eye scanner, and they electronically marked your bag for destination, even at the bullet train stations. The terrorism and nutcase threats had subsided, and randomized full-body checks managed those small remaining risks. His number had been called once, and even that run through the chemical monitors and a few questions were fast.

Once they were in the waiting area, they started bumping into more of their classmates. You could tell the Nupurs from the rest – they weren't pudgy. Also wristbands were on display. It looked like the group was about fifty-fifty.

Lara motioned she was going to hit the bathroom. "Me too." That gave him some time to think.

He hadn't been in a bricks-and-mortar package store in a couple of years. When he was climbing Nutt Mountain with his friends, he just ordered things off the net for next day delivery. The one-hour FEDEX drop was just too expensive. The old alcoholic drinks were also too heavy and therefore too expensive to have delivered. They'd pick up those at a package shop.

It was kind of embarrassing to be walking into a hedonic-molecule package shop, but he was in a hurry to catch the train. Keeping his license in effect was also breaking the rules. The eye scanner at the door checked his license.

He remembered how proud he was to max his licensing exam at age eighteen. That allowed him to order from the virtual stores and visit and buy stuff at the package stores. Sammy, his best friend from high school, also maxed the exam and got an early start on imbibed hedonism.

Sammy had gone to school on the East Coast, but was having a hard time with the Mountain. He'd gone all the way up to heroin and was now getting calls from the treatment folks about his addiction. Adam hoped it'd working out.

At the store the molecules were displayed along the white tile walls in order of their addictive powers. The intoxicants to the right. Salt, sugar, and coffee you could still buy at the grocery stores. The high taxes the food processors and restaurateurs paid for the spices had pretty much eliminated them as ingredients. Those taxes also put salt shakers and sugar bowls back on everyone's table. Medicines were still at drug stores. The package shops carried tobacco, alcohol, and the other intoxicants, from poppers to fentanyl.

Branding, using the original fonts and logos, was allowed on the otherwise white packaging. There was no display advertising. Indeed, there was also no mass-media advertising of the substances either. Each package had copious information about effects and side effects and warnings on the back. When you checked out, each purchase was nano marked to deter use by others, particularly minors.

Three things had worked to kill all the alcohol ads on television during the 2020s. First came the NFL reports of concussion brain damage. The League had tried all kinds of helmets and rule changes, but the fans just lost interest. Kids stopped playing. The sports heroes and role models were guys like Mike Trout.

Then, after the federal government eliminated its restrictions on marijuana, the pot producers sued in the states to allow mass-media advertising like the brewers, vintners, and distillers. The courts ruled that the discrimination was illegal, and the legislators passed laws banning mass-media advertising, including pop-up ads on the Internet, of all psychoactive substances, even added salt, sugar, and caffeine.

Finally, the Internet killed TV advertising, which took the money out of political campaigns, which in turn took most of the corruption out of politics. Truth mattered again. Candidates didn't have to repeat the fundamental lie, "No. Campaign contributions do not influence my votes." All these changes were slow moving, with a few prominent hallmarks in technology, the courts, and in Congress.

"We've got a few minutes. Let's stop at that chocolate bar. They've got fresh cherries, airfreight Rainiers from BC."

"They'll be better in a couple of weeks when we come back through," Lara answered.

"Come ooon!" Adam entreated. They ordered and sat down. He doused his cherries with unsweetened theobromine #9. She sprinkled.

He asked, "What are you most interested in seeing in Israel/Jordan?"

"After we finish the program, I'm taking a week to visit the sites with some friends. I'm a Christian, so I'm arriving a couple days early. Now that Bethlehem, Galilee, Jerusalem, and Calvary are open 24/7, we're going to catch them while we're working off the jetlag. After the program we're heading down to Elat for some Red Sea scuba diving and a visit to Petra. We'll finish up at the Disney park at Gaza. I know it seems silly and ethnocentric to go half way around the world to see Disneyland. But I'm interested in how they adapted the rides and characters for both Arab and Israeli visitors. One of my soccer teams when I was a kid was the Blue Jasmines."

"Blue Jasmines. Nice. Because of my running, I'm gonna go by both the Olympic Stadium in Jerusalem and some of the other sites for the games. My plan is to run the marathon course on the fifteenth.

"I'm also going to finish the trip at Disneyland. Last year I wrote a paper on how the prospective Olympic Games and a Disney park helped stop the violence in the region. Arabs and Jews started working together again. Tourism has always been the greatest draw, the real commercial opportunity. Now the infrastructure can handle the millions of Christians, Jews, and Muslims that want to see the places Jesus, David, and Mohammed walked.

"The two great Jewish peace offerings can be juxtaposed as a powerful message. Almost a hundred years ago, the Israelis maintained the Dome of the Rock atop the Temple Mount and the Wailing Wall. Throughout history the conquerors had always raised the cultural icons of the conquered. Now both sides have used the debris from the walls separating Israel and Palestine to construct the Olympic Stadium in Jerusalem."

Lara said to herself, "Hm. This guy's got beauty and brains. Hmmm!" Then she said to him, "Let's see if we can find some more time together during the trip."

"Better yet, let's see if we can negotiate adjacent seats. We've got more to talk about."

They played cribbage and laughed on the long flight. They watched *Zorro* and *Zhivago*. He had flipped the pill into the trash in the men's room.

> *"Can you remember your first taste of spice?"*
> *"It tasted like cinnamon."*
> *"But never twice the same... It's like life – it presents*
> *a different face each time you take it."*

FRANK HERBERT, *DUNE*

[Index]

About the Author

J ohn L. Graham spent nine years as an officer with the Navy Underwater Demolition/SEAL Teams. Since leaving the military, he has focused his work on promoting peace.

Graham studied marketing and cultural anthropology in his doctoral program at UC Berkeley. He has collaborated with colleagues in international marketing in twenty-four countries.

Formerly a professor at the University of Southern California, Graham is now professor emeritus and director of the Center for Global Leadership at the Merage School of Business at UC Irvine.

Graham has published articles in the *Harvard Business Review*, the *Journal of Marketing*, the *Journal of Consumer Research*, the *New York Times*, the *Los Angeles Times*, and other prestigious publications and has been interviewed on national and foreign broadcast media. In addition to *Spiced*, he has written six books on international marketing and global negotiations. For information on his books and upcoming projects, visit Graham's websites: www.orangetreepartners.net, www.spiced.world, www.inventivenegotiation.com, www.globalnegotiationbook.com, and www.allinthefamilybook.us.

Made in the USA
San Bernardino, CA
13 March 2019